About the Author

Peter Stephenson has specialised in professional career transition consulting since 1990, although he first became involved in the field some 25 years ago designing and marketing career self-assessment instruments. He is currently Director of Davidson & Associates in New South Wales and Australian Capital Territory.

Before joining D & A, Peter worked in a number of company director positions in Australia, Canada and England. He was the founding Managing Director of Deloitte Consulting Group, one of Australia's 'Big 6' management consultancies, founding Managing Director of Hospital Extension Services, Director and General Manager of Lucas Marine and Divisional Chief Executive of a food group.

He has extensive management consulting experience in the ASEAN region, South Asia, Japan and the People's Republic of China.

Peter has an exceptional understanding of the issues involved in corporate restructuring and its impact on executives and staff. He has worked with many of Australia's top 100 companies on planning and implementing organisational change and on providing career management counselling and coaching for directors and executives.

Educated in the UK, Peter holds a Postgraduate Diploma in Management Studies (specialising in behavioural sciences). He is a Fellow of the Australian Institute of Management and of the Australian Institute of Company Directors.

the bulletproof executive

the bulletproof executive

**Armour-plated Strategies
For Career Success,
if you're employed or not!**

Peter Stephenson

HarperBusiness
An imprint of HarperCollins*Publishers*

HarperBusiness
An imprint of HarperCollins*Publishers*
First published in Australia in 1997
by HarperCollins*Publishers* Pty Limited
ACN 009 913 517
A member of HarperCollins*Publishers* (Australia) Pty Limited Group
http://www.harpercollins.com.au

Copyright © 1997 ADVANTAGE 2000 Pty Ltd, ACN 003 131 744

This book is copyright.
Apart from any fair dealing for the purposes of private study, research, criticism or review, as permitted under the Copyright Act, no part may be reproduced by any process without written permission.
Inquiries should be addressed to the publishers.

While every care has been taken in the preparation of material for *The Bulletproof Executive*, the information contained herein is not intended to serve as a substitute for competent legal or professional advice and should not be relied upon as such. The anecdotes and case studies in this publication are based on real life cases, although names and details have been altered to preserve client confidentiality.

HarperCollins*Publishers*
25 Ryde Road, Pymble, Sydney, NSW 2073, Australia
31 View Road, Glenfield, Auckland 10, New Zealand
77–85 Fulham Palace Road, London W6 8JB, United Kingdom
Hazelton Lanes, 55 Avenue Road, Suite 2900, Toronto, Ontario M5R 3L2
and 1995 Markham Road, Scarborough, Ontario M1B 5M8, Canada
10 East 53rd Street, New York NY 10032, USA

National Library Cataloguing-in-Publication data:

Stephenson, Peter, 1945-.
  The bulletproof executive: armour-plated strategies for
  career success, if you're employed or not.
  Bibliography.
  ISBN 07322 58901.
  1. Executives — Training of. 2. Success in business.
  3. Leadership. 4. Management. I. Title.
658.4

Illustrations by Carol Stephenson
Set in Garamond Book 10/12.5
Printed in Australia by Griffin Press on 79 gsm Bulky Paperback

5 4 3 2 1
01 00 99 98 97

This book is dedicated to all those executives and managers — currently employed or not — who are seeking to be successful in their careers in today's precarious organisational environment and turbulent employment marketplace.

Foreword

It is an uncertain and competitive world in which all of us now live and work. Every one of us knows someone whose career has ended recently or at least faltered, through no readily apparent fault on their part. This is causing younger managers, in particular, to regard our major corporations as very temporary berths indeed for their talents. It is therefore the case that the publication of Peter Stephenson's book is extremely timely.

It provides an easily read and cleverly combined 'road map' and 'health check' for the management of a modern career at any age or stage.

Lord Blyth of Rowington, Deputy Chairman and Chief Executive
The Boots Company PLC, Nottingham, United Kingdom

If there is any message to executives resulting from the corporate restructuring and organisational upheavals of the 1990s, it is that to win in the career game, it will be essential to understand what is involved in managing a career. It is no longer possible to leave management of one's career in the hands of an organisation, no matter how well-intentioned that organisation may be.

The reason is that the probability of an individual losing their job, at least once in their career, is close to 100 per cent. The reasons for this are the underlying drivers of change, the impact of technology, significantly altered management philosophy which has led to such a phenomenon as evaluation of an organisation's core competence and the resultant outsourcing of all non-core elements, the move to corporate globalisation, as well as the increasing incidence of mergers and acquisitions. All of these trends will accelerate in the decade we have ahead of us.

In these circumstances, it is essential that individuals understand the principles of career management as well as they understand the principles of managing a business. Yet to my continued amazement and puzzlement, I and others of my colleagues working in the field of career transition management, continually encounter individuals who have no career strategy and are not actively promoting their careers.

They have not kept themselves up to date in what is involved in management of the asset which is going to yield the highest to them in the years ahead — that is, the career capital, the asset that they have in their head, accumulated expensively and often through hard experience over a long period of time, but about which they know little in terms of how it is converted to productive career outcomes, both in a monetary and non-monetary sense.

Peter Stephenson in his book has gone a long way towards providing the answers to individuals on how they can win in the career game and still provide outstanding service to their own organisations.

Frederick Davidson, Chairman
Davidson & Associates Pty Ltd, Melbourne, Australia

the bulletproof executive

It seems like only a few years ago that looking after one's career meant little more than graduating from school with a useful degree, getting hired by the right company, and serving loyally until retirement. The rapid disappearance of this scenario is no longer news, of course, since thousands of workers who thought they had jobs for life have found themselves making involuntary career transitions. By now, the science and art of the job search has been the subject of endless helpful articles, books, tapes and seminars. Somewhat less common, however, is sound information on managing one's career while fully employed.

Now that we know that no job is inherently secure, it only makes sense to do all we can to make ourselves valuable to the organisations in which we work. Above all, this means being experts on the business goals that are driving company strategy at any given time. It means measuring everything we do against this standard, designing initiatives that bring people and operations into alignment with these goals, and communicating relentlessly about the positive impact of these activities on the top and bottom line. It means not only developing our own leadership skills but those of the group and department managers throughout the organisation. The more effective we become at moving ideas from concept to reality within newly flattened and decentralised structures, the more we have demonstrated our command of the potentials of the new paradigm — and our contribution to profitability.

Similarly, the executive or manager who understands the value of providing systematic career management assistance to all employees, gains a critical advantage in aligning individual and company goals and in leading change initiatives that can succeed at all levels. Using internal career management as a strategic tool also supports achievement of recruitment and retention objectives and enhances morale, loyalty and productivity.

Anyone who can take credit for the cost-effective utilisation of human capital has made a powerful case for his or her own long-term, measurable value to the organisation. As we see it, this is part of the new reality of managing one's career, about which Peter Stephenson's book provides timely new insights and strategies.

Richard J Pinola, Chairman and Chief Executive Officer
Right Management Consultants, Inc., Philadelphia, United States

Contents

Foreword	ix
Introduction	xvi

Part One — Why It's A Battle-zone! 1

Chapter 1 Executives And Managers 'Under Continuous Fire' 3
- Causes of the Casualties 4
- Jobs Under Siege 5
- The Career Environment: A Minefield! 7
- How to Return the Fire and Survive 8
- Summary 9

Chapter 2 The Four Triggers Of Executive Failure 10
- The First Trigger: Job Performance 10
- The Second Trigger: Personal Performance 12
- The Third Trigger: Change Management 13
- The Fourth Trigger: Chemistry and Fit 14
- Summary 16
- Further Resources 16

Part Two — Armour-plated Strategies For Career Success   17

Chapter 3 Improving Your Job Performance — Business Results! .. 19
- Management Practices 19
- The New Core Competence for Effective Staff Management ... 25
- Primary Business Drivers 28
- Futures 29
- Summary 33
- Further Resources 33

Chapter 4 Improving Your Personal Performance — Self-motivation! .. 34
- Occupational Interests 35
- Motivational Capabilities 36
- Values 37
- Career Areas 39
- Implications 40
- Summary 41
- Further Resources 41

Chapter 5	**Developing New Millennium Leadership Traits**	42
	The Search for Leadership Traits	42
	Examples of Leadership Traits	43
	Defining Leadership Traits	45
	Closing the Gap	46
	Summary	47
	Further Resources	47
Chapter 6	**Excelling At Teamwork, As Member Or Leader**	48
	Behaviour — the Driver of Operating Style	49
	Major Categories of Operating Style	49
	Teams and Executive Success	52
	Summary	55
	Further Resources	55
Chapter 7	**Improving Personal Chemistry And Fit**	56
	Material Needs	57
	Structural Needs	57
	Behavioural Needs	57
	Emotional Needs	60
	Summary	62
	Further Resources	62
Part Three	**Leading The Charge Of Change And Winning The Challenge Of Transition**	63
Chapter 8	**Managing Restructures And Succeeding As A Leader of Change**	65
	Anatomies of Restructuring — Worst and Best Case Scenarios	66
	Leadership of Change Competencies	70
	Best Principles and Best Practice in Downsizing	72
	Selecting the Best Outplacement Provider	75
	Best Principles and Best Practice in Rebuilding	78
	Summary	80
	Further Resources	80
Chapter 9	**Avoiding 'Slash-and-Burn' Staff Dismissals (Only To Hire Again Later!)**	81
	Reasons for Dismissals	82
	Alternatives to Economic Reasons for Dismissals	83
	Alternatives to Dismissals for Reasons of Capability, Motivation and 'Not Fitting In'	85

Outcomes and Implications	90
Summary	91

Chapter 10 Nurturing Talent In This Era Of 'Hire And Fire' ... 92
Selection of Talent	92
Career Alignment of Talent	93
Summary	97
Further Resources	97

Part Four Creating And Controlling Your Own Career Destiny ... 99

Chapter 11 Focusing On Your Future And Targeting Your Ideal Career 101
Taking Stock of Your Career	102
Key Elements of the Career Environment	103
Transitioning Through Today's Employment Market	105
Creating Your Own Opportunity	107
The Self-employment Option	107
Summary	109
Further Resources	109

Chapter 12 Marketing Yourself Successfully And Winning That Ideal New Job ... 110
Changing Your Current Position	110
Preparing Your Personal Profile or Resume	110
The Covering Letter	113
Using Your Contacts	115
More Than Meets the Eye	116
Your Game Plan	117
The Interview	117
During the Interview	119
Closing the Deal	121
Summary	122
Further Resources	122

Chapter 13 Surviving The Pressures Of Your New Work Environment And Succeeding In Your Career ... 123
Stress and Burnout	124
Your Idiosyncracies	124
Stress Management	125
Career Stages	126
Through the Year 2000	129
A Final Word of Encouragement	130
Summary	130

Part Five — Selling Yourself, Networking Allies And Negotiating Your Way To Success 131

Chapter 14 Winning Hands Down At Power, Politics And Influence — 133
- Power 134
- Influence 136
- The Business of Personal Selling 136
- Knowledge, and the Psychology of Personal Selling 137
- Time Management and Prioritisation 140
- The Importance of Selling Yourself Externally 141
- How to Source New External Leads 143
- One-on-One Communication 144
- Group Communication 145
- Speaker Styles 147
- First Impressions Count 148
- Summary 149
- Further Resources 149

Chapter 15 Selling Yourself Outside The Organisation And Motivating Audiences — 150
- Approach Planning 150
- The Meeting 152
- Structured Versus Personalised Approach 154
- Use of Visuals in Personal Selling 154
- Closing 155
- Closing Techniques 156
- How to Develop Successful Speeches and Group Presentations 156
- How to Grasp the Audience's Attention 158
- How to Build Curiosity and Trust 159
- How to Deliver the Main Thrust of Your Speech and Gain Audience Acceptance 160
- Ending with Impact 162
- Summary 163
- Further Resources 163

Chapter 16 Beating Your Competition With Powerful Self-promotion And Group Presentation Techniques — 164
- Meeting the Needs of Your Allies 164
- Expanding Your Influence 165
- Major Ally Management 167
- Promotional Techniques for Executives and Managers ... 168
- Developing Writing Effectiveness 170

Speech Aids 172
Use of Visuals in Group Presentations 174
Summary 176
Further Resources 176

Part Six   Your Executive Armoury 177

Chapter 17   Focusing These Strategies Into A Winning And Enduring Bulletproof Theme 179
Ranking of Career Success and Failure Factors 180
Survey Results 181
Other Career Success and Failure Factors Cited 182
Difficulties and Dependencies Regarding the Rankings 185
How to Develop Your Own Priorities 186
Summary 187

Weapons At Your Disposal 189
1. Four Triggers Risk Assessment 191
2. Management Practices Survey 194
3. Primary Business Drivers 217
4. Optimising Job Fit, Self-motivation And Personal Performance ... 226
5. Defining Leadership Traits 229
6. Operating Style And Teamwork 233
7. Personal Chemistry And Fit 235
8. How To Plan And Manage Restructures 237
9. How To Select An External Outplacement Provider 241
10. Factors And Questions For Selection Interviews 244
11. A Bulletproof Career Planning And Strategy Development Process ... 248
12. Financial Planning 253
13. Your Own Business 256
14. Career- And Capability-oriented Resume/Profile 261
15. A Bulletproof Networking System For Career Search 268
16. The Convincing Communications Clinic: 39 Steps to Success ... 274
17. Eleven-point Plan For Preparing Group Presentations 294
18. Meeting Room Layouts 296
19. Develop Group Presentation Techniques By Auditing Others ... 298

The Executive Panel 301

Bibliography 305

Index 307

Introduction

My career had been progressing so well:

- A flying scholarship, private pilot's licence, and head of my house and cadets at high school
- A 'distinction' in a tertiary business qualification and a postgraduate diploma in management studies, specialising in behavioural sciences
- Production manager and personnel superintendent in a leading food company in my twenties
- Director and general manager of a group of industrial companies in Europe at age 30
- My own successful management consulting practice in North America, travelling the world in my thirties
- Managing director of a 'Big-Six' management consultancy in Australia in my early forties
- Divisional chief executive back in industry at 45.

Then 'bang!' my abysmally handled retrenchment some six months later . . .

I never knew what hit me. I had always been successful, always added value to organisations. Why did my job come to an end so abruptly at the pinnacle of my career? Then I began to realise I was not alone. The market was saturated with unemployed, confused executives with similar war-stories.

In the words of Charles Handy, in his book *The Age Of Unreason*, I 'reframed' my thinking about my future career. I decided to specialise and make another type of contribution, by becoming a career management and outplacement consultant. More than halving my salary to get started in this 'new' profession, five years later I am privileged to have been working with the pre-eminent firm in this field, Davidson & Associates Pty Ltd, as director responsible for New South Wales and the Australian Capital Territory.

I have worked with over 300 executives and managers and I have been able to look back and examine what made them effective, what made them succeed and what made them fail. This book summarises the highly surprising results of my assessment, as verified by an 85-member Executive Panel, and provides warnings, revelations and winning strategies for all those executives and managers seeking to be successful in their careers and as contributors to their organisations.

Some may currently be working but feel themselves to be 'under siege' in today's rapidly changing and uncertain employment environment. Others may feel less threatened but are aiming for even greater career success. Others may be casualties — perhaps one of the approximately 25 000 executives and managers who have lost their jobs in the manufacturing sector in Australia since the turn of the decade, or one of the 20 000 or so who have been retrenched from the finance and banking sector.

For these and other casualties, repositioning their thinking about their future careers, targeting and attaining that next new career position, surviving the inevitable

Introduction

probationary period in the new job, progressing and achieving, are all of paramount importance.

Help is now at hand! This book represents the survival and success guide for executives and managers finding themselves in each of these situations. The Bulletproof Executive can be a reality.

Part One of the book explains how it is a battle-zone out there and explores what is happening to executives and managers who may feel the world of work and careers has been turned upside-down on them. It also examines why difficulties and individual failures occur at the executive and managerial level. And surprisingly, it's not just all about job performance, which accounts for only a small proportion of the total career success formula!

Part Two uncovers a range of armour-plated strategies for career success, including how to excel at job performance, personal performance, chemistry and fit, teamwork and desirable new millennium leadership traits. All critical success factors for executives and managers under continuous fire in today's turbulent work climate.

Part Three presents a different class of weaponry to tackle the war out there in organisational life! 'Leading the charge of change and winning the challenge of transition' is the theme, and a range of new and essential management functions are reviewed, including: how to manage restructures, downsizings and rebuilding activities; required leadership of change competencies; how to avoid 'slash-and-burn' and having to dismiss staff — only to find you are hiring again six months later; and how to nurture talent successfully in this era of 'hire and fire' — all in all, how to make your organisation a sought-after employer and generate a motivated, productive environment.

Part Four in essence represents the executive 'flak jacket' and when followed through creates inner confidence and external resilience robust enough to withstand all the worst vagaries of organisational life. The focus is on how to establish and control your own career destiny — the days of the organisation looking after you, if they were ever really there, have long since gone. Setting career objectives which are reflective both of you as a person and the developing employment market place, marketing yourself successfully to attain that ideal new job, and strategies for surviving the pressures of, and for succeeding in, your new work environment are all explained, with a continuing emphasis on practical solutions.

Part Five completes the bulletproofing by providing definitive guidelines on how to sell yourself, develop allies and negotiate your way to career success. The rationale is simple, but the solution is not easy. All executives and managers need to win at power, politics and influence. This requires exceptionally well-honed personal selling and group presentation capabilities.

Part Six provides you with your 'Executive Armoury' — a veritable arsenal of tools, techniques and associated weaponry for you to use, which when applied consistently, virtually guarantee career success. Also, all the armour-plated strategies reviewed in this book are focused into one winning, bulletproof theme, the concept for which was developed with the assistance of an 85-member Executive Panel, who not only verified and ranked the various career success and failure factors for executives and managers addressed in this book, but who also provided a range of powerful additional insights into executive and managerial career success.

the bulletproof executive

Good reading! Fight the good fight and here's to your ongoing career success!

My thanks go to the four contributors to the Foreword and Executive Armoury, to the members of the Executive Panel (some of whose jobs will undoubtedly have changed by the time this book is published), and to my highly tolerant, supportive and loving family: to Barbara, my wife, whose work in compiling the manuscript for this book has been invaluable as it was a colossal task, and to my children Jackie, Carol and Paul — all key success factors in my executive career.

A special thanks to Carol, too, for her outstanding illustrations.

PART ONE

Why It's A Battle-zone!

Battle-zone — An area of extreme danger wherein opposing forces engage in warfare and all human resources are liable to come under fire, be they adversaries or merely innocent observers.

1

Executives And Managers 'Under Continuous Fire'

'Please come in, Peter, and sit down. How are things going? I'm afraid I have to tell you the board has lost confidence in you and I need to decide what to do about it. I don't think you can continue with us. What do you think? What do you feel we should do?'

Lies, damn lies! The full board had not yet met me. How could they have lost confidence if they didn't even know me? Besides, I'd only just started in the role of divisional chief executive officer some five months earlier.

Three hours later, after some heated and fruitless discussion with the group CEO, I returned home late for a 'Murder' party we were hosting. Simultaneously I was expected to launch myself into cold food and humorous play acting, without any appetite for either. My wife and friends could sense that I was 'not on good form' — the end of another tiring week, perhaps!

Our guests left late and there was no time to discuss the bad news with my wife, as we were leaving very early the next morning for the Prawn Festival at Hawks Nest on the Central Coast. The three-hour drive with kids and dogs to a 'fun-filled weekend' with family friends was again not the time and place to vent my grief, anger and frustration. Did I ever feel like a boiled prawn!

Two weeks later my fate was decided and I joined the ranks of the executive unemployed, fortunately on quite a good separation package. But what was going on? Everywhere I went I met other executives and managers who had been on the receiving end of 'the bullet' for a wide variety of reasons. There were similar patterns. Most had joined companies in professional or technical positions, but — beholden to the parental concept of 'getting on in life' and slaves to the company job evaluation systems which award more points (and hence more salary) to managerial positions — they had all progressed into management. Had this been a wise move when viewed retrospectively?

A 1996 American Management Association survey of 1000 large and medium-sized US companies found that 50 per cent of them had shed jobs, middle manager generalists being some of the hardest hit. Meanwhile, professional and technical jobs were being created 50 per cent faster than they were being cut. Judith Sloan, director of the National Institute of Labour Studies, is reported as finding similar patterns in corporate Australia — managerial positions on the wane, while professional positions have been on the increase.

As Thomas A Stewart, writing for *Fortune* magazine in January 1996, put it: 'In the vortex of the maelstrom, whirling faster than anyone: you. So you're now on your own, beholden to no one, the future as bright as your mind is quick and your courage deep. It would be nice, though, to feel less marooned.' It is not nice feeling marooned as an executive or a manager, or indeed anyone, particularly when out of work.

G J Meyer in his book *Executive Blues* describes how nearing 50 he was retrenched from McDonnell Douglas, having been heralded as a 'prodigy' from a working-class background in his early career. When following up resumes by phone, he found it very difficult to get past the blocking techniques of the efficient secretaries in his quest for interviews. As this happened again and again it began to unnerve him.

As John A Thompson and Catherine A Henringsen point out in their book *The Portable Executive*, no executive (or manager) today is immune. Your marketable skills and experiences are your only true job security. But the good news is that the opportunities are unlimited for 'portable' executives — those who are independent and self-directed.

Causes of the Casualties

As I further analysed the causes of executive and managerial unemployment, I discovered that some people had become casualties as a result of the recession in the early 1990s, when cost and head-count reduction developed with a vengeance after the good times in the 1980s. Others had been the victims of process re-engineering exercises in their companies, when efficiency and effectiveness rule, whereas employees, mere pawns, are readily disposable resources.

After the growth (and greed) in the latter half of the 1980s, returning to the core competencies of the organisation and selling off or contracting-out non-core assets and processes, has been and still remains another minefield for staff at all levels. However, the contracting-out option has created employment opportunities in smaller companies feeding on the crumbs, while the big fish concentrate on what they are good at.

Globalisation has also created a blood bath. The number of 'secure' companies who have lost out to the insurgence of new players from overseas competing in their own backyards seems to grow year by year. Executives can also lose out on the other dimension of globalisation, when companies here compete elsewhere. Large numbers of senior people find they have nowhere to go within their companies when they return to their homeland, following their overseas postings.

Company mergers, acquisitions and divestments have also caused major redundancies. However, information technology and telecommunications (IT & T) can probably represent the greatest threat to executive and managerial job tenure and survival, for the unwary. They have enabled organisations to cut out whole layers of middle management and supervisors. The personal computer is now the main device for monitoring and controlling operations and for communicating with staff. *Human* eyes and ears, and interpersonal communications, have been replaced, in no small part, by electronics. If executives, managers and indeed all staff are not keeping up to date in the fast-paced IT & T rollout, it is only a matter of time before they find themselves ambushed again by a machine or a piece of software.

Such technology has also had a profound impact on the rate and pace of change as it relates to organisational life cycles. The various phases of start-up, early growth, secondary growth, adolescence ('the turbulent years') and organisational maturity have often condensed from years into months, requiring changes in skill-sets, and therefore people, far faster than ever before. The average job tenure for a CEO is now under four years.

Jon Isaacs, chief executive officer of the Royal Blind Society, puts it this way: 'There is a need for all organisations to become much more technologically literate and competent. Unless all staff from the CEO down have a love affair with technology, the organisation (as well as the country) will find it difficult to survive.'

Some of these trends are acknowledged by David Birchall and Laurence Lyons in *Creating Tomorrow's Organisation* (much of their case study material coming from The Future Work Forum at the Henley Management College in the United Kingdom). However, they note that while IT & T provides opportunities for organisational improvement and development, there is also the danger of applying pat solutions, often to non-existent problems, and launching IT & T projects which do not always recognise or declare the full extent of their side effects, either inside the organisation or elsewhere.

Jeremy Rifkin, author of *The End of Work: The Decline of the Global Labour Force and the Dawn of the Post-Market Era*, promotes a different emphasis. He believes we are entering a new stage wherein we will experience a gradual reduction in the number of conventional jobs. Indeed unemployment across the globe is already at its highest since the 1930s. Information technology, telecommunications, robotics and other new technologies are taking over from humans in every area of the workforce. Many occupations are becoming extinct and others will follow. He predicts production will move towards virtual full automation by the middle of the next century.

Jobs Under Siege

So finally, in terms of the external causes of executive and managerial vulnerability, we are witnessing the demise of the job. The job, as we know it today, has been around for less than 100 years in Australia. Most people prior to this, if not employed by the government, were travelling workers primarily employed in agriculture and mining.

The mid-1900s saw huge growth in manufacturing, construction and utilities, while primary industry diminished rapidly. Now as we approach the year 2000, distribution, government and community services are projected by many to be the largest areas of the economy, followed by manufacturing, construction and utilities (although still declining), with information-based sectors the third and fastest-growing category.

However, the net effect is fewer jobs: whether technology drives organisational downsizing, or a host of other reasons, job reductions are very real and have been going on for quite a few years, internationally as well as in Australia. Witness the international score-card of redundancies in the 1990s as reported by *The Bulletin*: General Motors, December 1991, 74 000; IBM, July 1993, 60 000; AT & T, January 1996, 40 000; Boeing, February 1993, 28 000; Digital Equipment, May 1994, 20 000; McDonnell Douglas, July 1990, 17 000; Philip Morris, November 1993, 14 000; Chemical / Chase Manhattan Bank, August 1995, 12 000.

The Australian score-card in the 1990s? By the end of 1996 almost 50 000 managers had lost their jobs from the finance, banking and manufacturing sectors alone — myself included. Also, according to Charles Brass, executive director of the Future of Work Foundation (as reported in *HR Monthly*), more than 30 per cent of working age Australians do not have jobs, while numerous surveys reveal that at least 30 per cent of those who have 'jobs' hate them and want to leave — the job concept is not working for more than half our population.

'You hate everybody, and, worse, everybody hates you. You are in a living nightmare. You are working in a job you hate,' recounts Jenni Lans in her book *If it Wasn't for the Money I Wouldn't be Doing This*. The sad point she makes is that when something goes wrong in one section of your life (your work), chances are that it will start leaking into other parts of your life.

The outlook? Continuation of the status quo. The Future Focus Committee of the IACMP (International Association of Career Management Professionals) summed it up this way in their *Report on Trends and Issues Affecting the Career Management Industry*: 'Many companies are hiring and downsizing at the same time. A transformation is occurring in many industries. This affects individuals and organisations, as organisations strive to remain competitive. Technology is changing the way people work. Updated education becomes increasingly important as new skills are required in the workplace.'

Concurrent with these trends and projections, we see the continuation or emergence of the following themes:

- a shift away from regional and rural locations towards the capital cities
- males progressively becoming displaced in the workforce by females
- dual-career families and reverse-role families, where the previous breadwinner is now the housekeeper
- more part-time and contract jobs and a more geographically mobile workforce
- the increasing vulnerability of the baby boomers (those born at the end of the Second World War) now in their mid- to late forties and comprising a substantial proportion of the workforce
- the shifting of career streams by sector (for example, away from manufacturing and banking towards the business and personal services sectors and independent business); by size of organisation (the reduction in size and number of large organisations and the birth and development of a myriad of small ones, the niche and subcontract operators who, fortunately, *are* hiring!); and by job (the decline of middle management generalist positions and the growth in specialist or professional positions and self-employment).

(Source: *Jobshift: How to Prosper in a Workplace Without Jobs*, William Bridges, Nicholas Brealey Publishing Ltd, London, 1995.)

Get ready! It is not just particular jobs and careers which are disappearing; the whole idea of having a job may disappear, according to William Bridges in *Job Shift: How to Prosper in a Workplace Without Jobs*. This provocative statement addresses a growing concern.

Harry S Dent Jr in his book *Job Shock: Four New Principles Transforming our Work and Business* takes another tack by stating that the most fundamental aspect of the work revolution is simply having workers (executives and managers included) become more customer- and results-oriented, and being measured for such results. This means an end to the concept of conventional jobs and entitlements; it also means rewards becoming based on profits generated by teams, rather than on mere activities.

The Career Environment: A Minefield!

Given all of this, it is no small wonder the career environment for executives, managers and indeed for all employees has changed far faster than the rate at which most of us have been able to adapt. This poses a constant threat for the unprepared. Smaller, flatter organisations, fewer promotional opportunities and continuing organisational change have all caused confusion and concern, often adversely affecting morale, productivity and any sense of well-being, let alone a sense of career direction and control. Additional related problems are caused by the following:

- *Lack of competence*. Fast-developing roles and jobs often create a competency gap through insufficient knowledge, experience, training or skills. Broadened spans of control — increased numbers of staff reporting directly to managers — create staff management nightmares. Coping with and managing others at times of change and uncertainty represents a new management science, if not an art-form.
- *Waning self-motivation*. This is often caused by an individual's slowness to adapt to change, a lack of satisfaction in newly restructured roles, and a growing lack of trust in employers.
- *Deteriorating chemistry and fit*. This is a result of strained interpersonal relationships with new bosses, peers and direct reports; personal traits, characteristics or attitudes which may have been satisfactory in the past, but which now may be perceived to hinder job or personal performance; and the apparent need for more flexible, more 'modern' styles of behaviour, yet which are often poorly defined by the employer.
- *Increased stress*. Charles Handy, Fellow of the London Business School and author of *The Age of Unreason*, *The Empty Raincoat* and other books relating to the career environment, says: 'Half as many people, paid twice as well, producing three times as much' has become the order of the day, creating increasing — and in some cases intolerable — work pressures and stress for executives and managers, and indeed for all staff in many cases.

The effects of these problems vary. In some cases, there can be slow or even lack of recommitment by individuals to the new ways of work and the new career environment. There can be emotional misalignment between individuals and their employing organisations. There can be a plateau or tapering-off of job or personal performance. And there is a growing army of discontent: those executives, managers and others out of work and unable to get back in, let alone commence their careers, as many young adults are finding out.

There can also be the flight of talent from organisations to 'apparently' greener pastures, led by those who are most easily employable elsewhere and who find it easiest to jump ship. But the message is: 'Beware!' Those 'apparently' greener pastures may well turn out to be just as barren as the pasture you have left, if not more so, and the new horse in the pasture can find it hard to survive, particularly when the conditions are extreme.

How to Return the Fire and Survive

The first thing to realise is that organisational change is here to stay. It is increasing, and will continue to increase, at such a rate and pace that we are now in the era of organisational 'revolution' rather than evolution. In this, the organisation has become a variable rather than a fixed entity and cost, and anyone can be on the receiving end of the effects of that variability in the form of a bullet! As David Habler, national manager human resources of the Australian Stock Exchange, puts it: 'Ability to adapt to changing circumstances might require the acquisition of new competencies.'

Accordingly, do not rely on convention: career paths which were winners for most of this century are often no longer providing much success; increase your competitive drive; set high standards, develop a desire to win, and never stop trying to grow. Lifelong learning is increasingly necessary for success, says John P Kotter in *The New Rules*.

Returning the fire and surviving also dictates the need to:

- put yourself first and the organisation second — heresy in yesteryear!
- realise that your job security is only the length of your pay period or the termination notice provisions in your employment contract
- continue to develop yourself so that you remain employable, no matter who your employer may be
- not only learn about these external causes of your vulnerability and build your defences accordingly, but also study the career success strategies articulated throughout this book — your armoury for survival and success
- above all, contingency plan! Nothing will ever again be certain in organisational life. Be certain about your personal future through your development of fall-back options, and in this, enjoy a developing inner sense of self-preservation, personal security, confidence and control.

SUMMARY

Chapter 1 raises the following key issues:

- Executive and managerial life is open warfare. You are in the battle-zone, so always be ready to receive and to return fire.
- Organisational change will continue and accelerate unabated, impacting on jobs and the career environment.
- This is causing organisational 'revolution' rather than evolution.
- Executives and managers are continually at risk.
- Put yourself first, your employer second.
- Learn and apply Bulletproof Executive success strategies.
- Develop your contingency plans and always have fall-back options.
- With contingency plans in place, develop and enjoy a greater sense of personal security.
- There is no such thing as job security!

2

The Four Triggers Of Executive Failure

In the 1980s there was a huge stigma about being fired from work. Hushed conversations at dinner parties about 'John losing his job' were accompanied by speculation as to what had really happened. John was seen as having an 'illness' which might be catching. Avoid John, don't talk about it and it might just go away! Poor John didn't know what to do. His job defined his position in life, much of his reason for being. His confidence was shattered. But at least there were plenty of other vacancies in the 1980s.

Today, with tens of thousands of executives and managers having lost their jobs over the past few years, the stigma fortunately is far less. We all know people who are out of work and many of them never really know what hit them. Restructuring, a merger, a new chief executive, new technology, not fitting in, or 'a need for new blood' are often the stated reasons.

'But why me?' the exiting executive asks. 'Where do I go to today, with so many other executives and managers out of work?' Sponsored by their former employers, departing staff can go to a career management and outplacement firm like Davidson & Associates (the leaders in this field in Australia and the Asia-Pacific region) with whose assistance there is every probability that they will target and attain their next career steps within a few short months.

'But need it have happened in the first place? How can I make sure it doesn't happen again?' Based on my work with over 300 executives and managers over more than five years as a career management and outplacement consultant, and as verified by an 85-member Executive Panel, I have found that the reasons for career success and failure centre around a range of quite complex factors. I will now reveal what I perceive to be the four main triggers of executive and managerial failure, and later I will detail the essential strategies for career success.

The Bulletproof Executive is not a myth but a reality, if individuals put into practice the principles and approaches revealed in this book.

The First Trigger: Job Performance

'George Stratton runs our Consumer Division. He never went to business school, and it shows. He doesn't seem to understand or apply the basic principles of accountability, responsibility, authority, delegation and motivation, let alone plan, coordinate and monitor the performance of his team — he just lets it happen. Also I doubt if he understands what the primary "drivers" of performance are in his business unit, let alone the emerging trends and projections in the market place. He should have remained in sales where he personally excelled. Once a salesman, always a salesman. But it's probably too late to turn the clock back. I fear for his survival as a general manager, and I doubt if he ever really wanted the job.'

Yes, even the most basic management principles and practices can be missing at the executive or manager level, but you do not have to go to business school to learn them. Short courses abound, but there has to be at least some basic motivation and organisational support to bring new knowledge back to the workplace and convert it into applied skills. There also has to be quality time devoted to the process of staff management, which in itself can be a challenge, given the shortage of time in today's climate of 'doing more with less, faster'.

Compounding this, over the past few years, spans of control for executives and managers — the number of staff directly reporting to them — have increased and widened substantially, as a result of decentralisation and the 'de-layering' of organisations. This means, in effect, that there is a danger of the manager being spread too thin and spending a disproportionate amount of time on non-essential matters.

This, coupled with a failure to prioritise the primary 'drivers' of the business — be they financial, physical or human (usually a combination of the three), can result in the executive or manager operating across too broad a front, rather than being focused on the main result areas. They often fail to succeed as a result.

The Duck's Foot Pistol
The Duck's Foot or 'Mob' Pistol was designed in the 1700s. It had four barrels each set at an angle, so that 25 to 35 degrees of horizontal spread was attained. The four barrels simultaneously fired four .45 calibre heavy lead slugs and offered adequate fire-power to defend against a gang at close range.

The pistol was highly effective in this regard and was used by ship's captains, bank guards and prison officers whose ongoing survival and success depended on defence against a range of adversaries at any one time, much like today's executive or manager and the four triggers of executive failure!

Additionally, with all the organisational change and restructuring which has been occurring and which will continue to accelerate as we move towards the year 2000, executives and managers can often become too inward-looking within the organisation and fail to realise what is developing in their external environment, be this at the customer or competitor level.

The fast-developing environment within which the organisation operates presents opportunities and threats, and resources and priority attention need to be dedicated to the assessment of these external 'futures' and the development of appropriate business strategies. *However, less than 20 per cent of executive and manager dismissals, excluding genuine job redundancies, are triggered by straight job performance inadequacies in the areas I have described. More than 80 per cent of failures result from one or more of three other triggers described later in this chapter.*

Finally, many executives and managers fail to attract and develop staff of the highest calibre available, as a result of:

- selection and development practices which do not ensure 'career alignment' — the alignment of the goals of the individual with the goals of the organisation
- a draconian 'slash-and-burn' approach to downsizing and staff reductions
- a 'hire-and-fire' mentality towards staff.

Clearly, executives and managers need to ensure the organisation has a favourable public image and is a sought-after employer in order to attract talent — the starting point of exceptional job performance for individuals *and* their line managers.

The Second Trigger: Personal Performance

> 'Marian Shorter heads up our Technical Support function. She seems to perform satisfactorily in terms of business results. However, Marian seems to have "reached a plateau" in her personal performance. She coasts through the week, often arriving quite late and leaving early, and she doesn't seem particularly motivated either. I'm not sure what's going on, but I think she may be bored, unchallenged and needing a change. We've always valued her contributions in the past, and if we don't do something quickly, I think she might leave. I think she's in the wrong job and worried about her future career with us.'

The second trigger of failure is when the executive or manager is perceived not to be performing at their personal best. The business results may be there, but the individual seems not to be giving of their all and is perceived as 'going through the motions' at work. Self-motivation seems to be the problem. Left unattended, the situation can deteriorate into a separation, be this voluntary or involuntary.

On closer examination, the reasons for this second trigger of failure often relate to the fact that the individual's main occupational interests are not represented in the job. We all have different interests — for some it may be helping people; for others it may be being persuasive; for others, problem-solving. If your interests — what you ideally like to do — are not to be found in your job, then job satisfaction can be adversely affected, as well as self-motivation and personal performance.

The same can be said of your capabilities — what you excel at. If the capabilities you were born with, or which you have developed over the years — and, in particular, those capabilities you enjoy using ('motivational capabilities') — are not represented in the job, then the situation can again deteriorate in terms of job satisfaction and self-motivation. Capabilities include numeracy, fluency, reasoning ability and several other categories.

The same is the case with your values — what you believe in. Values are the beliefs we uphold at work, at home and in the way we live. Integrity, security, financial success and a range of other values can exist in differing mosaics in us all. If our values are not upheld in our work, dissatisfaction often results. These values become less negotiable as the years unfold and so are particularly significant at the executive and managerial level. Additionally, most people these days perceive their employers with mistrust. 'The days of the career for life employer are over.' 'Cradle to grave is a thing of the past.'

Yet, ironically, executives and managers usually spend more time planning their holidays or home extensions than their careers. Few have replaced mistrust and a sense of vulnerability, with a sense of personal confidence and control, through career direction and 'ownership'.

The missing ingredients so often are the tools for personal career planning and necessary self-development, which together can make senior people impervious to the vagaries of organisational life and continuously employable (no matter who your future employer may be!). Developing a sense of control over your own career destiny in this way, significantly improves self-motivation and personal performance with your current employer.

The Third Trigger: Change Management

'Ron Clarke runs our manufacturing plant. Ron's just fine if things simply roll along and remain the same. Where Ron has difficulties, is when we have to make internal changes as a result of what's happening in the economy or market place. He resists change because he feels exposed and he can't seem to manage his team well at times of restructuring and uncertainty. I don't think he's flexible enough, and he's neither persuasive nor convincing when communicating with groups. Also, I think his engineering background causes him to be too risk averse. And from time to time it all gets to him and he just appears to give up and go back to the old ways of doing things. How can we centralise and restructure the group while Ron's at the helm of manufacturing?'

Change is here to stay. Technology has accelerated the various phases of the organisational life cycle — start-up, early growth, subsequent growth, the adolescent/turbulent years, maturity and decline. Change in organisations has advanced faster than anyone's expectations and will continue to do so. This, coupled with the return to the core competencies of the organisation, process re-engineering, mergers, acquisitions and divestments, and never-ending changes in the external market place, have meant that change is a major part of ongoing organisational life.

Executives have to be able to embrace change personally rather than resist it, and to lead others at times of change, uncertainty and turbulence. Indeed, executives and managers have to be 'leaders of change'. Yet, how many executives and managers are born with these characteristics, and how many have had help from their organisations in developing the required competencies? What are these leadership of change competencies? Where do you start?

Certainly adaptability will help, as will more of an entrepreneurial approach. A dogged streak of perseverance when the going gets rough will also be needed as organisations continue to flex and adapt to the fast-developing external environment. Additionally, understanding the various phases of restructures and how to manage them requires competencies very much in vogue for as far into the future as anyone can see.

Leaders of change always need to prioritise the human factor, avoiding staff dismissals whenever possible and continuously seeking to select, align and retain talent. An organisation, its executives and managers are only as effective as their people.

Finally, leaders of change require skills in proactive, open, two-way communication. This includes group as well as individual communication. At times of change, in particular, executives and managers need to be able to generate presentation impact in the way they communicate with groups. However, most presenters concentrate too much on the 'content' of their speeches and too little on 'delivery' — the real driver of impact. In fact, delivery accounts for more than 90 per cent of the group presentation success formula.

The Fourth Trigger: Chemistry and Fit

> 'Joan Robinson runs our Hospital Division. We thought she was fairly conventional and she looked as though she'd fit in, when we interviewed her. Now, some four months later, I'm beginning to wonder. I don't think she likes our fairly assertive management style and organisational culture, and I think she wants more autonomy than the CEO is prepared to give any of us. You know we are a fairly conservative and traditional group of executives. The way she sometimes behaves is too academic, too textbook and too naive. Her behaviour in this context is so different to the rest of us and we do have a fairly political environment here, which can be very hard if you don't carry much influence. I know we'll all persevere with her, but I'm still concerned about her future with us.'

In looking at chemistry and fit, in addition to whether the executive or manager 'fits' in the conventional sense, the organisation's culture and management style, or 'atmospherics', need to meet the expectations and needs of the individual in order to maximise personal effectiveness. For example, if the bureaucrat tries to develop a career in an entrepreneurial environment, or the entrepreneur in a government bureaucracy, they don't fit.

It goes further than this, in fact. Atmospherics also include material benefits, interpersonal relationships and the need to achieve. If individual motivational needs in these areas are not met, it can cause a negative and even stressful reaction on the part of the individual, which is then perceived by others to be a chemistry or fit problem.

Secondly, organisations often expect quite specific types of traits in their executives and managers, often seeking 'modern' leadership traits to help propel them into the future, and at the same time discarding, via dismissals, the 'old' style of leadership traits. Modern leadership traits include a visionary approach, open-mindedness, a customer service orientation, and an emphasis on developing people. Old-style traits often are more autocratic, bureaucratic, unaccepting of diversity in people, and emphasising supply and production.

Executives and managers also need to be perceived to be making a significant contribution to the team, by exhibiting and adding value through different personal operating styles, perspectives and viewpoints to their colleagues. Yet so often we see the case of the 'mirror-image' effect at times of hiring — the CEO recruits an executive of similar operating style, causing in the worst case scenario a cloning of the executive team. Initially, the new recruit may well 'fit' in the team, but as the months go by the individual's team contributions may not be seen to add significant value — too much 'me too'.

Time and again, researchers reveal that the best-performing senior executive teams are balanced in terms of the operating style of the members — some, perhaps, great analysts, others more creative in their approach, others more results-oriented, and yet others focusing on the human perspective. But even *with* balanced team composition, some team members seem preoccupied with jousting with each other — a potentially destructive rather than synergistic activity — whereas others just sit on the fence!

Finally, executives and managers may fail to understand or respond appropriately to organisational politics, power and influence. For example, they often fail to realise that those in real power may not be those in the senior ranks. In this way they may also fail to sell themselves, to develop a supportive network of allies and to negotiate their way to success.

Like it or not, politics, power and influence are alive and well in even the most results-oriented environment, and executives and managers need to learn how to play this game constructively, and win!

SUMMARY

Chapter 2 raises the following key issues:

- The four triggers of executive and managerial failure are job performance (business results), personal performance (self-motivation), change management, and chemistry and fit.
- Job performance accounts for less than 20 per cent of these potential failure factors and is at risk if staff management practices, 'primary business drivers' and external 'futures' are not prioritised, or if in the first place, talented people are not attracted, retained and developed in ways which align their personal goals with the goals of the organisation.
- Personal performance can be at an optimum when an individual's occupational interests, motivational capabilities and values are represented in the job and working environment, and where the executive or manager has developed a sense of career destiny and control.
- Change management — a relatively new executive and managerial function — requires expertise in managing restructures, as well as competencies in the areas of adaptability, entrepreneurism, perseverance, and proactive, open, two-way communication (one-on-one and with groups, where the process of delivery is even more important than the content).
- Chemistry and fit, the most complex area, requires that the motivational needs of the individual are accommodated by the 'atmospherics' of the organisation, as far as possible.
- 'Modern' leadership traits also need to be exhibited by senior people, as do personal value-added contributions to mutually supportive teamwork.
- Finally, executives and managers need to sell themselves, network and negotiate their way to success in an environment wherein politics, power and influence still, and always will, flourish.

Further Resources

Section 1 of your *Executive Armoury*, which you will find at the back of the book, provides a risk assessment exercise for the four triggers of executive failure, which will help you to determine which chapters you should read first.

PART TWO

Armour-plated Strategies For Career Success

Armour-plating — Protection for human resources liable to come under fire, originally in the form of heavy and cumbersome armour, but now in lightweight and flexible material affording maximum protection and counter-attack efficacy.

3

Improving Your Job Performance — Business Results!

> 'Robert Johnson is chief executive of our plastics company. He has that uncanny knack of knowing where to look and what to concentrate on, to tease every last ounce of financial performance from his business unit, without draining it. Additionally, the fact that he manages his people and operations well, and is able to predict future trends in our market and industry, undoubtedly explains how he has been able to develop and grow the company over the past three years, with exceptional bottom-line performance.'

According to Greek mythology, Midas, King of Phrygia in Asia Minor, wished that everything he touched be turned to gold. This wish was granted by Dionysus, god of wine. Unfortunately, wishing does not seem to get the same results for executives and managers, yet some of them do seem to have an uncanny knack of being able to generate superb profits in the world of business! To do this requires capacities in the areas of management practices, business 'drivers' and external 'futures'.

Management Practices

Most executives have had some type of management training and development, and 'management' is one of the most widely written-about subjects in business texts the world over. At the end of the day, it must be remembered and realised that in working with over 300 executives, I have found it is the *basic* management practices which can either make or break executives when it comes to job performance and business results. However, with the corporate restructurings and downsizings which have flourished over the past few years, most executives and managers find themselves having to 'do more, with less, faster', creating huge time management pressures, and often causing the 'basics' of good management to be neglected.

Bruce Robertson, trustee of the Royal Botanic Gardens and director of a number of community and sports boards, and previously chairman of the Zoological Parks Board of NSW and executive general manager, divisional general manager and subsidiary director of James Hardie Industries, places a different emphasis on staff management practices. He broadens the topic to 'people' management practices and remarks: 'Modern business will use less staff (ie full-time company paid) and more consultants, contractors, part-time and outsourcing of work. Therefore, it's the successful handling of people in general, rather than control of staff, which will be important.'

Here are the descriptions of the basic management practices of planning, organising, monitoring, decision-making, motivating, delegating and a new core management competence. However, John Matthews, deputy general manager group human resources, Commonwealth Bank, provides a word of caution: 'Good practices can produce good managers, but over-attention to process can stifle leaders.'

Planning

The best planner I have come across is Rosemary Langton, chief executive of a regional airline in Europe. In running an organisation with complex logistics, customer and regulatory requirements, Rosemary has to be adept at planning, including objective setting and the strategies to accomplish them.

With her management team, Rosemary specifies what is to be attained, and how, and takes into account required physical, financial and human resources. She anticipates problems in progressing from planning to implementation. Rosemary personally monitors, controls and reviews monthly progress as each annual departmental plan is implemented, and ensures the update of plans according to progress, making any necessary changes. Objectives are quantified and address: what, when, where, why, how much, how often and by what means? In establishing budgets, Rosemary ensures they are stretching yet attainable.

Rather than being too rigid, Rosemary allows plans to be adjusted as they are implemented, according to prevailing or projected external circumstances: the economy, the market, competition and customers — all so volatile in the airline industry. She ensures departmental plans are complete and coincide with overall corporate goals and objectives. She also makes sure staff are involved in the planning process, thereby buying ownership of them, and so that they understand what is expected of them in terms of implementation.

Finally, when asked to comment on the key elements of successful business planning, Rosemary offered the following points:

* Being proactive rather than reactive — in other words, projecting and planning for external changes, rather than being caught on the back foot and having to react to them.
* Plans need to specify not only where the organisation is headed but how it will get there. This includes a mission or purpose statement, objectives and goals, strategies, principles and policies, processes and methods.
* Planning needs to be ongoing rather than a once-off or annual event. Continuous monitoring of performance and external factors will require plans to be modified as they are implemented.
* Those involved in the planning process need to be good conceptualisers with a capacity to think about the future and unknown territory. They also need to be creative and to think outside of convention, 'outside the square'. An external perspective is also needed — an understanding of where the company currently resides in the industry and market place and where it plans to reside in the future.
* Successful planning requires top management commitment of the necessary time and resources for planning, and this commitment needs to be communicated to all staff, who should feel involved in the planning process.

❖ The best plans consider both effectiveness and efficiency, the former focusing on outcomes and achievements, the latter on inputs and processes.

Organising

Harold Limmer served his time in the armed forces before moving into the private sector defence industry. He now heads up the sales, services and support group of a major aircraft weapons systems supplier. In advising Harold about future career directions I undertook a multi-level survey of his management practices and found that his peers, superiors and direct reports rated him highly in his organisational ability.

In terms of organisation, Harold ensures that all relevant parties understand the structure and reporting relationships, which are designed to organise people in the most effective, efficient and yet flexible manner to attain desired goals and objectives. Rather than the more 'rigid' structure with which Harold was well acquainted earlier in his career in the army, he ensures maximum flexibility and cross-fertilisation, relying heavily on multi-disciplinary project teams and matrix management. However, with these approaches he has long since recognised that clarity of organisational and reporting relationships is a prerequisite for success.

The vital theme of coordination is enhanced by Harold ensuring that all parties understand who is responsible for what and who is accountable to whom, with those responsible and accountable having the necessary authority to attain their goals and objectives. Jobs are well defined but 'broad-banded' and flexible enough for individuals to adapt to changing operating conditions.

Harold makes sure that span of control — the number and types of job positions reporting to each line manager — is neither too broad (a common complaint in the 1990s and causing the manager to be spread too thin) nor too narrow (causing replication of work and effort). Also, he makes sure that people are clear about with whom they need to liaise and to whom they report, be this reporting in 'line' (to their boss), liaising in a 'functional capacity' (with any functional specialist who may be responsible for how the function is performed), or liaising within 'matrix'-based teams, so often used in the sales and service environment.

Harold ensures that opportunities for delegation are maximised, but avoids 'abdication'; that organisational arrangements maximise morale; and that teams are comprised of people with different operating styles, rather than 'clones' of the leader. Finally, Harold's teams feel empowered, encouraged as far as possible to be self-directing, with a clear understanding of the role of the leader, who often acts as a resource and facilitator, rather than as a proactive 'micro manager' of the 'old style'.

Monitoring

Georgina Reynolds heads up sales and customer service in one of Canada's largest telecommunications groups. I had the opportunity of once sitting in on a training session led by Georgina for new sales and service team leaders. This is what she had to say about monitoring, by way of introduction to a half-day training session on the subject, as part of a new supervisor's training program:

'Monitoring of progress ensures that goals and objectives are attained according to plan and is orientated towards **preventing** *problems, rather than having to* **solve** *problems.*

Preventative monitoring helps your sales and customer service staff know in advance what is expected of them in terms of quality, quantity, time and cost. It also enables them to know their job parameters: scope of responsibility, authority and accountability; policies and procedures; availability of support and advice; relationships with others — in a way which offers them maximum freedom to achieve, rather than confinement.

Maintenance monitoring focuses on major result areas signalling when progress to plan is adverse, major result areas being specific and including orders, units, errors, complaints, dollar volumes and dollar costs. As you are aware, each member of staff has up to nine major result areas in our organisation.

Preventative and maintenance monitoring takes the form of your on-the-job supervision; concentration on major result areas; systematic, periodic and random personal inspection; management by exception; and taking action when it is needed through your staff.

The individual performance standards for each major result area are established and agreed between you and your staff, coincide with overall corporate objectives, and have to be specific. Our performance appraisal processes regularly monitor individual performance compared to these standards, identifying development needs and enhancing the further deployment of strengths.

Development needs of staff are quickly and effectively met through necessary counselling, coaching or training, which is your responsibility, backed by our training and development specialists.'

Decision-making

I once had the opportunity to appraise the performance of several competing teams in a residential management course based on a rather complex computer-based business case study. I was particularly interested in comparing the decision-making approaches of the various teams. The following summarises how decisions were made in the winning team, and based on my experience of 'real life' situations, I believe these approaches represent good value. The following is in fact an extract from the final report the winning team wrote on what they had learned about decision-making during the case study:

'Decision-making seems to be most effective when it is selecting a course of action from a **variety** *of alternatives.*

Decision-making starts with fully defining and understanding the problem or opportunity and collecting all the available facts that may impact directly or indirectly on the decision. These facts need to be analysed, evaluated and interpreted in the context of the problem or opportunity.

A range of solutions to the problem or options for exploiting the opportunity is developed, and alternative potential decisions addressed. These are compared and ranked, the overall ranking determining the decision.

In defining a problem, the root causes as opposed to the symptoms need to be addressed, and in collecting the facts, they have to be true and valid facts, rather than guesses, opinions or lies.

In examining the possible solutions, creative, "outside the square" thinking is encouraged, problems and opportunities are shared, and all relevant parties are encouraged to contribute in the decision-making process.

In fact, it seems a "bottom up" as well as a "top down" approach to decision-making makes most sense, and we can see this approach as being particularly successful in the corporate setting.'

Motivating

Earlier in my career I worked for an American-owned food company which was one of the most motivated work environments I can recall. In examining why motivation levels were so high, I am able to conclude the following:

- From the chief executive down, management style seemed to enhance the self-motivation of direct reports and others, the executives having created an operational climate of trust and integrity encouraging personal development and advancement.
- Management style was more democratic than autocratic, and was consultative, participative and delegating.
- Employees were satisfied with their remuneration levels and were interested in, and satisfied with, the breadth and content of their jobs, finding them responsible and meaningful.
- Employees were recognised in public for a job well done, and were counselled in private when they were not attaining their standards of performance.
- Employees felt themselves to be achieving their own goals as they achieved corporate goals. In other words, there was a strong alignment between the future of the individual and the future of the company. In this, employees also felt informed and involved in planning and decision-making.
- Employees felt free to monitor themselves and to accomplish goals and objectives within defined parameters, and experienced a sense of self-direction and empowerment in so doing.

❖ Finally, an egalitarian atmosphere prevailed. Anyone could approach and talk to the managing director on first name terms. There was *one* cafeteria for all, *one* first-come-first-served car park, an open plan office environment with workstations and no doors on the few offices used by senior executives, and all clocked in and out on time cards (including the managing director!), winning a 10 per cent good timekeeping bonus in so doing!

Delegating

Helen Spencer runs a large government department, having previously held a range of management positions in several government agencies. She is an excellent delegator, and she allowed me to interview her and develop the following guidelines based on her delegating techniques.

> *'I believe that effective delegation is probably one of the most important management functions in running large organisations. All the other functional areas of planning, organising, monitoring and so forth can only be effective if the manager is a capable delegator.*
>
> *I see delegation as a four-step approach: decide what needs to be delegated (and in this context "more" rather than "less" can and should be delegated in most cases); decide to whom the responsibility for such activities should be delegated; explain the reasons for and objectives of the delegated responsibility; and provide sufficient resources and authority for the responsibility to be carried through and for the required activities to be accomplished.*
>
> *Based on my experience, some of the rules for effective delegation include:*
>
> - *Only delegate if you are prepared to take some risks, which can be minimised through effective monitoring.*
>
> - *Only delegate when you are prepared to put in sufficient time and effort to make delegation work successfully.*
>
> - *Delegate in those areas where you are conducting activities which do not use your greatest competencies and capabilities.*
>
> - *Delegate to save time which can be used on activities which cannot be undertaken by direct reports.*
>
> - *Delegate only when you have confidence in your direct reports to assume delegated responsibilities and accomplish the required activities.*
>
> - *Delegate to improve the involvement of your direct reports which can enhance their motivation and personal performance.*

* *Delegate in order to develop your direct reports for increased responsibilities.*

* *Provide sufficient authority to the direct report to whom you are delegating and define the parameters of this authority.*

* *Establish priorities and time-lines for completion of tasks and for progress reports.*

* *Relinquish sufficient control for your direct reports to buy ownership of your delegation and to have freedom to act.*

In my experience as a senior executive, manager and administrator, effective delegation throughout the organisation frees up the bottlenecks and allows executives to concentrate on higher-level matters, for which after all, they are being paid an executive salary. Providing these guidelines are followed at all levels, the organisation can move forward with greater involvement, commitment, speed and effect.'

The New Core Competence for Effective Staff Management

Of course, some models of required management competencies go even further than what I have addressed here — planning, organising, delegating, monitoring, decision-making and motivating — and include such elements as:

- leadership, participation and personal assertiveness
- interpersonal skills, influence and discipline
- initiative, controlling and communicating
- time management and personal and subordinate development.

All of these competency areas are in fact addressed elsewhere in this book, where I have been able to position them within other key subject areas for greater impact and relevance, rather than representing them as just one long list. Even the six competencies I have discussed in this chapter are quite difficult for executives to prioritise and concentrate on, given all the other pressures of organisational life. Accordingly, I have examined the principal causes of success and failure by executives and management in the area of management practices, and I have been able to consolidate my findings into one new core competence for effective staff management: *motivational delegation*.

Motivational delegation embraces three main themes: the individual executive or manager delegating to direct reports effectively, creating a motivational environment, and the organisation creating a motivational environment.

The individual executive or manager delegating to direct reports effectively

The key success ingredients comprise those articulated by Helen Spencer earlier.

The individual executive or manager creating a motivational environment

The key success ingredients for this include:

- selecting and developing staff on the basis of a strong work ethic and high personal standards in terms of results
- creating challenging jobs which in themselves create satisfaction, enjoyment and self-motivation
- developing an external image and internal identity of the organisation based on clearly articulated values, principles, mission and goals, with which employees can identify enthusiastically and in which they can visualise their own success
- encouraging employees to be involved in goal-setting (which buys their ownership of such goals and enhances their self-esteem), offering freedom to, and support in accomplishing such goals, especially where their own goals coincide with the goals of the organisation
- creating a positive, active and mutually involving working environment, with a sense of dynamism, progression and 'change for the best', with a commitment to excellence and winning, and encouraging a sense of self-direction and empowerment
- creating an environment where personal power (which is earned) and influence (which is also earned) prevail, rather than formal authority (which is often mandated)
- praising in public, and counselling and taking action for poor performance in private, each *at the time* such performance is recognised, and with consistency in terms of application across all direct reports
- meeting the motivational needs of each individual as far as possible, be they *material* (remuneration, safety and security), *structural* (degree and type of structure, bureaucracy and systems), *behavioural* (management style and interpersonal relationships), or *emotional* (trust, social, self-esteem and self-realisation)
- creating an environment where the executive or manager's style is based on integrity, is more democratic than autocratic, is consultative, participative and delegating.

The organisation creating a motivational environment

The key success ingredients for this include:

- a deliberate and continuous attempt to establish and develop an egalitarian climate wherein status differences are minimised
- while reporting lines and authority are understood well, cooperation and a team-based ethos is even more apparent and promoted
- open two-way communication prevails both laterally and vertically
- job specifications and grades are broad-banded to maximise flexibility, cooperation and teamwork
- spans of control are never so narrow as to impose a regime of very close top-down management and supervision
- shared values and aligned goals are emphasised, as is group-based decision-making

* a climate of trust, fairness and co-operation prevails — employees trust each other and their managers (whom they perceive to be fair)
* creating an environment where mutually supportive teamwork helps people to synergise and have more effect *co-operatively* than they would otherwise have *independently*
* creating an operational climate which encourages personal development and advancement
* creating an environment where the management style in the organisation maximises self-motivation, morale and productivity.

Motivational delegation is summarised in the model in Figure 3.1, which needs to be examined twice: first, in the context of delegation and *the individual executive or manager* creating a motivational environment; and secondly, in the context of delegation and *the organisation* creating a motivational environment.

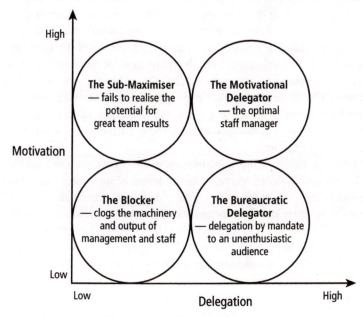

FIGURE 3.1
The New Core Management Competence:
Motivational Delegation

However, whether including yourself or your organisation in this analysis, your direct reports will always perceive *you* as the source of delegation and a creator or otherwise of a motivational environment. This is why the labels and descriptors in the model refer to you. Don't take offence. If there is a problem, it may in fact be caused by the organisation.

Finally, what do some of the members of the Executive Panel say about the components of my proposed new core management competence? Tony Harbour, independent management consultant and formerly group personnel director of the

Ocean Group PLC in the UK, comments: 'Although I ranked staff management practices as number ten, I see significant importance in the areas of motivation and delegation.'

Robert C Stephenson, my brother, who is local divisional manager of SCA Molnlycke AB in the UK, and previously managing director of Sancella Ltd and Northfleet Terminal of Scott Ltd, agrees: 'Delegation and motivation are clearly the key elements here.'

'Motivating and delegating are important. But it's difficult for highly focused managers to allow others freedom [to make errors],' comments Carol Limmer, chief manager, executive development and recognition, Commonwealth Bank of Australia.

Primary Business Drivers

'If pushed to choose a single factor, I believe I would opt for understanding the primary business drivers,' says Peter Herborn, group general manager, development of Tower Corporation Holding Limited in New Zealand, previously a partner of Deloitte Touche Tohmatsu. 'I suspect that if you have a clear view on these, you will at least have a chance of achieving the required ends of the organisation, even if this happens without all the preferred style or finesse. If you keep focused on these ends, then you will adapt your behaviour according to the circumstances of the moment.'

One of the biggest problems in business today is the breadth of responsibility held by most executives and managers, exacerbated by the stripping out of middle management positions. Whereas in days gone by, management science suggested that seven direct subordinates (each representing a discrete management function) was about an ideal span of control, it is not uncommon today to see senior executives with a dozen or more direct reports.

Even if an executive or manager has a smaller team than this, compare today's breadth of additional responsibility to ten years ago in terms of such time consumers as equal employment, age discrimination, unfair dismissal, protection of the environment, enterprise bargaining, occupational health and safety, quality accreditation and so forth. The list goes on and on and is seemingly endless. Senior people often feel spread too thin. Time and effort is dispersed across too broad a front. Primary business drivers are insufficiently attended to, as secondary business drivers and time consumers predominate.

Clearly, executives and managers need to withstand being sucked into this vortex, determine what the principal business objective is and devote maximum time, effort and resources to the primary business drivers which will best deliver this objective. 'It is essential to understand the business, and in particular, your role in contributing to business success. It is pointless being a good leader, motivator or role model if the business is going backwards,' says Michael T Duffy, senior manager group human resources at the Commonwealth Bank of Australia.

Paul Lilley, general manager human resources (Australian Banking Group), Westpac, formerly human resources director, Rothmans Asia, explains: 'To me, this is probably the biggest determinant of likely success in an organisation: the ability to understand the breadth of the business environment in which one operates, identify the priority issues and get on and fix them. This does not, however, mean that by definition one only recruits people who have a knowledge of one's industry — paradoxically they are often too close to the issues to make the more difficult calls. The broader definition of this factor would be around a method of thinking: the ability to gather relevant information, sift out the important facts and focus activity in the most appropriate area.'

Bruce Coates, general manager employee relations Ampol, believes an understanding and application of primary business drivers is critical. 'If you don't have these sorted out, you'll waste a lot of time and energy doing the less important things.'

'Concentrate on the important, not the urgent!' says John Baker, independent consultant and associate of Davidson & Associates, previously president Australia and New Zealand of Marion Merell Dow Pty Limited.

Developing this further, what is your single most important business objective right now or in your last executive or managerial position? You are only allowed one objective, the most important one! What are the two main drivers of your principal business objective — in other words, the two activity and result areas which will have the greatest impact on attaining your principal business objective? Which secondary drivers drive your two main drivers? Which supporting drivers drive your secondary business drivers? Which of all these drivers, if prioritised, can be most improved and will have the greatest impact on your principal business objective?

This approach, which I refer to as the Hierarchy of Business Drivers, leads to a better understanding of the *primary* business drivers, usually found at the secondary, or other supporting levels, which can have the greatest impact on overall business results.

'Profit is not a dirty word — drivers of business performance consistent with a desired strategic outcome, has to be Number One,' says John Marlay, chief general manager, Australian Building Materials Division, Pioneer International.

Section 3 of the *Executive Armoury* contains a complete example of how primary business driver analysis can work to your advantage.

Futures

The same reasons which prevent executives and managers from determining and concentrating on primary business drivers — too much to do, too much an internal focus on time-consuming activities, being spread too thin — prevent many of the same individuals from remaining alert to the emerging changes external to their organisations.

'Becoming too inward looking is dangerous,' remarks Meredith Hellicar, managing director TNT Logistics Asia, previously executive director of the NSW Coal Association. Greg Brinkley, state director Queensland of Davidson & Associates and previously deputy general manager of the Queensland Federation of Industry, agrees: 'My observations suggest to me that managers can become too "standing on the shores looking inward instead of outward".'

'It is imperative that we understand the external environment and how we fit in. The person or firm who can capitalise first on changes, will win,' says Rob McPaul, human resources director Australasia, Reckitt and Colman. Bruce Coates, general manager employee relations Ampol agrees: 'It is difficult to allocate the time, but essential for long-term survival and success.'

'Forecasting and adjusting for the future is a key role for CEOs — and a role often only CEOs can play,' says Tony Thirlwell, chief executive of Tourism New South Wales, previously managing director of the Australian Tourism Commission.

In these rapidly changing times, we can no longer assume that past trends will repeat themselves in some predictable cycle. It is highly likely that the future will bear little or no resemblance to the past. In order to assess futures, we must look forward, not backwards, to try to get an idea of where the future opportunities will be in the context of several external areas: *technological*, *economic*, *political*, *social*, *customers* and *competition*.

Technology

There seems to be no disputing the fact that the rapid growth of technology is having, and will continue to have, a dramatic impact on executive management. What new kinds of businesses will new technologies create? Where will future business opportunities lie? Which sectors will experience growth in the years ahead? Which sectors will experience decline?

The impact of technological change must be viewed in relation to your own organisation and executive and managerial aspirations. For example, the continuously increasing trend towards automation in offices and factories has shifted the focus from manual to mental skills. Specialised knowledge, skills and decision-making abilities are in demand more than ever, and those organisations and individuals possessing and developing them will hold the power, as others come to depend on their expertise.

How can you make sure that you will be ready to respond to the technological and indeed other changes when they arrive? You can do this by keeping a close watch on the environment for 'signals'. The futures model in Figure 3.2 illustrates the stages of technological advance but is relevant to any aspect of 'futures'.

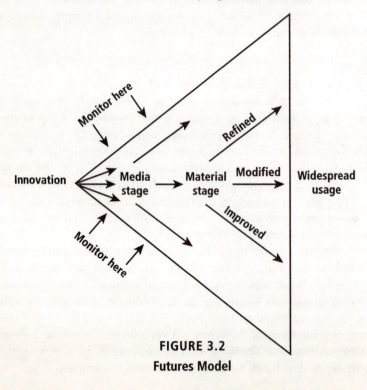

FIGURE 3.2
Futures Model

It commences with *innovation*, when someone or a company develops some form of breakthrough or discovery. Next is the *media stage* when it is written up in publications, papers, or other forms of print and media (for example, radio and TV announcements). This is the time to be alert and monitoring such indicators of future developments.

Next is the *material stage* when prototypes, models or pilot batches take the innovation concept to a more material form, often a test launch or limited initial release. Again, careful monitoring is needed. The next stage is that the material form becomes *refined, modified* or made more *effective*, and indeed is produced and made available on a wider scale. The final stage is *widespread usage* — in other words, market acceptance, and by now it is history!

By monitoring at the *media stage*, and then at the *material stage*, you may well be able to predict futures, to your own and your company's advantage.

Thus the impact of innovation can be determined years before it actually affects your business or yourself in any major way. All it takes is to be aware of developments around you, stay up to date with your reading, talk to people who are involved with technology and other forms of innovation, and know what the predictions are and how they may affect your business plans or you. Constant monitoring is essential, in order to plan effectively to take advantage of future business and personal opportunities.

Economic variables

Economic variables in the environment can certainly affect business performance, as some of us are painfully aware today. For example, a prolonged recession causes many people who might otherwise upgrade their buying patterns and behaviour, to stay put. It is precisely in times like these that previous contingency planning pays off, because it provides options not available to those who neglected to plan ahead. Knowing how to prepare for economic conditions will lessen the chances of your organisation or yourself being 'left out in the cold' when hard times hit, or when the economy swings upward again.

In looking at the economic environment, we are basically looking at those factors which influence the demand for your products or services, their supply from other sources, and the competition for marketing them in the economy. Too many executives ignore the fact of economic cycles when business planning. In good times the tendency is to reap the benefits of demand with little concern for the future. Then, when the hard times hit and the demand falls off, there is a struggle to develop new products and services, which should have been developed earlier in anticipation of a downturn in the cycle. This all takes its toll in time, money and frustration. Economic cycles and a variation in demand are a fact of life.

Political variables

In developing business plans, it is becoming more and more necessary to take into account political and legal implications. As we are all aware, the various levels of government are affecting our lives to an ever-increasing degree. For example, tax legislation has a great influence on personal lifestyles and business performance. It can also affect such business decisions as whether or not to develop and launch new products.

Social variables

Environmental shifts in social attitudes, behaviour and values should be taken into account in business planning. Understanding social trends puts the executive or manager in a better position to take advantage of potential business opportunities. For example, we see an increasing number of dual-career marriages, where the career plans of one partner must take into account the career aspirations of the other. We also see a switching of 'breadwinner'/'housekeeper' roles, with more men tending families while women provide the family income. Such social trends can affect your business performance, but should be seen as opportunities rather than threats, with careful business planning and full consideration of futures.

'I believe social fabric and environment should be added to futures, not only local and national, but international, as we live in a world which technology has made so small,' adds Bruce Robertson, trustee of the Royal Botanic Gardens and director of several boards.

Customers

The life-blood of any commercial organisation, customers — and their requirements from your organisation — are also affected by the four external areas already mentioned. Being aware of the impact and how it converts into customer demand is perhaps the single most important area relating to futures. Continuous customer monitoring and evaluation is needed, rather than an assumption that they will continue to purchase your products or services in the same or increasing volume as in the past and through the same methods of distribution.

'The area of "futures" has always been a problem with production-driven businesses, especially as they attempt to become more market driven without adequate marketing resources,' comments Donald Ross, general manager Sydney Ports Corporation, and previously managing director of Stegbar. This applies to small business, too. Take the example of food products. The increasing tendency of dual-career marriages has created exponential demand for eating out, fast food and pre-prepared dishes. An example of this in Australia is the launch of freshly prepared and packaged fruit salads and ready to heat and eat meals, now available at the supermarket.

Competition

Competition is also affected by all these external factors, in terms of competitor responses to the changing market place, and their reactions to your organisation as a competitor. Unless you are carefully tracking your competitors, it is only a matter of time before you get caught out. Yet it is surprising how poor competitive intelligence can be, or how quickly it can become outdated. Continuous tracking is required both formally (perhaps via external specialists, who may be better placed to do this) and informally through the eyes and ears of customers, suppliers and staff.

'If you can't work out why your business should win, you can't win!' says Philip Twyman, finance director of General Accident plc, Scotland, previously chief general manager AMP Society.

SUMMARY

Chapter 3 raises the following key issues:

- Basic management principles and practices — so easily overlooked while operating in crisis mode (a phenomenon of many executives in the 1990s) — include:
  — planning, organising and monitoring
  — decision-making, motivating and delegating.
- Of these, delegating and motivating are by far the most significant in terms of optimising executive and managerial job performance, leading to the new core management competence of motivational delegation.
- Business 'drivers' are usually a combination of activities engaging financial, human and physical resources. Just what the primary drivers are in a given business situation often eludes even the most experienced executives, who, invariably 'spread too thin', find much of their available time preoccupied with low-priority rather than primary driver activities.
- 'Futures' are external to the organisation and include emerging changes in customer requirements, technology, research and development by competitors, and a range of other external threats and opportunities. Given today's pressures for organisational change, executive and managerial focus can often be too introspective rather than external, the tracking of futures requiring continuous commitment and priority attention.

Further Resources

A do-it-yourself multi-level survey is enclosed in Section 2 of your *Executive Armoury*, designed to help you assess your performance with regards to management practices, including motivational delegation. An example of how to go about identifying primary business drivers is provided in Section 3.

4

Improving Your Personal Performance — Self-motivation!

'Chris Dean runs our Customer Service Centre. She always goes that extra mile in terms of effort and hours worked. I don't know why she's so committed, but I think it's something to do with that expression "job fit". Clearly she enjoys her work, is inspired by its challenges and sees it almost as a way of life, not solely a job.'

Job fit is a prerequisite for job satisfaction, self-motivation and personal performance. When in place, job fit creates a situation where you look forward to going to work and are perceived to be 'giving of your all' rather than coasting or 'going through the motions' at work. Selection of job fit is critical for those considering changing their jobs or who have had that decision imposed upon them.

'Job fit is a critical consideration,' says Geoff Wright, former state director Western Australia, Davidson & Associates. 'You won't get hired unless there is a solid match, and for the individual, it should be spot on.'

'History tells us that any mistakes in job fit between the individual's capabilities and job demands will cost the individual and the organisation dearly — productivity, morale and so forth,' says Lawrie Horder, head of human resources, business financial services NSW and ACT, National Australia Bank.

This theme is developed further by Donald Ross, general manager of Sydney Ports Corporation: 'Jobs should not only be hard work, but should also be fun. Incorrect fit is not fun!' R V Matthews, human resources director of Goodman Fielder International, sees job fit in another light: 'I do not believe this ranks highly. Truly successful executives can weather poor job fits in their gathering of different experiences.'

It is interesting to note that of those hundreds of executives and managers with whom I have worked on outplacement programs, about half change industry sector, some one-third change job function, and about one-quarter go into some form of business for themselves (often contracting or counselling). In so doing, job fit is an essential success factor, and ensuring this occurs requires considerable forethought, as well as self and job analysis.

One of the most demanding challenges relating to this, is the plight of middle manager 'generalists' who have been leaving organisations in their droves, owing to flatter, more competitive structures, as well as personal computers replacing people in the monitoring of human performance. Such generalists often need to dig deep into their minds to work out their interests and transferable skills and where they are ideally headed job-wise, which is highly unlikely to be to other middle management generalist positions, most of which are gone forever. For them, therefore, it is all about selecting job fit — 'what new type of job will suit me best?'

'Recruitment consultants are interviewing managers every day; and the majority of managers are not gaining job satisfaction,' points out Graeme Duhs, managing director of Davidson & Associates Limited New Zealand, and formerly director of Cook Duhs & Associates Ltd, a recruitment consultancy.

Job fit depends on two very different components: the nature of the work itself, and the fit with certain personal characteristics. When these two components match each other, this generates outstanding fit, self-motivation and personal performance. The personal characteristics representing one side of the job fit formula include occupational interests, motivational capabilities and values. The nature of work representing the other side of the formula is described in the form of 12 discrete career areas.

Occupational Interests

As mentioned, one side of the job fit formula is personal characteristics, which include occupational interests. The 12 main occupational interest areas can be summarised as follows. (Note that these are *interests*, and not necessarily *abilities*, which are noted later.)

1. *Scientific:* an interest in facts, particularly relating to the natural sciences; a desire to work out how things occur, why they occur and what results from them; an interest in finding things out, perhaps by using laboratory techniques or doing research; and analytical and investigatory activities.
2. *Social:* an interest in people rather than things; an interest in listening to other people and a genuine concern for their troubles and problems; and an interest in supplying services which others need and will be happy to receive.
3. *Persuasive:* an interest in meeting and convincing people, and promoting your ideas, beliefs, projects or sales; an interest in influencing people in some way, their attitudes or behaviour; and an enjoyment in persuading people, in discussion, debate or argument.
4. *Literary:* an enjoyment of writing and words; an interest in any activity that needs the use of imaginative verbal descriptions; a love of books, reading or reciting; and an interest in writing or speaking originally and imaginatively.
5. *Artistic:* an enjoyment of visual art, design or drama; an interest in colour and artistic activities with a desire to create something of imagination or beauty; and a keen interest in your surroundings or in some aspect of design.
6. *Clerical:* an interest in administration, office or clerical work, often based on a routine requiring accuracy and precision; and an interest in recording and filing, coding and classifying, where detailed numerate, scientific or technical knowledge may not be needed to any great degree.
7. *Practical:* a liking of being 'good with your hands'; an interest in repairing and making things; a preference for learning by doing rather than by reading; a liking for working with tools and materials rather than with words; and an interest in constructing or building things.

8. *Musical:* an enjoyment of, or interest in, any type of music, playing musical instruments or singing; an enjoyment of listening to people play music; and a love of going to musical concerts, films or shows.
9. *Computational:* an interest in working with figures; an interest in dealing with numbers and mathematical problems and concepts; an interest in using mental arithmetic or formulae; and an interest in proving or disproving things with figures.
10. *Outside:* an interest in being or working outside, sometimes involving considerable physical activity and/or travel; a dislike of having to work inside the whole time, and of routine work or regularity; and an interest in animals, in growing crops or plants, or in moving from place to place.
11. *Technical:* an interest in work which entails dealing with anything technical, such as machines, engines, tools, computers, or electrical and electronic equipment; a preference for operating anything technical; and an interest in how and why technical items work.
12. *Medical:* an interest in medical and biological subjects; an interest in healing and caring for sick people; a desire to investigate the causes of and to relieve the effects of illness and disease; and an interest in various aspects of mental or physical health.

Clearly, some interests relate more to certain career areas than to others, and your major occupational interests need to be represented in your job to enhance self-motivation and personal performance.

Motivational Capabilities

As noted earlier, motivational capabilities are those capabilities — whether you are born with them or whether you develop them through learning and application — which you enjoy using. They also form part of personal characteristics and one side of the job fit formula. They can be summarised as follows:

- *Memory:* an ability to remember, to retain things in your mind and to recall things from the past; a good memory perhaps is better at remembering certain things — for example, faces rather than names.
- *Verbal comprehension:* an ability to understand accurately the meaning of words — both written and spoken; an ability to read and understand 'difficult' books or reports, and to differentiate between words with closely similar meanings; and having an extensive vocabulary.
- *Numeracy:* an ability to understand and express ideas by way of numbers; an ability to understand mathematical concepts and numerical problems; and an ability to understand statistical tables, gambling or betting 'odds', or technical data.
- *Spatial ability:* an ability to see and understand shapes or objects in more than one dimension; an ability to understand complicated diagrams or technical drawings in three dimensions; a good sense of direction; and good at puzzles where you fit or disentangle complicated objects and shapes.

- *Perception:* an ability to perceive or notice things in detail, or to understand situations; and an ability to notice quickly if something is wrong, or to pick up important details or information which others can miss.
- *Fluency:* an ability to express your views or meaning in the correct spoken words; a good communicator with an ability to argue or persuade; well able to make your meaning clear in discussion; and good self-expression.
- *Reasoning ability:* an ability to reason, to progress from the known to the unknown by using logic and drawing conclusions; an ability to solve problems, to see when people contradict themselves in a discussion or argument; and an ability to resolve complex matters through logical reasoning.
- *Creativity:* an ability to produce a stream of new, useful or creative ideas; an ability to be inventive or creative and to think of more than one way of looking at a problem or answering a question; and being good at art or design, or at creative problem-solving, or at computer graphics.
- *Social ability:* an ability to get on well with other people from a wide range of backgrounds, beliefs or views; an ability to get other people to accept your views, to trust, confide in you and to do things for you; and a capacity to mix with anyone socially.
- *Clerical speed and accuracy:* an ability to be quick and accurate with anything clerical: spotting typing mistakes, filing, cross-checking columns of figures, note-taking, etc; and good at office-type activities, typically undertaken in administration.

As with occupational interests, some motivational capabilities relate more to certain career areas than to others, and again they need to be represented in your job if your self-motivation and personal performance are to be maximised.

Values

Values — in other words, those ideals which are important and virtually non-negotiable (particularly as the years unfold!) in the way you live and work — represent the last component of personal characteristics on the same side of the job fit formula. They cover a broad range, including:

- *Employment conditions:* high levels of salary, benefits and other elements of compensation; or security of employment and job stability; or an organisation where you can acquire a stake in the equity, or become a partner.
- *Prospects:* an organisation in which you can develop your career through promotions; or a job which requires and recognises qualifications.
- *Importance:* a job which has status and which is respected; or a job in which you can lead or influence others.
- *Responsibility:* a job which helps others within the community; or a job within an organisation which has a respect for the environment.
- *Fulfilment:* a job in which you feel you can achieve; or a job within a competitive environment; or a job within a challenging environment.
- *People orientation:* a job which interacts with people; or a working environment based on trust and integrity.

- *Autonomy:* a job offering independence and autonomy; or a work environment where you can be entrepreneurial or operate your own business.
- *Technical/ functional:* a job which requires finely honed skills and competencies; or a job which involves research and development.
- *Lifestyle:* a job offering variety and change; or a job which allows you to balance work and home life; or offering a reasonably short working week.

The degree to which your values are met in your career depends not only on the job itself, but also on the working environment; different jobs and environments match different value-sets. You may have other values, as this is not an exhaustive list. What are they?

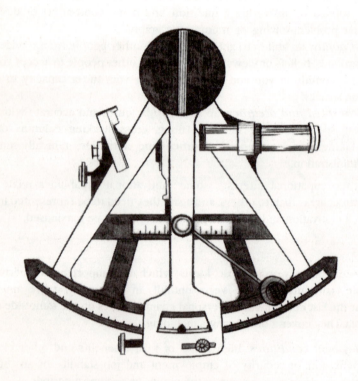

The Sextant — For Use In Determining Where You Are
The optical instrument known as the sextant is able to determine exactly where you are. It was developed in the mid–1700s for purposes of navigation, and enabled the user, through two mirrors, to measure the angular elevation of the sun and other planets and stars, which determined the exact longitude and latitude of the navigator's position.

If off course, the compass was used to determine an appropriate heading to correct your course of direction, but unlike the sextant — which relied on several celestial bodies, in other words a range of inputs to determine your precise position fix — the compass is solely a direction finder.

Career Areas

The other side of the job fit formula is represented by 12 major career areas. Each career area relates more to certain occupational interests and motivational capabilities than to others. While these career areas represent an open field of choice for people at the start of their careers, it is surprising how people — as I did — can make career changes late in their careers, in order to maximise job fit and other criteria.

Do not try to match up the following career areas to your interests and motivational capabilities at this stage. In the *Executive Armoury*, you will find a far more efficient process to enable you to do this!

Practical careers are for practically-minded individuals who like to work with their hands, and this can often include outdoor work. This type of work often suits people who have a spatial ability. Typical careers include: the armed services; manufacturing and distribution; building, civil engineering and land services; agriculture, horticulture, forestry and parks, fisheries; clothing industry; and metal and printing industries.

Technical careers are for practical *and* technical individuals, sometimes with outside and/or medical interests, and they often require a good memory, a capacity for thinking spatially — in three dimensions — and sometimes numeracy. Perception and reasoning ability are also often required. Relevant career areas include: health and hospital services; science; engineering; management services; media services; metal and printing industries; building, civil engineering and land services; and agriculture, horticulture, forestry and fisheries.

Analytical careers are for the computational- and sometimes clerical-minded individual. Abilities include memory, numeracy, spatial, perception, reasoning, and sometimes clerical speed and accuracy — often a detail person. Analytical career areas can be found in a range of business sectors and are often located in the management services functional area of organisations.

Scientific careers are for the scientifically and sometimes social welfare or computational-minded individual, sometimes with medical interests. Ability requirements often include a good memory, numeracy, spatial, perception, reasoning and creativity. Career areas include science, and health and hospital services.

Creative careers are for the literary, or artistic, or musical individual, sometimes with persuasive or practical interests, often with spatial ability, perception, creativity, and sometimes verbal comprehension, fluency or social ability. Career areas include: creative art, fashion and design; entertainment and recreation; and media and publications.

Careers in design include artistic, technical and sometimes practical or computational interests. Requirements often include a good memory, spatial ability, perception, reasoning, creativity and sometimes numeracy. Career areas include: creative art, fashion and design; technical design; media and publications; and building, architecture, civil engineering and land services.

People-oriented careers are for the individual who has social welfare and sometimes persuasive, practical or medical interests. Perception, fluency, reasoning and social ability are often key requirements. Relevant career areas include: teaching and cultural activities; catering and personal services; health and hospital services; social work; human resources management; and transport, travel and materials handling.

Managerial careers are for the more persuasive and sometimes social welfare-oriented individual who often has good perception, fluency, reasoning and social ability. Career areas include: the armed services; management and administration; inspection; security and protective services; and transport, travel and materials handling.

Enterprising careers are for the individual who is persuasive and sometimes social welfare-oriented. The individual is perceptive, fluent, has good reasoning ability, is social, and is sometimes spatial and creative. Career areas usually include a marketing orientation in a wide variety of different businesses and sectors.

Entrepreneurial careers — the 'entrepreneur' is often a persuasive and practical individual who is perceptive, has good reasoning abilities, and is sometimes fluent or creative. Careers include independent business and sales.

Administrative careers are often for the individual with clerical and sometimes social welfare and computational interests, and often require a good memory, verbal comprehension, perception, reasoning ability, clerical speed and accuracy, and sometimes numeracy and social ability. Careers in administration can be found across a wide range of business areas.

Professional services careers often suit individuals with persuasive and sometimes clerical and computational interests and often require a good memory, verbal comprehension, perception, fluency, reasoning, social ability and sometimes numeracy. Typical career areas include: law; finance and accounting; and management or business consultancy.

Clearly, some career areas relate more to certain occupational interests, motivational capabilities, and in some cases values, than to others, and ideally your existing or new job will offer a good match in this regard.

In summary, a high level of job fit should enhance the prospects of your feeling self-motivated in the work you do, enhancing your personal performance. A low level of job fit will have the reverse effect and if this is the case, you need to consider your options.

Implications

Based on my work with more than 300 executives and managers over more than five years, I am amazed by how many of them have been in jobs and work environments which do not fully accommodate their interests, motivational capabilities or values. Not only does this often mean that through lack of self-motivation they fail to perform at their personal best, but it also means that a large proportion of their lives — executives and managers working some 100 000 hours in their careers — is unfulfilled.

One of the most exciting parts of my professional work is to help executives and managers realign themselves in this context and to see them self-motivated and performing at a personal optimum, reaping the rewards of greater job satisfaction, improved personal output and enhanced remuneration, at the same time being seen to be contributing more fully to their organisations.

SUMMARY

Chapter 4 raises the following key issues:

- Executives and managers need to ensure their major occupational interests match the job. Interest areas include:
  - technical, computational, practical, medical
  - scientific, social, persuasive, literary
  - clerical, musical, outdoors and artistic.
- Similarly, major capabilities — particularly those capabilities which you enjoy using ('motivational capabilities') — also ideally need to be represented in your job. Capabilities include:
  - memory, verbal comprehension, numeracy
  - spatial ability, perception, fluency
  - reasoning ability, creativity
  - social ability, and clerical speed and accuracy.
- It is also important to ensure personal values are accommodated in the job and work environment, particularly in the case of the more mature executive or manager (values become less negotiable with the passage of time). Values include:
  - security, integrity, social
  - community and environmental responsibility
  - personal financial success, prestige and variety.
- Types of work, the other side of the job fit formula, vary considerably and each category orientates itself towards specific occupational interests and motivational capabilities. The major categories of work include:
  - practical, technical, analytical, scientific
  - creative, design, people-oriented, managerial
  - enterprising, entrepreneurial, administrative and professional.
- Job fit, self-motivation and personal performance will usually be best if interests, motivational capabilities and values are met in the job and work environment.

Further Resources

Refer to Section 4 of your *Executive Armoury* for some further guidelines on optimising job fit, self-motivation and personal performance.

5

Developing New Millennium Leadership Traits

'Stan Graham is general manager of our Construction Materials Division. His business results compare satisfactorily with other divisions, but what separates Stan from his peers is that he displays the types of leadership traits which will help to propel us as a company into a promising future: a creative approach to strategy development rather than simply "continuation of the status quo"; a customer focus; and a visionary management style with utmost respect for his team and a focus on individual development. Indeed, Stan is an inspirational leader of people rather than simply a manager of ongoing operations.'

Desirable leadership traits needed to carry the organisation forward into the future often need to be more clearly specified, selected in new hires, and developed in executives and managers with the help of the organisation. Any senior person needs to know what is expected in terms of desirable leadership traits in order to survive and succeed. The only problem is that organisations may not be able to articulate what these desirable traits should be!

The Search for Leadership Traits

Determining ideal leadership traits has been the quest of academics and authors alike, throughout this century. As far back as 1916, H L Gantt wrote about industrial leadership and in 1935, Ordway Tead wrote about the art of leadership. In the 1950s and 1960s there was a rush of further 'definitive' guidelines, including *How to Identify Promotable Executives* by C Wilson Randle, *Appraising Executive Performance* by Carl Heyel and *How to Select Executive Personnel* by Edith S Sands.

This has continued through to the present day, with a widening variety of academics and authors endeavouring to define ideal leadership traits and related 'soft' competencies with such titles as *Real Change Leaders* by J Kazenbach, and *Roses and Rust: Redefining the Essence of Leadership* by D Clancy.

Today in Australia, many executives and managers are seeking to digest, learn from, and implement the findings and recommendations of David S Karpin who led an Industry Task Force to report on leadership and management skills in Australia in the context of 'Renewing Australia's Managers to Meet the Challenges of the Asia–Pacific Century'. *Enterprising Nation*, or *The Karpin Report* as it is more often called, took some three years to complete and proclaims itself as the 'most comprehensive insight ever into the way Australia prepares its managers for work and leadership'.

Gary Hamel and C K Prahalad's book *Competing for the Future* is an international bestseller. In the context of some of their work, desirable leadership traits may be deduced as follows:

- *As an inspirational leader* — not being overly directive, putting the team before self, relating well to groups and individuals, and having a customer and people development focus.
- *As a visionary strategist* — having a big picture perspective, being less conforming, less structured, and a creative problem-solver, and using initiative in trying to create the future.

In reality, however, many organisations may not yet have reached the point where they can specify *desirable* leadership traits, but they can often react negatively when *undesirable* traits are being exhibited. These can be as germane as executives and managers being too production (rather than customer) oriented; too autocratic; not supporting equal employment or promotion; exhibiting racism, sexism, harassment or discrimination; being involved in unfair dismissal; making preferential appointments; not engaging in adequate two-way communication; and not being prepared to delegate or change.

Says Michael T Duffy, senior manager group human resources at the Commonwealth Bank of Australia, 'In this day and age, profile is extremely important. If you are perceived as a "dinosaur" or as someone unresponsive to change, you *and your team members* will probably suffer.'

What seems to be lacking today is a simple conceptual model or framework which can be understood and applied by individuals and organisations in their identification, pursuit and adoption of ideal or desirable leadership traits. I will propose and describe such a model shortly, but first are a few examples of people displaying desirable and perhaps less desirable leadership traits: *K P Singh*, *Kentaro Iwamoto*, *Marcel Pinot* and *Peter Hardwick*. You be the judge as to whether their traits are desirable or undesirable!

Examples of Leadership Traits

K P Singh is a senior executive responsible for a significant sports footwear production plant and distributorship in Kuala Lumpur. He is well qualified, having both an MBA and a first degree in economics. He believes he is a specialist in sports footwear, emphasises low-cost production and tight centralised control, and he personally gets involved in the detail of operations which he has divided into three strategic business units. He excels at administration, has good local knowledge and perspective, always conforms with head office, and expects his subordinates to operate by the rule-book.

Although market demands change quite rapidly — sports footwear now being predominantly fashion items — Singh believes in the 'continuation of the status quo': develop and update the product according to customer needs, but produce and distribute it conventionally. Clearly, K P Singh is production-driven. When confronted by operational problems, he personally gets involved in solving them and he is seen as a logical problem-solver.

the bulletproof executive

In Paris, *Kentaro Iwamoto* runs the French operations of a high-tech office equipment company. He is seen as being very considerate of his 3400 staff, displaying a caring attitude and relying very much on natural attrition rather than retrenchment for downsizing as the organisation flexes its way through the second half of the 1990s. The firm pays its staff quite well and has the best employee sickness benefits, health insurance, and personal disability and life cover in its industry.

However, Iwamoto is also considered autocratic. He believes in discipline (he doesn't always seem to trust his staff), tight control and firm directive management. He has taken great pains to develop a formal and hierarchical organisation structure, where jobs, reporting relationships, accountabilities and authority are all very clearly defined and rigidly adhered to. While he seeks to communicate with staff, he relies heavily on selectively 'transmitting' information top-down, but the opportunities and processes for his 'receiving' information bottom-up are less evident.

As an individual, Iwamoto is fiercely competitive with his peers, and he is often thought to be too self-promotional, putting himself rather than his team first when he visits his superiors in Japan for quarterly business reviews.

Marcel Pinot works in London as a senior executive in the publishing industry. He has lived in several countries, and this seems to have equipped him with a global perspective and knowledge. He is considered by his industry peers to be a nonconformist, taking a highly customer-centred and entrepreneurial approach to the strategic development of his publishing 'mini-empire', although at the same time understanding, committing to, and deploying the core competencies of his organisation as much as possible.

Taking a flexible approach and believing in decentralised control, Marcel and his team quickly respond to change and are considered to be pioneers and pathfinders in their industry. Personally, Marcel is financially astute, uses a lot of initiative, and is perceived to be a creative problem-solver with broad-based general management capabilities.

Peter Hardwick runs a software development company in Vancouver. He is considered to be a natural and inspirational leader of people, be they employees or customers. Being both customer-oriented and empowering his employees, he has a track record of unparalleled software development success in his field, being the 'first to market' with true innovation, only accomplished by defining customer needs and by relying on a committed team to convert concepts into real solutions.

When questioned at an industry conference about leadership styles, Hardwick emphasised his beliefs in flat organisational hierarchies, open two-way communication, learning, people development, and the need for leaders to relate well to both groups of people and individuals.

An article on his company in a business periodical reported an interview with several of his staff. They said he was trusting of employees, unstructured, certainly not directive, and always seemed to put the customer and his team first, rather than himself. They also applauded his creativity — his capacity to think outside the square — and his ability to enthuse others with his innovative approaches and solutions.

Four very different sets of leadership traits and, in each case, very successful people! Which traits are more desirable, and which are less desirable? What are the common threads in each subset of traits? Of course, the degree of desirability or undesirability is defined by the orientation and perception of the beholder. Some of us do not trust staff, others believe in firm discipline, while others believe in more of a hands-off or creative style.

Similarly with organisations, some companies have a culture wherein K P Singh would be perceived as exhibiting highly desirable leadership traits, whereas other organisations may prefer the traits exhibited by Marcel Pinot. Yet other organisations, particularly the larger and more decentralised, may identify well with a blend of three or even four different subsets of traits. Invariably, flexibility is sought in most executives and managers, rather than rigidity.

In the ideal setting, both individuals and their organisations must come to some agreement on what they mean by desirable leadership traits for executives and managers to be successful. To enable this to happen, they need to develop a common language to describe this other 'make or break' area of executive and managerial success.

Defining Leadership Traits

Two dimensions together define the major categories of leadership traits in the examples I have cited. The first dimension relates to the *degree of people orientation* versus the *degree of output orientation*. Clearly some executives and managers are highly oriented towards *output*, tasks and production, whereas others are more oriented towards *people*, be they employees or customers. Some executives are a blend of the two, or verge towards one orientation or the other.

The second dimension relates to the *degree of control* versus the *degree of creativity*. Again, some managers are very dominant — they often seek to be in control or impose controls on others, and they are likely to be intensive in their approach. Other managers think much more outside the square and are more interested in a hands-off and creative environment.

These two dimensions can now be joined to form a matrix, as shown in Figure 5.1.

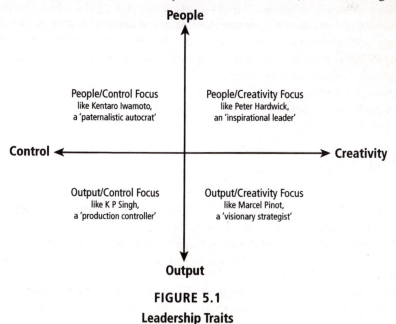

FIGURE 5.1
Leadership Traits

Increasingly it seems, desirable leadership traits are perceived by employers as a dual orientation towards people and creativity, not ignoring the need also for visionary strategists. This is because many organisations have been through a period of unprecedented restructuring and downsizing — managing the costs — when a production and control mentality was highly relevant.

Today, in this time of low inflation and high competition, many of these same organisations are seeking to regenerate and grow, perhaps into entirely new profitable areas, or by being very different to their competitors. This will only come about through an increased orientation towards people (both employees and customers) and creative approaches.

'Say goodbye to the "controlasaurus" — the control freak,' says David Benn, managing director Australasia of Korn/Ferry International, a leading executive search firm, as he quotes from a study entitled *Developing Leadership for the 21st Century*, prepared by the Economist Intelligence Unit in cooperation with his firm. 'Providing vision is perhaps the most critical task.'

Phillip Hart, executive director, Red Cross New South Wales, puts it this way: 'Unless executives listen to staff, customers and clients, and synthesise the material for creating the vision, the chances of developing an organisation for yesterday and not today, are high!' Sue Bussell, general manager employee relations of Qantas, declares: 'Understanding your business now, and investing time in understanding the future direction, is what separates out the "business leaders" from the "managers".'

'Managers and executives must be open-minded, keen to know and understand their customer needs, and capable of inspiring others to follow. Conflict management skills are also vital for effective performance management,' says Lawrie Horder, head of human resources, business financial services NSW and ACT, National Australia Bank.

Another desirable leadership trait is suggested by Christopher Conybeare, independent consultant and associate director of Davidson & Associates, previously secretary (CEO) of the Australian Department of Immigration and Ethnic Affairs: 'I would add: being perceived by all levels of staff to be able to add value and enhance the external reputation of the organisation.'

Kenneth J Roberts, company director of ATG, CSL and AGEN and formerly chairman and managing director of Wellcome Australia, emphasises: 'A strong influencer, negotiator and presenter of ideas is also crucial.'

Closing the Gap

If there is a gap between what is sought and your own traits, then the alternatives are:

- *Ignore it.* Hope that the gap will go unrecognised. However, in today's smaller and flatter organisational structures, every single cog has to be moving in harmony with every other cog. In the heavy machinery of old bureaucratic structures the occasional rusty cog could survive unnoticed, but today, every rusty cog is exposed and vulnerable.
- *Attack it.* Refuse to change and buck the trend, but beware! Organisations, rather than individuals, usually win out.

- *Change the organisation.* Try to change organisational requirements for leadership traits more towards your own traits — but how movable are mountains!
- *Change your attitude.* View the problem as an opportunity rather than a threat.
- *Change your traits* so that they coincide more with the expectations of your organisation.
- *Retreat.* Move to another part of the organisation or remove yourself altogether from the organisation.

> **SUMMARY**
>
> Chapter 5 raises the following key issues:
> - Desirable leadership traits to carry organisations forward into the future may not be clearly specified by employers but are increasingly likely to include the need for inspirational leadership and visionary strategists.
> - Undesirable leadership traits may be as germane as executives and managers being: unsupportive of equal employment and promotion, minority rights or diversity; not engaging in fairness or adequate open two-way communication; or being unprepared to delegate.
> - They may also include being too production (versus customer) oriented, too autocratic or too controlling.
> - Any executive or manager needs to be clear about organisational expectations in this regard, and perceptions by others regarding any differences compared to their own traits.
> - When differences exist, the executive or manager has six alternatives: ignore it, attack it, change the organisation, change your attitude, change your traits, or retreat!

Further Resources

In Section 5 of your *Executive Armoury*, a process is provided for assessing your own or your colleagues' leadership traits compared to organisational expectations.

6

Excelling At Teamwork, As Member Or Leader

'When Susan Hardie was promoted to planning and logistics director and joined the senior executive team, I was uncomfortable, as were some of my colleagues. She seemed different in her outlook and approach, and many of us had difficulty in understanding where she was coming from. Now, four months later, I believe Susan represents the best addition to the team for years. Whereas most of us are conservative and perhaps overly structured in our approach, Susan inspires us with her flashes of intuition — her capacity to "think outside the square" — on reflection so lacking for so long in the team.'

'The sustainable strength of the organisation's performance and ability to cope with major changes, will be critically dependent on effective teamworking,' emphasises John Marlay, chief general manager, Australian Building Materials Division, Pioneer International.

'I've always found that having the right team, well motivated, is the biggest support factor in ensuring success — you can't do it on your own,' says Meredith Hellicar, managing director, TNT Logistics Asia.

'Team skills are essential to ongoing managerial and executive career success,' remarks Lawrie Horder, head of human resources, business financial services NSW and ACT, National Australia Bank. 'We measure it as a set of behaviours essential to excellent leadership.'

Kenneth J Roberts, company director of ATG, CSL and AGEN, takes an interesting tack regarding teamwork: 'Leaders need to guard against being over dominant, ie to submerge their own ego and thereby become an equal member/facilitator in teams!'

'Teamwork is one of the hardest areas for modern managers, as they are giving up their control and power. The team outcome provides better results,' comments Donald Ross, general manager of Sydney Ports Corporation.

Psychologists and behavioural scientists the world over agree that winning senior executive or management teams need to be balanced in terms of composition as it relates to the various operating styles of team members. In other words, those teams generally perform best whose members between them represent all the main operating styles associated with human behaviour.

In this, the 'gurus' have developed countless models depicting differing personal styles, behaviour or personality. Drawing on much of this thinking and on my dealing with over 300 executives for more than five years, I have been able to produce a new model which bridges conventional wisdom with my practical experience, and which first provides some primary guidelines on behaviour, secondly enables the observer to determine their own and others' operating styles quickly and precisely, and, finally, can be used in analysing team composition.

Behaviour — the Driver of Operating Style

Visualise two very different individuals, Mary Hunter and Paul Wong. Mary Hunter is operations manager in an airline catering and food service organisation in London. She is described by her colleagues as being highly 'hands-on' and action-oriented. She talks a lot to her staff, actively giving them instructions as they go about their work. She seems preoccupied with results and displays a strong output orientation. Mary exhibits highly 'proactive' behaviour.

Paul Wong is the employee relations manager in the sales and service centre of a major consumer electronics manufacturer in San Francisco. He is seen to be 'hands-off', believing that line managers and supervisors need to be the primary interface with hourly-paid employees. John appears to be calm in nature, he is an excellent and 'active' listener, and is regarded as extremely friendly and approachable by all. John evaluates situations with care and with special consideration of the human factor. He exhibits highly 'receptive' behaviour.

Major Categories of Operating Style

Most of us are in fact a mixture of 'proactiveness' and 'receptiveness' in the way we behave. Indeed, there are several different operating styles when blending proactiveness and receptiveness together:

High proactiveness and low receptiveness

This is somewhat like Mary Hunter, but perhaps not to her extreme. The label I give to this style is Commander/Doer, the key characteristics being hands-on, action, talking, results, and above all, an output-orientation.

Commander/Doers both direct others, often quite forcefully, and are people of action. They are always on the go and can never sit still. They put a lot of effort into things and like to keep on the move. They can be very energetic and they find it hard to relax. They take a down-to-earth attitude, relying on commonsense approaches. They prefer tangible, concrete objects rather than 'airy-fairy' ideas or feelings. They learn by doing rather than by reading. Also, they are confident in meeting new circumstances or strange situations alone. Commander/Doers are happy to rely on their own capabilities in any environment or in tackling any matter.

High receptiveness and low proactiveness

This is somewhat like John Smart, but perhaps not to his extreme. The label I give to this style is Empathiser/Humanist, the key characteristics being hands-off, reflective, listening, and above all, a people-orientation.

The Empathiser/Humanist is able to understand other people, their ideas, attitudes or behaviour and is affected in mood or behaviour by others — what people say or do. People of this style enjoy listening to others, are cooperative, and enjoy their company.

Empathiser/Humanists allow and encourage others to have their say. They believe in majority decisions, but not to the disadvantage of minorities. Also, they dislike unduly forcing or asserting themselves over other people.

High proactiveness and high receptiveness

This is a combination of styles in the direction of both Mary and John's. The label I give to this style is Responder/Initiator, the key characteristics being a capacity both to get involved and stand aside; to act and to be reflective; to talk and to listen; and to seek tangible results but also to be oriented towards people.

The Responder/Initiator tends to exhibit good levels of both proactive and receptive behaviour. Indeed, people with this style of behaviour usually display great enthusiasm in working with others, being both active listeners and enthusiastic talkers. They sell themselves well, are usually good presenters, and in the social setting are the people that can really get the party going!

Low proactiveness and low receptiveness

The label I give to this style is Evaluator/Detailer, the key characteristics being neither particularly hands-on, nor overly action-oriented, nor an active responder nor initiator. Such people tend to remain alone or detached rather than engage in too much group or individual interaction — they tend to stay out of the limelight. They are often non-committal, yet invariably factual and analytical — classic planners and detailers, in fact.

In this regard, the Evaluator/Detailer takes a lot of care over things; is painstaking in doing things; sometimes is seen as cautious; likes to do a job well; and does not like sloppiness or a casual approach. People with this style take a consistently steady approach to all situations, are unflappable, are neither easily aroused or stimulated nor provoked, and are often thought of as cold and unemotional. Evaluator/Detailers tackle things in a controlled way, are quite happy with their own company, and are self-sufficient.

A mixture of low and high proactiveness and low and high receptiveness

This is the Idea generator, who is a combination of the previous four styles and who can nimbly dart from one operating style to another operating style, often exhibiting extremes of behaviour and flashes of inspiration and creativity, seeing 'endless possibilities'.

Idea generators are very concerned with the 'big picture', knowledge and theory, often forgetting practical application. However, they do jump in and apply themselves enthusiastically when committed to a course of action. People of this operating style usually are interested in the future and the longer term, perhaps more than the 'here and now'. Idea generators often change their minds, or courses of action; and enjoy variety.

Idea generators also have a preference for 'doing their own thing'; they do not always agree with or conform to other people, their wishes, ideas, attitudes or behaviour; and they enjoy freedom of choice.

A mixture of a reasonable degree of proactiveness and a reasonable degree of receptiveness

This is the All-rounder, who also occupies all four quadrants (see Figure 6.1), but seldom if ever shows extremes of any type of behaviour, exhibiting more of a balanced, yet flexible style. All-rounders often represent the stabilising factor in teams and can make good chairpersons. They can help the team reach consensus and are able to compromise. While not usually seen as the life and soul of the party, they are usually quite popular and their opinions are often sought. They usually give others a fair hearing.

All-rounders are well able to identify with all the other styles and converse with them easily, providing extremes in behaviour are not evident, which can cause them some difficulties. Indeed, when others are exhibiting extremes in behaviour, All-rounders often act as moderators.

These six different operating styles are noted in Figure 6.1, which represents a model for assessing behaviour and operating style.

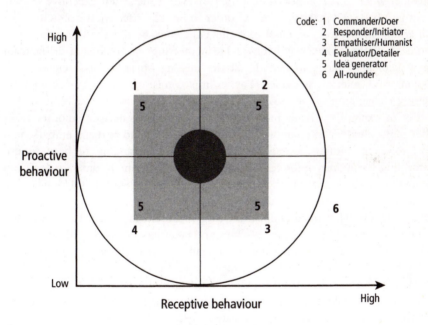

FIGURE 6.1
Operating Styles

One way of assessing other people's operating styles is first to gauge the degree of proactiveness and receptiveness of the person in mind, in terms of the way that person behaves. How proactive and how receptive are they? This approach may lead you to operating style definition more easily. Also, anyone can display a combination of operating styles, but they will usually exhibit a main style, perhaps along with a subordinate style.

Operating styles can also vary depending upon circumstances — for example, the main style of an individual working under stressful conditions may be very different to their style at home under more relaxed conditions. Clearly, for our purposes in this book, we need to concentrate on the work situation.

Teams and Executive Success

This approach can also be used as a road-map to plot the positions of the operating styles of others in your existing, future or most recent team. Be careful not to assume that the team leader or chairperson automatically occupies the All-rounder or any other specific style position. Formal leaders can in fact be of any operating style, providing the senior team has members who between them display each of the six operating styles described, preferably as their main styles, but if not, then as a combination of their main and subordinate styles.

Lower-level or specialised teams, however, may not need such a balanced composition and indeed may benefit from being unbalanced and biased towards one or more operating styles — for example, a sales team may need a bias towards Commander/Doers or Responder/Initiators. However, if the senior executive team is deficient in a balanced make-up, then in order to be fully effective it needs to make special arrangements to compensate for this deficiency, be this through new hires, secondment of others to team activities and team meetings, or, not least of all, the team taking a deliberate stance to include all the missing operating style elements in discussions and relevant activities. For example, this can be accomplished by appointing a 'champion' of the missing style to ensure due consideration is given to it.

By way of example, a team may be missing an Idea generator. Another team member may volunteer to champion this operating style and perhaps embark on a creative thinking training course to develop an understanding of how to use brainstorming techniques in the team setting, which from time to time are deployed when significant matters are being addressed and require detailed and 'outside the square' assessment before resolution.

Clearly, with a well-balanced senior team, each member can be seen to make a valid and different contribution to team activities and meetings, enhancing the prospects of individual executives or managers and team success. However, this is often mitigated by the 'mirror-image' effect in hiring, and the 'clashing' of operating styles causing interpersonal relationship problems. The mirror-image effect is well known. The hirer, usually the boss, prefers to hire someone of their own operating style. The individual joins the organisation and initially is seen to fit in well with the hirer and other team members — themselves perhaps hired or promoted into the team under the mirror-image effect. As time goes by, the new hire, and indeed other 'clones', are not perceived to be making significant contributions to team activities and meetings. There is too much agreement and insufficient challenging debate, fresh ideas and innovative input. This can result in the team performing poorly and in sideways moves of individuals perceived not to be adding value, or may even lead to demotions or dismissals.

The message? As an individual executive or manager operating as a member of a senior team, assess your existing team and if you find yourself part of the cloning, try to take a deliberate stance and adopt one of the six missing operating styles — but *only* do this after discussing it with the team leader and members. Circulate this book and suggest that the other team members read this chapter or, better still, buy them their own copies! They will probably appreciate reading the other chapters also.

If you are joining a new senior team, try to determine your team role in advance and meet team members to assess their operating styles. If you feel you are a clone, then 'caveat emptor' — let the buyer beware! Would you really want to be part of a badly imbalanced senior team, or a team full of clones, anyway?

If you are the leader of the senior team, or about to become one, then clearly you now have the understanding and process to assess team make-up and to ensure that you lead and develop a well-balanced team which will succeed in its endeavours. In so doing, the success prospects of your fellow executives or managers and yourself will be enhanced.

By now you may be asking yourself if this theme of well-balanced senior team make-up is real or just hot air? I can assure you that at the executive and managerial level, it is *real*. Time and again, studies and real life examples have shown that well-balanced senior executive or management teams, and their individual members, succeed best!

However, sometimes even when team make-up *is* well-balanced, some of these very different operating styles can 'clash' against each other like knights jousting at a tournament, particularly when the team is working under pressure. This can cause difficulties in interpersonal relationships and become destructive rather than synergistic. There are two requirements in such cases:

1. Share this information on team make-up, with a view to all team members knowing and recognising each other's main and subordinate operating styles, and understanding the importance of a balanced make-up. This chapter can again be used to good effect in communicating and demonstrating this.
2. Ensure that an All-rounder operating style is present and preferably is able to chair or intervene at meetings. This may be difficult when the leader or official chairperson is not the All-rounder — which often is the case. Under these circumstances, while the leader or chairperson may facilitate the execution of the agenda and ensure that priorities and objectives are attained, the All-rounder needs to be given sufficient 'air-time' to ensure that the strength in the style differences within the team is utilised positively and synergistically.

Stephen R Covey in his book *The 7 Habits of Highly Effective People* sums up synergy by saying that its essence is valuing the difference between people (and team members). The key to valuing these differences is to realise that all people see the world not as it is, but as they are. These differences in perceptions, when shared and understood, lead to new possibilities and new alternatives.

Clearly, clashes and poor interpersonal relationships are not what individual executive, manager or team success is about. Nor is team success about rook-like behaviour, where participants sit on the fence and wait and watch which direction the flow is going, before going with the flow! The bottom line is that successful teamwork is all about 'fit'.

Clones, Knights, Rooks and Henchmen!

Clones, from the biological perspective, are genetically identical to one antecedent, or from the botanical perspective, are the transplants from one original seedling. Clones in the work or team setting usually result from the 'mirror-image' effect of hirings, where the comfort level of the hirer is increased if the hiree is of the same ilk. Knights were originally men of noble birth and are often thought of as medieval warriors wandering the land in search of chivalrous adventures. But knights also took part in pageants where they would joust by charging at each other with lances on horseback in an endeavour to dismount their combatant and win the tournament. A veritable 'I win–you lose' outcome!

Rooks, often mistaken for crows, are very common in Europe where they live in large colonies or rookeries. Rooks rarely venture forth on their own, preferring to stick with their colleagues and go with the flow. Indeed, rooks really are 'fence-sitters' and only commit to a course of action if it seems to be the way all the other birds in the rookery are headed.

Henchmen historically were squires or pages of honour, and could always be trusted and relied on. Whatever the needs of an individual or team, henchmen would endeavour to support and provide for them, enhancing the overall effectiveness of the group.

Teams need to be comprised of henchmen. In today's fiercely competitive environment, there can be no room for clones, knights and rooks!

'Fit is a very important concept in working with a management team,' says Mark C Kershisnik, managing director of Eli Lilly Australia Pty Ltd, and formerly director of manufacturing, Lilly Germany. 'This is not to say we eliminate diversity and use a "cookie-cutter" approach, but without fit, the politics go out of control as protective behaviours and one-upmanship take hold, or just plain withdrawal of participation occurs.'

Successful teams need to avoid all these potential difficulties and be comprised of mutually supportive 'henchmen', each doing their utmost to support their colleagues. As a team member or leader, by avoiding the pitfalls and using the approaches suggested regarding team make-up, success prospects for one and all are enhanced!

SUMMARY

Chapter 6 raises the following key issues:

- A senior executive or management team ideally needs to be comprised of members displaying, between them, the following operating styles:
  - *Commander/Doer:* usually directs other people and works energetically to get results.
  - *Responder/Initiator:* seeks to understand others, communicates very well and leads enthusiastically.
  - *Empathiser/Humanist:* the people- rather than production-oriented individual, with an amicable style.
  - *Evaluator/Detailer:* the analytical, logical, and meticulous planner and organiser.
  - *Idea generator:* the conceptual and creative thinker who can see endless possibilities and who often shows extremes in behaviour.
  - *All-rounder:* the balanced individual who has a flexible style, yet does not show extremes in behaviour.
- Senior teams comprised of all six styles usually perform best. Other teams may benefit from being unbalanced and biased towards one or more operating styles.
- At the senior team level, or where the 'mirror-image' effect in hiring causes teams to become cloned, the main style of the most senior executive, the formal leader of the team, often dominates team make-up.
- When team make-up is well balanced, some of these very different operating styles can 'clash'. This can be rectified if all team members know and recognise each other's main operating styles, and how they can be used synergistically, rather than destructively.
- Team members need to engage with each other, rather than sit on the fence.

Further Resources

Further guidelines are provided in Section 6 of your *Executive Armoury*, on how to assess your own operating style and the styles of other team members.

7

Improving Personal Chemistry And Fit

> 'Mary Pearson is our human resources director. She has settled in well over the past six months. Not only does the management team feel she fits in superbly, but according to Mary, she is motivated by the way we operate, our culture, and our balanced management style which has a dual emphasis on business results and employee development.'

In addressing personal chemistry and fit, 'I would say this is a critical factor,' says Paul Lilley, general manager human resources, (Australian Banking Group) Westpac. 'I have seen a number of examples of highly successful individuals recruited from similar organisations, failing due to a misfit with the style or culture of a business. I believe that in moving to a new organisation, an executive has to learn a new set of "rules of the game", and success will depend on the individual's capacity to adapt to, and enjoyment of working with others within those rules. I would also postulate that this factor becomes more important further up an organisation, and further into an executive's career.'

'Finding an organisation where values and culture match the individual is probably the prime reason for success. Sometimes it happens by accident. How much better if it could be "caused to happen",' remarks Tony Harbour, independent management consultant and formerly group personnel director of the Ocean Group PLC in the UK.

'We need diversity and it's good to be different, but constant tension between the individual and the organisation saps energy and enthusiasm,' suggests David Learmond, personnel director of Unilever Australia.

'Organisational fit is a critical area for long-term satisfaction and personal motivation,' agrees Donald Ross, general manager of Sydney Ports Corporation. 'The right person in the wrong organisation is a flawed combination.'

'Organisational fit is a key success factor. An executive can have all the other desirable leadership traits but without organisational fit, will not achieve major success,' says Karen Robinson, director human resources, BZW Australia Ltd.

Organisational fit is, in fact, quite a complex subject. In addition to the usual chemistry and fit assessments by individuals at times of hiring, major organisational or 'atmospheric' needs of individual executives and managers — to maximise their self-motivation and personal effectiveness — include a range of characteristics of the organisation, its culture and its management style:

- *material needs:* remuneration, safety and security
- *structural needs:* degree and type of structure, bureaucracy and systems
- *behavioural needs:* management style and interpersonal relationships
- *emotional needs:* trust, social needs, esteem needs and sense of achievement.

Executives and managers need to assess their own atmospheric needs and ensure they are appropriately accommodated in the organisation, if at all possible. If not, self-motivation and thereby performance are unlikely to be at an optimum.

Atmospherics are a critical element of chemistry and fit, and yet are often ignored in management or executive selection and development, where an orientation of 'will the candidate fit in with us?' rather than 'are we right for the candidate?' usually applies.

Material Needs

Material needs relate to the base-level needs as described by the well-known behavioural scientist Abraham Maslow. They include all the basic needs for living and working:

- remuneration for food, clothing, shelter, health and education
- safety and security at work, and even
- 'comfort' at work, be this the office environment, cafeteria arrangements, style of car, or fringe benefits.

Clearly, if the material needs of an individual are not satisfied, this may create, on the one hand, self-motivation to progress within the organisation and via promotion to improve material returns to a more acceptable level; or, as is often the case, cause dissatisfaction, poor morale and poor performance, potentially leading to a voluntary or involuntary separation.

Structural Needs

Structural needs relate to the way the organisation is structured, which can include degree of centralisation versus decentralisation and levels of autonomy accorded. Other factors include:

- degree of bureaucracy and red-tape versus a more free-wheeling environment
- complexity and intensity of management reporting and supporting systems
- degree and type of computer-based information versus paper-based, and requirements for computer literacy
- rigidity or otherwise of policies, rules and regulations.

Again, the organisation, in terms of structure, may either meet the motivational needs of the individual, or may be diametrically opposed to them, causing an adverse, reactive and often stressful behaviour, and apparent 'poor fit'.

Behavioural Needs

Behavioural needs start to get more complex and can become somewhat of a moving target because of the coming and going of senior people in corporate life to whom an individual reports. For example, an executive may be hired by a chief executive who displays ideal behavioural characteristics for the individual newly hired.

However, chief executive job tenure now spans less than four years and so there is a strong chance that any executive is likely to report to a new boss — it is simply a matter of time! That new boss may display very different behavioural characteristics from the original hirer, and these characteristics may not meet the motivational needs of the individual.

However, behavioural needs are not only met (or not met) by the senior executive to whom one reports, but also by the culture of the organisation, and so these needs and how they are satisfied are well worthwhile examining in detail. Behavioural needs, in fact, fall into two main categories: management style and interpersonal relationships.

Management style

Management style encompasses such aspects as *planning*, *organising*, *monitoring*, *decision-making*, *motivating*, *delegating*, *adaptability*, *entrepreneurism*, *resilience* and *communication*, which are summarised below in the context of assessing atmospherics:

- *Planning* — the degree to which and how senior executives plan, set objectives, develop strategies, monitor, control and review the performance of direct reports; how 'top-down' or 'bottom-up' the planning processes are within the organisation; and how fixed or flexible plans are during implementation. Some executives and managers are motivated and perform well in a highly planned environment, whereas others operate better in a more spontaneous setting.
- *Organising* — in addition to the structural aspects of the organisation as addressed earlier, individual senior executives clearly have an impact on 'organising' — for example, the degree of formality or informality in terms of team structure, reporting relationships, responsibility, accountability, authority, delegation, and span of control. Some executives and managers prefer a well-organised environment, while others prefer a more informal or 'loose' setting.
- *Monitoring* — the degree to which the monitoring of performance is preventative or maintenance; the number and specificity of major result areas and standards of performance; the form of monitoring, be it on-the-job supervision or hands-off, via reporting and information systems; and how individual development and learning needs are identified and addressed. Some executives and managers perceive close and formalised monitoring as an unpalatable invasion of their autonomy, whereas others see this as the norm and need regular feedback about their performance.
- *Decision-making* — the degree to which: decision-making is involving of direct reports or imposed; problems and opportunities are fully defined or understood; a range of prospective solutions is developed and assessed; root causes as opposed to symptoms are addressed; and how much creative thinking 'outside the square' is encouraged in the development of best possible decisions. Some executives and managers need an environment where decisions are made quickly, where there is neither ambiguity nor 'shades of grey', whereas others prefer and operate better in a more reflective environment, where there is ample time for decision-making, particularly when complex issues are being addressed.

- *Motivating* — the degree to which a motivational environment is created, through: a climate encouraging personal development and advancement; democratic rather than autocratic leadership; trust and integrity; job interest and satisfaction; recognition of individual or group contributions; alignment of personal and corporate goals; and an egalitarian as opposed to status-based culture. Some executives and managers need, and can only survive in, a motivational environment, while others are more self-motivated.
- *Delegating* — the extent to which senior executives delegate in terms of: being clear about what and to whom responsibilities are delegated; sufficient resources and authority being provided so that the delegation can be carried through effectively; delegation to maximise the skills and personal development of direct reports; and delegation to free up internal bottlenecks and to allow senior executives to concentrate on higher-level matters. Some executives and managers have an insatiable appetite for delegated responsibilities, whereas others prefer to work to their own agenda and perceive an environment where there is a lot of delegation, as one where being continuously on the receiving end of 'passing the buck' adversely impacts on personal freedom, initiative and autonomy.
- *Adaptability* — the degree to which senior executives appreciate and offer variety and change, adapt to changing circumstances rather than resist them, and take a flexible management and leadership style depending upon the competence of direct reports and the urgency of tasks. Some executives and managers thrive on change, while others resist it to the hilt (and it can become the cause of their undoing!).
- *Entrepreneurism* — how far the organisation is prepared to experiment with new ways of doing things, innovate in terms of products, services, processes or systems, and display a certain amount of daring in this (yet balanced by an appreciation and application of risk management). Some executives and managers need to work in a highly entrepreneurial environment, whereas others fit best in slower-paced or more predictable settings, and perhaps in bureaucracies.
- *Resilience* — the degree of resilience in senior executives in the form of handling and managing stress, capacity to persevere when the going gets tough, seeing change as a way of life rather than a hindrance, and generally displaying that 'dogged streak' of perseverance at times of particular difficulty or uncertainty. Some executives and managers fit best in a 'tough' or resilient environment, whereas others prefer a 'softer' work setting.
- *Communication* — the degree to which people engage in open, two-way communication, seek to understand the other party's point of view, minimise the physical and behavioural barriers which can so often detract from effective communication, and are considered approachable by direct reports. Some executives and managers thrive on open two-way communication and indeed need this to be effective, whereas others prefer a more traditional hierarchical setting, and are more used to communication which is primarily top-down.

Executives and managers need to be very clear about their needs regarding management style, be this in the senior executive to whom one reports, or from more of a management culture perspective across the organisation. If such needs are met, self-motivation and performance are invariably enhanced. If such needs are not met, this will likely cause difficulty and, in the extreme case, a negative stress reaction. Yet, how many employers even are aware of or consider chemistry and fit from this 'reverse' perspective?

Interpersonal relationships

For the purposes of considering atmospherics, executives and managers need to assess the operating styles of the senior executives to whom they report, which may include one or a combination of the following:

- *Commander/Doer* — usually directs other people and works to get results.
- *Responder/Initiator* — seeks to understand others, communicates very well and leads enthusiastically.
- *Empathiser/Humanist* — the people- rather than production-oriented individual, with an amicable style.
- *Evaluator/Detailer* — the analytical, logical and meticulous planner and organiser.
- *Idea generator* — the conceptual and creative thinker who can see endless possibilities and who often shows extremes in behaviour.
- *All-rounder* — the balanced individual who has a flexible style, yet does not show extremes in behaviour.

We may have preferences regarding the operating styles of others and to whom we report, and yet we may not always be able to choose our bosses in organisational life! But even understanding that there are differences in operating style, and that these differences in the senior team setting are actually needed in order to provide for balanced team composition, all helps. However, in selecting a new role within your existing organisation or a new job outside it, there may be some extremes in operating style you might be better to avoid. *You* have to decide!

As mentioned earlier, although the initial focus in assessing the degree to which your behavioural needs are met is the senior executive to whom you report, and although this executive may change and be replaced by another, many of the elements of management style and interpersonal relationships also relate to the culture of the organisation, and so need to be assessed in this dual context: will my behavioural needs be met by the person to whom I report; will they be met by the culture of the organisation?

Emotional Needs

In considering the final category of needs, emotional needs, we revert to Maslow and the higher levels of his hierarchy of needs, which include trust, social needs, esteem needs and sense of personal achievement.

Trust relates to the organisation being seen as fair and reasonable in its approach to dealing with staff, that senior management is trustworthy, that results will be rewarded, and that there will be no undeserved penalties or dismissals. *Social needs* encompass the theme of individuals feeling they 'belong' and are part of a group.

Esteem needs are satisfied by executives and managers being recognised as individuals, and for their contributions, capabilities and achievements. *Sense of personal achievement* is where the executive or manager feels a sense of high-level accomplishment in terms of attaining what has been strived for, which brings great personal satisfaction and self-confidence.

Most executives and managers need an environment where their emotional needs can be met in one or more ways, and yet in today's era of organisational turbulence and uncertainty, even large, apparently well-managed organisations seem to have lost the plot with many in their senior-level ranks.

Trust has walked out the door as a result of a hire-and-fire mentality. Social interaction has deteriorated as individuals in the group jockey for survival and the apparently fewer opportunities for promotion in today's flatter organisation structures.

Esteem needs may be only partly met as achievements go less recognised, the pressures of 'doing more with less faster' leaving little time for such pleasantries and a sense of achievement becoming an even more elusive butterfly.

Since it has been estimated by some career management experts that more than 50 per cent of unsuccessful executive career episodes are caused by the atmospherics of organisational life being at variance with the motivational needs of the individual, executives should therefore:

- determine their main atmospheric needs from the various categories and items noted above
- endeavour to position themselves in organisations, and under people where their atmospheric needs are best attended to
- judiciously select new roles or new employers with the same considerations in the forefront of their minds.

When the atmospherics are seriously out of alignment with individual needs, prepare and implement a defensive strategy which may include better understanding and accepting the situation; changing your own needs and expectations; communicating with others about your concerns with a view to changing the atmospherics in the organisation; 'attacking' it (but who is likely to win, the organisation or the individual?); or 'retreating' — moving on within the existing organisation or moving out. Getting atmospherics right helps to create an 'I win–you win' situation for both the individual and the organisation. Getting it wrong can cause grief and lead to casualties.

'Jobs may change — but the culture, style and quirks of the organisation are with you for as long as you are there,' says Martin Prentice, vice president training and education of a major consumer product manufacturing and marketing organisation in the United States. He continues:'It's not worth being too specific on what the next job will be: just concentrate on being in the right organisation fit, be prepared to learn something out of every job you're in, and a career will unfold . . . !'

R V Matthews, human resources director of Goodman Fielder International, agrees: 'Very important. A fit with an organisation is the basis for further success. As one of my early mentors told me, "Find me someone who fits [with the organisation] and we shall soon teach them what they need to know to do the job".'

Christopher Conybeare, independent consultant and associate director of Davidson & Associates, suggests an alternative approach regarding organisational fit: 'Important — but the individual also needs to make some compromises/concessions, or undergo training and development, or seek appointments in a different organisation.'

Meredith Hellicar, managing director of TNT Logistics Asia, has yet another point of view: 'My own experience would say that one can be very successful despite having a very poor fit with the organisation, if personal drive and all other factors are present.'

SUMMARY

Chapter 7 raises the following key issues:

- Executives and managers have differing motivational needs of the organisations for which they work. They include:
  - *material needs:* remuneration, safety and security
  - *structural needs:* degree and type of structure, bureaucracy and systems
  - *behavioural needs:* management style and interpersonal relationships
  - *emotional needs:* trust, social needs, esteem needs and sense of achievement.
- Most of these needs can be satisfied or frustrated by the senior executive to whom you report, as well as by the organisation itself — each has to be assessed in this context.
- Where your motivational needs are not met, the reaction is likely to be a negative or even stressful one — often perceived by others as a chemistry or fit problem of the individual.
- Your options when on the receiving end of adverse atmospherics (when your needs are not met) are: to better understand/accept it; to change your own needs and expectations; to communicate the need for, and seek to change the atmospherics; to attack it; or to retreat — move on or out.

Further Resources

In Section 7 of your *Executive Armoury*, you will find a profiling system designed to enable you to test the degree to which the atmospherics in your own organisation meet your motivational needs.

PART THREE

Leading The Charge Of Change And Winning The Challenge Of Transition

Transition — The process and passage of moving from one situation or stage of development to another, usually accompanied by uncertainty and a desire to identify, understand and quickly attain the next stage. A time for leadership and resolve.

PART THREE

Leading The Charge Of Change And Winning The Challenge Of Tempion

8

Managing Restructures And Succeeding As A Leader Of Change

'John Smart runs our Information Technology and Telecommunications Group. He always seems to be able to go with the flow. In fact, he appears to welcome change, sees uncertainty as a challenge, and maintains the morale and productivity of his staff even at times of significant organisational restructuring. We can always count on John and his team to attain their performance improvement objectives, whenever we restructure, which is more than can be said for many other divisions of the company.'

During the recession in the early 1990s, restructuring of organisations largely centred around 'downsizing' to effect cost savings. However, this tended to hide what also has been happening to organisations:

- *Globalisation*. As companies have expanded their international horizons, their competitors have become more evident in their own home markets.
- *Computers*. Not only has information technology enabled organisations to 'delayer' (strip out levels of management and supervision), but it has also shortened the various phases of the organisational life cycle, and opened up new 'reveal all' communication channels with customers and suppliers.
- *Management*. Greater competition and increased customer and shareholder expectations have driven managers and their organisations to become highly responsive and adaptable to the external environment.

The impact of all this on organisational life is 'revolution' rather than 'evolution', the rate and pace of change accelerating to the extent that we now have the 'variable' (rather than the 'fixed') organisation. The variable organisation anticipates change, and flexes and adapts to the needs for change.

'Change is the one constant,' says Kit Middleton, general manager human resources, Tandem Computers. 'It's absolutely critical to be able to live within this context — adaptable, flexible, meet the competition, etc.'

Restructures are also here to stay, to the extent that many organisations hardly complete one set of organisational changes before being forced into yet another restructure by external pressures.

Anatomies of Restructuring — Worst and Best Case Scenarios

Two-thirds of restructures are estimated not to achieve the objectives of restructuring within the desired timeframes. Peter Scott-Morgan, in his book *The Unwritten Rules of the Game: Master Them, Shatter Them and Break through the Barriers to Organisational Change*, verifies this from a detailed survey of 350 major companies across the United States undertaken by his company. Nearly every organisation seemed to be undertaking some form of significant change, be it cost reduction, improving efficiency or expanding sales volume. Such activities are usually inspired by a new CEO, a new strategic direction, pressure from competition or financial performance.

On the other hand, less than 20 per cent of such companies seemed to be satisfied with the outcomes of these changes, and more than one-third were in fact dissatisfied with the terms of performance improvement or the timeframe.

Take the case of the food factory relocating some of its production lines to a new factory in another state. Unfortunately, I was involved in this exercise as a consultant too late to have any impact on the outcome. Two years earlier, the accounting and administration departments had moved from the site to head office, an exercise which was far harder and which took far longer to implement than senior management had believed possible. The casual observer might have thought that management had learned some lessons from this, but they obviously had not, for the relocation of the production lines turned out to be an even more unsatisfactory experience, for *all* parties.

The problems started when employees perceived that managers appeared to 'go missing'. For some reason, weekly and daily routines started to change as managers attended extra meetings, some of them off-site. During breaks and in the canteen, employees from production, warehousing and distribution compared notes. Yes, senior managers across the company seemed to be involved in some sort of planning exercise. Could it be another restructure, or worse, a closure?

The signals were certainly there, that something 'big' was going on. The factory started to miss a beat or two as these signals converted to speculation. With unsettled minds on the shop floor, productivity dipped. Managers seemed not to notice. Meanwhile, a group of supervisors were heard to be talking in the canteen about the earlier centralisation of accounting and administration, and how it had never really worked out. 'Another bad decision by management!'

By the day of the announcement of the relocation of the production lines, speculation was so intense that when employees were assembled to hear the news, there was an air of inevitability and bad omen. The upcoming changes were announced and employees learned that the decommissioning and relocation of the three production lines would be phased in over the next 12 months, and production moved to a newer factory in Queensland. The critical point made by management was the need for continuing productivity, quality and output, as consumer demand for the product lines affected was increasing. The news was received with anger and scepticism. Not only were people going to lose their jobs, but also the plan for a running handover to the new factory clearly 'wouldn't work'.

Indeed this prophecy by the sceptics became a reality, as productivity dropped and quality problems soared during the transitionary period. It was clear that building the required stock levels by the time of the handover to the new factory was going to be an unsurmountable challenge.

Eventually, what the company had to do was to invest in completely brand-new production lines in Queensland, rather than phase in the relocation of the more modern process and packaging equipment from the existing factory. This was at enormous extra cost, and the whole exercise took more than two years to complete.

This anecdote represents the worst case scenario, summarised in Figure 8.1.

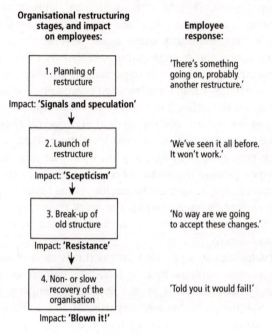

FIGURE 8.1
Worst Case Scenario

Here is additional evidence that organisations invariably do not attain their performance improvement objectives within an acceptable timeframe, post-restructuring. *Corporate Downsizing, Job Elimination and Job Creation*, a survey in 1996 by the American Management Association of more than 1000 medium-sized and large companies in the United States, found that some 70 per cent of them found no immediate increase in productivity and less than half of these organisations improved profitability the year after downsizing.

This was also found to be the case by Wayne F Cascio of the University of Colorado at Denver with his associates Clifford Young and James Morris, who examined whether changes in employment numbers affected company financial performance by studying more than 500 companies. Their findings showed that companies downsizing fared no better in terms of costs and profits, and that productivity improvement often was imaginary.

Other surveys, such as those conducted by the Australian Graduate School of Management and Professor Craig Littler of the University of Southern Queensland, point to the drawbacks of 'slash-and-burn' cost reduction and downsizing, which invariably lead to lower levels of morale and productivity. Richard D Freeman of the London School of Economics feels that such activities can even adversely impact on the ongoing health and longevity of companies. In his article in the *Economist* in April 1996 he says that one downside of head-count reductions is that organisations can suffer corporate amnesia from the loss of experience, background and knowledge that departs with the retrenched employees.

Going one step further, Dwight Gertz and Joao Baptista studied more than 1000 large companies and concluded in their book *Grow to be Great: Breaking the Downsizing Cycle*, that managers must move beyond the current rounds of downsizing, restructuring and re-engineering, and that they must grow to be great, arguing and demonstrating that growth opportunities are everywhere and across all business sectors — even in stable industries and companies 'too big to grow'.

David M Gordon, on the other hand, in his book *Fat and Mean: The Corporate Squeeze of Working Americans and the Myth of Managerial Downsizing*, says that downsizing at the executive and managerial level has not gone far enough, most companies having only gone halfway, being 'mean' but far from 'lean'. Indeed, most American companies employ more managers and supervisors than ever before, he claims, the overstaffing of management hierarchies being balanced by the inadequate compensation of workers who are prodded to work harder by instilling the fear of worker layoffs. US corporations have become fat and mean, he concludes, and need to become lean and decent.

However, restructuring can work well provided it is meticulously conceived and even more meticulously implemented. In fact, the anatomy of a more successful restructuring can be demonstrated by the insurance company which decided to contract out its information technology department and 'call-centre' (inbound and outbound telemarketing and customer service). Rather than rush this exercise, even though cost savings and other benefits appeared significant, the company decided to take a well-planned approach in order to minimise disruption, employee resistance, and the potentially adverse impact on customer service if things went wrong during the changeover.

Six months before initiating the contract-out option, management stepped up its proactiveness in the context of staff communication. Briefings were conducted on the 'changing face of the insurance sector', and information was shared about responses by competitors to these changes. Communication was two-way at these briefings, and feedback, questions and ideas were encouraged. ('Communication of change is done poorly in most large organisations,' remarks Kerri Burgess, chief of staff, Citibank Ltd.) Managers increasingly were encouraged to become more available to staff and a more open, positive and communicative environment developed. In this way, 'development opportunities' for the company were more regularly addressed and discussed, as was the need to 'move forward in response to external change'.

By the time the 'contract-out' plans were announced, the organisational environment was so fertile to receive such news, that even those directly affected seemed to accept the decision as being right for the company. What helped was the painstaking efforts by senior management to describe how this change tied in with the vision of where the company was headed, and the values or principles which drove how the exercise would be implemented, including extremely fair separation arrangements for those who would have to leave the organisation (some of them joining the two external contractors).

In the words of Jack Welch, CEO of General Electric, quoted in the book *Control your Destiny or Someone else Will* by Noel M Tichy and Stratford Sherman, 'Companies need overarching themes to create change. If it's just someone pushing a gimmick or program, without an overarching theme, you can't get through the wall.'

Back at the insurance company, from initiation onwards, the exercise was a success. All staff seemed clear about their changing goals and roles, and a 'can-do' atmosphere prevailed. As progress was made, staff not only cooperated but took the initiative and necessary modifications were made on the run in order to facilitate the changes. In this, managers seemed to be leading more from behind, staff often seeking and implementing their own solutions.

As the new information technology and call-centre arrangements settled into place, everyone felt themselves to be winners. Morale and productivity were at new heights, bottom line results flourished, and the size of annual salary increases recognised the efforts made by all and were funded by the cost savings.

The anatomy of a successful restructuring can also be summarised in diagram format, as shown in Figure 8.2.

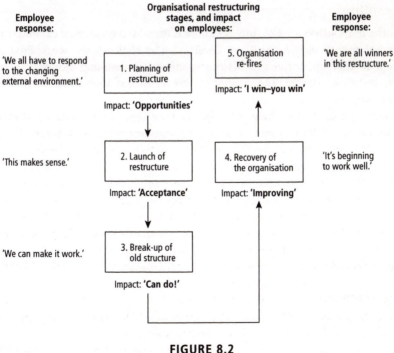

FIGURE 8.2
Best Case Scenario

In organisational restructuring, what usually separates the worst case scenario from the best case, is the capacity of executives to embrace change, and to lead others through change when organisational life seems so turbulent and uncertain.

Leadership of Change Competencies

'You have to be very conscious of the fact that change is going to accelerate,' says John T Ralph, former chief executive officer, CRA Limited, when interviewed about the book *Leadership, Australia's Top CEOs: Finding out what makes them the best*, by James C Sarros and Oleh Butchatsky. 'You may think that we've had a lot of change in the last ten years, but there is going to be more in the next ten . . . You can't bring about change in an organisation if you don't have the people prepared to accept change and work to respond to it in a positive way!'

'Change is the currency of today's environment,' says Joe Fischer, manager Human Resources Department and Regional Staff Coordination of Nestlé Australia Ltd. 'If an executive can't demonstrate capability to deal with change (for self and team) then he/she won't succeed.'

Besides knowing how to manage restructures, required competencies for the leadership of change include *adaptability*, certain elements of *entrepreneurism*, *resilience* and, above all, *open, two-way communication*. The following anecdotes describe executives whom I believe display particular capabilities in these required competency areas.

Adaptability

One of the most adaptable executives I know is Fred Morely, a senior executive in the information technology sector. When confronted by challenges at work, Fred is able to take a flexible approach to solutions, rather than assuming 'business as usual'. Indeed, he seeks variety and change at work, rather than routine, and when experiencing new situations, is curious and probing.

Although upholding corporate policy, Fred can be seen by colleagues as sometimes being nonconformist, adapting to changing circumstances rather than resisting them, comfortable with the unexpected and interested in the unconventional. Fred's management and leadership style changes according to the competence of the particular direct report and the urgency of the particular task, and is seen by direct reports as flexible rather than rigid in day-to-day operations.

In problem-solving, Fred thinks 'outside the square' and actively seeks input from others when confronted by changes at work. Kenneth J Roberts, company director of ATG, CSL and AGEN, describes it this way: 'Style flexibility and adaptability to changing internal and external non-controllable variables.'

Entrepreneurism

I would describe Susan Rheingold, marketing manager of a food service company, as an excellent example of an 'entrepreneurial' executive. She is good at experimenting with new ways of doing things and is successful at innovation, be this in the form of new products, services, processes or systems. Indeed, she displays a certain 'daring' and tries out brand-new concepts at work, not only taking the initiative, but also accepting accountability for the results from the initiative — good or bad.

Displaying an independent style and acting autonomously, Susan is as good at development as she is at straight maintenance of ongoing operations. This includes taking risks when the rewards are high, but also understanding the possible benefits *and* adverse consequences of taking risks. Indeed, Susan is good at managing risks, and at applying preventative monitoring appropriately.

'Sustained success will only be achieved when an organisation can exploit new opportunities and changing circumstances faster and more effectively than your competitors,' remarks Philip Johnston, director Cabarita Operations, Glaxo Wellcome Australia Ltd.

Resilience

John Baxter runs a medium-sized transport company. He can handle and manage stress: he avoids the negative impacts of stress at work, leaves 'troubles' at work rather than taking them home, and sleeps well and 'enjoys weekends' rather than worrying about work. Resilience also implies a capacity to persevere when the going gets rough. Indeed, John is considered to be extremely tough and forges ahead at times of adversity, getting the desired results even when confronted by difficult work situations.

John confronts change as a way of life rather than as a hindrance, and accepts change positively. Even though the challenge may be extreme when given a job to do, he completes it and is seen as a good ally by colleagues when the going gets rough and when everyone is up against it. Resilient executives like John Baxter have to have a 'dogged streak' of perseverance, particularly at times of change or uncertainty. Rodney Lester, managing director of AMP General Insurance, sums it up this way: 'Resilience is a key requirement — the capacity to bounce back when things do not pan out as planned.'

Open, two-way communication

Val Neilson manages a major public hospital. One of the secrets of her success is that she communicates well with direct reports, peers and superiors, keeping them informed as and when necessary. This includes understanding the other party's point of view before responding, and *listening twice as much as talking* in interpersonal communication.

The 'physical' barriers to effective communication are understood and minimised by Val — noise, outside interference, incoming phone calls and other interruptions; as are the 'behavioural' barriers — the expectations of other parties which may be different to Val's own and influencing what they choose to hear. Val's written communications are usually planned and well thought-out, rather than 'dashed off' too spontaneously. Similarly, her presentations to groups are well planned, with a clear objective of what is to be achieved with each particular audience.

At times of organisational change, Val communicates the changes to all affected parties, both in person and in writing regularly — she has found that communicating changes once or twice is not enough at times of restructuring. She agrees with

Robert Levering, a consultant with Arthur D Little and co-author of the book *The 100 Best Companies to Work for in America*, who believes that the better organisations encourage employees to ask difficult and even embarrassing questions. In his view, the human resources function should champion such mechanisms.

Finally, Val is seen as approachable by direct reports, encouraging questions and concerns and seeking to hear quickly about bad, as well as good, news.

Which executives and managers that you know display adaptability, entrepreneurism, resilience and skills in open, two-way communication? How do your leadership of change competencies compare? What can you learn, and how should you adapt your behaviour, to become an outstanding leader of change?

'All major corporations are looking for this trait. Certainly, at the moment it is the characteristic that is essential for promotion. It can cause enemies, of course, and in some cases, leads to the downfall of executives,' says R V Matthews, human resources director of Goodman Fielder International.

Lawrie Horder, head of human resources, Business Financial Services NSW and ACT, National Australia Bank, agrees with its importance: 'In a dynamic change environment, more than ever followers are needing effective leaders with strong skills in this area, and organisations are demanding it.'

'Change has to come from the top to be effective,' says Moira Holmes, director human resources, Hitachi Data Systems. 'If senior management is not comfortable with, and committed to change, it won't happen.'

Being an outstanding leader of change is inspiring others to embrace, cope with and indeed excel at times of change. This requires not only being a leader of change oneself, but developing a culture and a set of business processes within the organisation which stimulate change and experimentation, and celebrate risk-taking, according to Professor Jerry Porras from Stanford Business School and co-author of *Built to Last: Successful Habits of Visionary Companies*.

Yes, leadership of change is not about charismatic leadership. Rather, leadership of change embodies the capabilities described, *and* ensures that the necessary organisational environment exists to seek out, embrace and exert maximum leverage of the impact of the changing external environment, for the organisation, its objectives and its people.

Best Principles and Best Practice in Downsizing

Time and again, thunder-bolt 'slash-and-burn' staff cuts have not resulted in the desired cost reduction and other goals. The reasons often relate to the trauma caused by such draconian measures and the negative impacts on remaining staff in terms of reduced morale and productivity.

More enlightened organisations seek to attain any necessary head-count reductions in two ways. First, they do so by improving their forward planning and relying on natural attrition, internal redeployment to other more buoyant areas of the organisation, early retirement, leave of absence, study leave, secondments to other organisations, part-time work, pay cuts, job sharing and selective voluntary redundancy (retaining and rewarding talent, however).

Secondly, if they do need to move faster than this as a result of unexpected externally driven forces — for example, happenings in the market place or economy, then they do it according to what I call 'Best Principles, Best Practice' — BP^2. The leaders in providing specialised advice to help ensure BP^2 are Davidson & Associates, who have been developing their expertise in this area over the past 14 years in Australia, and more recently in Asia and New Zealand.

Leadership of Change on the Battlefield. On 25 October 1415, King Henry V of England, after winning the battle for the Port of Harfleur, was returning to Calais with his depleted and hungry army of 6000 men.

They were intercepted in a narrow valley by Charles d'Albret, Constable of France, and his army of 25 000 strongly armed men. Henry tried to negotiate a truce, but to no avail. The odds were against them and Henry was forced to think 'outside the square'.

Although his army was outnumbered by more than four-to-one, Henry devised what turned out to be a winning leadership of change strategy based on the following facts:
• Recent heavy rains had turned the narrow valley into a quagmire.
• The French were predictable in their use of heavily armoured, and therefore weighty, mass formations of cavalry to lead the charge, followed by infantrymen.
• The English were mainly lightly equipped archers and nimble foot soldiers.
• The archers were longbowmen. Would their light metal-tipped arrows penetrate the French army's heavy armour?

The challenge seemed overwhelming to Henry's soldiers until he addressed them with a rousing emotional speech and turned fears of defeat into a thirst and hunger for victory.

The French cavalry charged, became bogged down in the mud and were sitting targets for the archers, blocking the path of the infantry who also suffered from the continuous waves of arrows. The English foot soldiers made quick raids on the French as they stumbled in the mud, with no signs of leadership and no alternative defensive strategy. It became a bloodbath as the English overwhelmed their counterparts, killing 5000 with a loss of only 200 men.

Henry's deployment of what few strengths his army possessed succeeded in turning a demoralised brigade into one with fire in its belly and completely outmanoeuvred the French.

This English victory paved the way for the domination of most of France by the English for the next 35 years.

the bulletproof executive

Take the case of the finance company which decided it needed to centralise operations, reduce staff head-count and develop more of a customer focus. At the time I was called in, the company had not been performing well in terms of financial results and other benchmarks. It appeared to be overstaffed, and head office seemed to be unable to control the highly decentralised organisational structure and state-based operating business units. A recent customer survey suggested that the company was overly product-driven, and inadequate in understanding and attending to the real needs of customers.

A new managing director had recently been appointed from a consumer product manufacturing and marketing background. In his previous position he had turned a substantial food product group from a loss to a healthy bottom line by:

- successful new product development based on extensive consumer market research, supported by innovative 'above and below-the-line' promotional campaigns
- centralising operations and closing down marginal plants
- substantial head-count reductions, undertaken according to BP^2
- development of morale and productivity through his own inspirational leadership and the progressive implementation of a range of rebuilding initiatives.

Although the board of directors knew there was some risk in hiring a new CEO from a non-financial services background, they felt reasonably secure knowing that the company's senior executive team was comprised of excellent people with strong finance company track records. What they felt they needed was a strong new leader with a customer and employee orientation who could breathe new life into the organisation and turn around its performance through the development and implementation of innovative business strategies.

I recognised these qualities in Dan Small, the new managing director, when I first met him, and since then I have admired the way he approached what turned out to be an enormous task, the outcomes of which exceeded even the board's expectations. I was called in early enough to get involved in some initial business strategy development sessions conducted off-site, led and facilitated by Dan himself. In this way, each member of the senior executive team personally bought into the need for change, as well as the need for specific business development and profit improvement goals and supporting strategies.

My input concentrated on the human factor and the need for meticulous planning of the restructurings, and it was agreed by the team that anything less than BP^2 would be inadequate and unacceptable. The restructuring and downsizing was going to be significant, with some 350 people needing to leave over a 12-month period, from top to bottom in the organisation and throughout Australia.

The first phase of the restructuring process mirrored the earlier insurance company example: an ethos of open management was initiated by managers 'walking about' more, frequently articulating core statements about the state of the financial services industry and the need for change, along with the active solicitation of feedback to management from all employees. Concurrent to this, the organisation went into planning turbo-drive to ensure that all aspects of the change program were thought through and linked against timeframes, actions and responsibilities in a comprehensive master plan. A project planning software system was used to facilitate this.

An initial element of the schedule was my further coaching of the line managers in successful change management practices, and in how to communicate with their staff about their job losses, be they on a voluntary or involuntary basis. Included in this coaching was how to recognise and handle the emotional responses of departing staff at the time of announcing the restructure and job losses, how to risk-manage the exercise from humanistic and legal perspectives, logistics on the day of terminations, and how to communicate with and manage the 'stayers'.

The next phase looked into the dismissal avoidance strategies: natural attrition, early retirement, part-time work, job sharing and selective voluntary redundancy — all being fully considered and deployed where practicable. In fact, the voluntary redundancy option was offered to all employees for their consideration, but with no guarantee it would be granted in each case. Loyalty bonuses were promised to key staff where their requests for voluntary redundancy were declined, the bonuses payable after restructuring, and when the company attained its business growth and profit improvement goals.

As the restructure was launched, there was a dual emphasis on vision and principles for the stayers, and attendance on-site by my team of outplacement consultants for individual and group meetings with departing staff. These meetings focused on the staff themselves, allowing them to express how they felt about their changing employment status. A brief introduction was given to the outplacement programs which were to be provided.

In selecting an outplacement provider offering BP^2, Dan Small and his team attained exceptional results: 76 per cent of departing staff found new jobs within 16 weeks. Because such staff were treated well during their career transitions, they reported this back to remaining staff and customers alike, which as predicted, further enhanced employee and customer perceptions of the company, morale, productivity and business results.

Selecting the Best Outplacement Provider

Outplacement, which is now a much used strategy to facilitate the career transitions of leavers and help them target and find new jobs, is often poorly communicated in terms of content by providers, and is often poorly understood by companies in terms of the difference between 'tick and flick' exercises, and real, value-added and cost-effective outplacement interventions.

Outplacement is provided via individual one-on-one programs at the more senior level, and via group training workshops at the more junior level. At the very least, the following top ten elements need to exist in order to attain BP^2, as indeed they exist at Davidson & Associates.

1. A comprehensive phased outplacement approach to generate timely results

For those more senior people leaving the organisation:

- financial advice and health check-ups
- self and career assessment in order to define longer- and shorter-term career goals which are both appropriate for the individual and for the employment market place

- the development of, and coaching in, appropriate self-marketing strategies including references, resume development, networking, executive search and recruiters, advertised job recruitment, interviews and follow-up of contacts
- advice on the entrepreneurial or independent business option, or how to go about attaining non-executive directorships, or how to get into consulting or contracting
- support during the job search campaign in the form of use of private offices and library facilities (for researching companies), and secretarial, librarian and consultant input
- further advice at times of evaluating job offers, negotiating compensation packages, and settling into the new job and work environment during that critical induction period.

2. In-depth knowledge to minimise risks associated with terminations

In selecting a consulting company to assist in downsizing or restructuring, outplacement, career management and rebuilding programs should be the only business the provider is in — 100 per cent of the provider's focus and resources needs to be concentrated on these highly specialised professional service areas. The provider being both in recruitment and outplacement is a 'no-no'. It creates conflicts of interest, and the supposed internal referrals to recruiters just do not happen successfully. It also alienates other recruiters who see such dual-focus firms as competitors.

Being attached to an accounting firm is also a 'no-no'. Accountant partners invariably fail to see these services as a core area of their professional practice, and often fail to dedicate sufficient priority and resources to ensure BP^2.

3. Purpose-built programs to meet needs at every level

Many organisations require outplacement consultants to provide 'vertical' services from top to bottom of the organisation, and therefore need a wide range of programs to cater for CEOs and directors, senior executives, executives, managers, professional and technical staff, and blue- and white-collar staff.

4. Purpose-built segmented facilities designed to maximise candidate morale and progress

To maximise self-esteem and dignity, the outplacement provider needs separate office facilities in major city locations for outplacement candidates of different levels of seniority, each facility designed to meet the particular needs of its target audience: one self-contained office environment for directors and perhaps senior executives on individual outplacement programs; a similar facility for executives and mid-level managers as well as for senior professional and technical staff; and the third, for group job search workshops for operational staff.

5. The right environment to generate confidence and successful outcomes

Every outplacement candidate needs to be accorded an individual office rather than a workstation. This ensures confidentiality and further enhances dignity, self-esteem and career transition success. How can you make confidential phone calls in a noisy workstation environment? How would you feel if you were crowded into a 'corral' and only accorded the occasional use of a workstation during your job search campaign?

6. Career focus — the key to career management and transition success

Self and career assessment to develop career focus needs to be bolstered through the use of dedicated career profiling instrumentation (rather than broad-based psychological assessment which can overly emphasise *weaknesses*, at a time when outplacement candidates need to feel confident about and promote their *strengths*).

An example of such profiling is the Birkman Career Management Profile[SM] used by Davidson & Associates and developed by Dr Roger Birkman. It has a database of upwards of half a million individual profiles used for comparative analysis in career evaluation. The profiling technology accurately assesses occupational interests and the ideal work environment — each critical factors for career choice and success — as well as provides insights into the occupational areas which candidate characteristics appear to match.

7. Maximum face-to-face interaction — critical for early success

During the first phase of an individual outplacement program which typically covers self-assessment and career focus, seven to eight hours of one-on-one interaction between consultant and candidate is needed. In other words, the consultant should not simply hand a candidate a self-help manual or put them in front of a computer screen. Extensive face-to-face interaction with an experienced consultant is critical at this stage in order to attend to candidate emotions and to kick-start the career transition process.

8. Highly individualised treatment to hasten successful outcomes

All outplacement processes and programs should be driven by the needs of the candidate, who has to be treated on a highly individualised basis, rather than as part of a 'production line'. This also applies to group job search workshops, where course design, small group attendance and the skills of facilitators need to ensure a highly personalised approach for each participant.

9. Unfair dismissal dangers and remaining employee alienation to be avoided

Professional consultants of the highest calibre and experience in outplacement need to be used to minimise the risks associated with dismissals. BP^2 provides outplacement candidates with greater confidence and a more positive, constructive approach. This is reflected in conversations between candidates and remaining employees who see that their employer is providing the best support available to those who have departed from the organisation.

Anything less than BP² on the other hand, may lead to the greater potential for legal action and deep concerns in the minds of remaining employees, adversely affecting their morale and productivity, potentially at great cost.

10. Risks inherent in using under-experienced or inadequately qualified staff

Given these risks, outplacement providers should not use 'program supervisors' (often senior administration staff) for counselling or advice to candidates. The provider should only employ consultants whose qualifications, experience and expertise are recognised at the highest executive level.

Best Principles and Best Practice in Rebuilding

As the break-up of the old organisational structure was happening back at base with Dan Small's financial services company, the firm continued to adopt BP² by prioritising the key elements of successful leadership of change. Goals and roles were clearly identified and linked from the organisation to each individual. In moving to the recovery of the organisation, all managers — topped up with additional coaching — increasingly allowed their teams and direct reports to decide on and implement improvements 'on the run'. In fact, managers were by now truly leading from behind, rather than micro-managing from the front.

Additionally, at the break-up and recovery stage, my consultant colleagues and myself were called in to advise on, and provide progressively, a range of rebuilding interventions including *counselling, coping and managing, new team building* and *career focus*.

Time and again, organisations seem to underestimate the impact of restructures on remaining staff, which is why such rebuilding initiatives are invariably needed, in order to:

- facilitate the timely attainment of performance improvement goals after restructuring
- enable managers to cope with change better and manage others more successfully at times of organisational change and uncertainty
- offset the risks of remaining staff feeling betrayed or becoming angry, anxious, depressed or resentful about staff departures and necessary internal changes
- similarly offset the risks associated with such emotional responses, including reduced productivity and risk-taking, role ambiguity, increased absenteeism, and bailouts of talented executives, managers and staff (often the first to go when the organisation is in strife).

Thus the objectives of special rebuilding initiatives are based around rebuilding morale, productivity, performance and commitment. In this, *counselling* often represents the first step, as was the case with Dan Small's company. At the break-up stage I advised him that he would need to have counsellors available, both to advise line managers on how to attend to any anxiety, trauma or grief experienced by remaining staff, and to be available themselves for direct intervention where needed.

Coping and managing skills development was provided by my colleagues and myself in two forms. First, a skills development workshop was provided to all line managers which focused on:

- how to cope with changes personally
- how to manage others at times of change and uncertainty
- how to recognise and handle the predictable elements inherent in organisational restructuring
- how to minimise the intensity and timeframe of reduced productivity during transitions
- how to develop leadership of change competencies.

The outcome was a much more confident and positive management group, who in fact became a much better equipped and more effective group of leaders of change. Back-to-back with this, we provided half-day 'handling change' workshops for all employees, addressing very similar topics, yet from the employee's perspective.

The double impact of managers developing their leadership of change skills and employees developing their coping skills has a highly potent effect. In fact, Dan Small remarked that he felt these particular interventions enabled the organisation to accelerate through the break-up stage to recovery, far faster than he had seen in any other organisational environment at a time of restructuring, in his more than 20 years as an executive.

As new teams were brought together, we were able to assist through the provision of *new team building* profiling and group discussion sessions. The objectives and outcomes of these initiatives were the rapid development of interpersonal relationships between new team members, and the enhancement of team composition and processes.

Finally, as the organisation nudged towards the re-firing stage, and as the 'I win–you win' theme of improved motivation, productivity, organisational performance and individual reward was increasingly becoming an attainable reality, we addressed *career focus* by providing career management counselling at mid-to-senior levels in the organisation. Outcomes sought and invariably attained were a greater sense of control by executives and staff over their own destinies, the better development of ideas and strategies as to how to progress their careers within the restructured, flatter organisation, and a greater alignment between personal and organisational goals.

Dan Small's company re-fired and attained 'I win–you win' within its desired timeframes. End of story. No wonder the company quickly achieved sought-after employer status!

All companies can do what Dan Small's company did, and derive the same benefits. Out with slash-and-burn! In with restructuring Best Principles, Best Practice!

SUMMARY

Chapter 8 raises the following key issues:
- Major leadership of change competencies include:
  — how to manage restructures; adaptability
  — entrepreneurism (particularly the elements of experimentation, innovation and daring — balanced by an appreciation and application of risk management)
  — resilience; and, above all, open, two-way communication.
- For downsizing to work, it requires that Best Principles, Best Practice (BP^2) is applied in any necessary head-count reductions, which includes:
  — rigorous planning of restructures and meticulous attention to the human factor
  — coaching of line managers who have to inform staff they have lost their jobs
  — attendance by outplacement consultants on-site at dismissals to attend to the emotional needs of departing staff and to describe to them the career transition support available
  — provision of a range of outplacement programs.
- BP^2 also requires the provision of survivor management and rebuilding processes like some of those also provided by Davidson & Associates, which can cover:
  — the planning of rebuilding
  — alleviating anxiety in the workplace at times of restructures
  — training of managers in personally coping with, and managing staff at times of change
  — new team building
  — career evaluation programs for those executives, managers and staff unsure about their futures in the newly restructured, flatter, organisation.
- The whole exercise, if undertaken according to BP^2:
  — minimises trauma on the part of departing staff, the managers engaged in the exercise, and remaining staff
  — maximises the self-esteem and dignity of those leaving
  — upholds and enhances positive perceptions of the organisation by staff, customers and the public at large.

Further Resources

In Section 8 of your *Executive Armoury* you will find a step-by-step guideline on how to plan and manage restructures. Section 2 will help you to assess your leadership of change competencies. Section 9 can be used in selecting an external outplacement provider.

9

Avoiding 'Slash-and-Burn' Staff Dismissals (Only To Hire Again Later!)

'I must confess that on reflection, I used to have a "hire and fire" mentality towards executives and staff. We used to have a bad reputation for this. No wonder we always found it hard to attract, retain and develop people of high calibre. Fortunately, a few years ago we started to implement alternatives to dismissals at all levels and now we are reaping the rewards. These are in the form of consistently high levels of morale, productivity and job performance, and a steady stream of talent seeking to join our organisation.'

Leaders of change need to ensure that they retain, motivate and develop staff at all levels if they wish success for themselves and their organisations. An organisation is only as good as its people. Executives and managers with staff management responsibilities are also only as good as their people. It is teams which make organisations and individual executives and managers successful — a fact which people often lose sight of.

Ken Boag, managing director of Tower Life Australia Limited, puts it this way: 'Just as in buying property, position is the "P word", in a business it is the people — people will make or break you.'

'Good people can make even a poor manager look good!' says Martin Prentice, vice president training and education of a major consumer product manufacturing organisation in the United States. 'Having the talent is increasingly going to make the difference in a world which is becoming more complex and subject to rapid change,' remarks Bruce Coates, general manager employee relations Ampol. 'Good leaders must surround themselves with the best, and not feel intimidated by this,' says Brett Haly, general manager customer relations and organisation development, Tower Life.

I have come across many people whose dismissals — and the costs and trauma associated with them — potentially might never have happened, had some of the principles and practices in this book been adopted. The irony is that often such 'failures' end up working very satisfactorily and effectively for the competition, or are hired back later as contractors or consultants. Also, many organisations downsize only to find that six months later they are in hiring mode again!

The anatomy of a 'firing' often goes something like this. The individual's performance or fit becomes a concern and the boss perceives that 'things seem to be going a bit off the rails' — any one or a combination of the four triggers of failure start to emerge — without perhaps the boss or the individual really understanding the situation. Instead of talking about this in a constructive fashion, positions become polarised, two-way communication dries up, the situation goes from bad to worse, and . . . 'bang!' — a dismissal is the outcome.

'The easy way out, and the most costly, is to hire and fire,' says John Baker, independent consultant and associate of Davidson & Associates. 'An organisation with a hire and fire mentality will not obtain the necessary dedication from its employees,' says John Walmsley, production and engineering manager Masport Pty Ltd and formerly chief design and development engineer of Gas and Fuel Corporation.

Reasons for Dismissals

Before examining possible dismissal avoidance strategies in more detail, it is worth considering the more obvious reasons for dismissals from the employer's perspective. Broadly speaking, employers categorise dismissals into four main groupings:

1. *Economic*. In the recession of the early 1990s in Australia, and indeed since then while largely undifferentiated organisations endeavour to compete on the basis of 'low-cost', staff at all levels have been the target of an unprecedented volume of retrenchments. This has been exacerbated by international organisations seeking low-cost production and management, wherever this takes them worldwide. Economic rationalisation will continue into the foreseeable future for large and small organisations alike, as low cost continues for many to be the main competitive thrust — genuine 'differentiation' remaining an elusive competitive concept, let alone a reality, for so many companies.
2. *Capability*. This relates to whether or not an employee has the necessary experience, competencies, and in some cases qualifications to be able to do the job. If the base capability is not there, the tenure of the employee is at extreme risk.
3. *Self-motivation*. Capability is one thing, but putting into practice what you can do, really depends on the level of self-motivation through job fit and the degree to which the 'atmospherics' of the organisation attend to the motivational needs of the individual.
4. *Not fitting in*. If an executive or manager has difficulty with an employee who, for whatever reason, seems to have a personal chemistry or fit problem with the people and the organisation, then a replacement is usually sought rather than time and effort spent in trying to resolve the problem. One reason is because not many senior people are equipped with the necessary skills to deal with personal chemistry and fit problems.

However, the economic justification for firing 'misfits' has always been and remains highly doubtful given all the costs associated with it, and from a risk-management perspective, how can you guarantee that a costly replacement will perform any better, particularly when you consider the inadequacies inherent in most hiring and selection procedures?

Alternatives to Economic Reasons for Dismissals

Natural 'attrition', or natural labour turnover, can be a very cost-effective approach to head-count reduction, when economic reasons dictate this need. This cost-effectiveness comes about from not having to pay separation packages, as a result of resignation rather than dismissal. Clearly this minimises the trauma often associated with dismissal which can be experienced not only by departees, but also by those senior executives having to dismiss them, as well as remaining executives, managers and staff who wonder when the axe may be wielded in their own direction. This takes their eyes off the job, affects their morale and self-motivation, and results in lost productivity and lower job performance.

However, natural attrition may also have some drawbacks. This can include the wrong staff deciding to leave — in other words, the talent. Better-performing employees are more readily employable elsewhere, rather than those considered to be of lesser potential, who find it harder to secure alternative employment. Unfortunately, therefore, at times of organisational difficulty or uncertainty, it is very often the talent that moves on first.

Also, people may move on of their own accord at the wrong time. With the rate and pace of change in the external environment creating the need for head-count reductions, savings are often needed fast — or so it seems to the board of directors and CEO. Waiting for natural attrition may just take too long for them. However, if they really did their sums and costed out the full costs of separation, lost motivation and productivity, and potentially adverse public and customer image at the time of major downsizings, they might be surprised to find that natural attrition can actually be a far more cost-effective strategy.

But there is often more than meets the eye! Over the years, many organisations have experienced the dreaded salary 'bracket creep', when salary bands at various levels — often fuelled by over-zealous search and recruitment consultants whose fees are based on percentage of salary — have been soaring skywards, and this can be particularly costly at the senior staff level. The saving of removing, say, ten senior staff members, perhaps each with total annual compensation costs of $75 000 and not replacing them (but relying perhaps on a flattening of the organisation structure and redistribution of their job content), is $750 000 annually. Very tempting, even if the costs of removing them are high.

However, this may not be as cost-effective as it first may appear, as after their dismissals the new organisation structure can take a long time to recover and re-fire, and to really benefit from the savings. No small wonder some dismissed staff members find themselves back at the organisation working on contract, to help make this happen.

An alternative way to effect such savings, but at a reduced initial level, is to freeze the salaries of the employees in question, and even reduce their salaries following appropriate notice periods. But an across-the-board salary freeze or reduction may cause the talent to leave, and can damage morale and productivity over the longer term. Selective salary freezes or reductions may also be difficult to implement, but again need to be considered as options.

Indeed, the extent of this potential damage depends on how affected staff are managed at the time of, and after they have been told about, the change to their salary arrangements. For example, if they have been paid 'well over the top' as a result of salary bracket creep, then they are likely paid well over the external market rate. This can be confirmed by compensation specialists, recruiters and career management specialists to whom access by affected staff should be encouraged, to check this out independently.

Other forms of pay cuts can also be used — for example, decreasing the base remuneration and increasing the incentive element which can be based on both organisational performance and personal results. Pay cuts can also be made in return for shares in the company.

Other strategies as alternatives to dismissal for economic reasons include *early retirement*, *part-time work*, *job sharing*, *leave of absence*, *study leave*, *secondments to other organisations* and *voluntary redundancy*.

Early retirement and part-time work

Offering incentives for early retirement can often be much more cost-effective than dismissals, as may be the offer to move to part-time work. There are countless numbers of staff, perhaps in their fifties, who may have a partner working full or part-time, whose children are working, and who have perhaps inherited some family assets. Such people might leap at the chance to work four, or even three days per week, or seriously consider the early retirement option. Retirement counselling of the type offered by Davidson & Associates often facilitates this option.

Job sharing

Taking the part-time strategy on a broader basis, this may create the opportunity for some jobs effectively to be shared. This job sharing strategy certainly may not fit some organisations, but may be suitable for the larger organisation with sizeable and homogeneous staff groups.

Leave of absence

Leave of absence can also be offered, whether this be for study leave or a sabbatical. When offered in one company I can recall, employees retained their benefits and received government unemployment payments, and were 're-hired' when the fortunes of the company improved and they were needed again.

Secondment

Another approach is secondment to suppliers and customers, sometimes on a salary-sharing basis between the two companies. This offers the seconded employee the opportunity to develop new skills and better understand the operations and needs of companies in the supply and distribution chain.

Voluntary redundancy

These approaches offer humane, dignified and sensitive treatment to those affected, as does the voluntary redundancy option, which can be offered across-the-board or selectively. Across-the-board offers for voluntary redundancy may mean that the best employees — those more readily employable elsewhere — put their hands up and leave, denuding the organisation of talent.

Selective voluntary redundancy may take several forms, including specific employees or areas of the organisation, or following a broader invitation for expressions of interest in voluntary redundancy with no guarantee it will be granted in each case. Selective offers may back-fire, however, when those wishing to leave are in fact asked to stay and therefore feel penalised.

The story can go like this: 'You mean to tell me that you are letting others go, with golden handshakes, who really have not performed well over the years, whereas in my case, and I'll remind you that all my performance appraisals have always been rated "excellent", my reward for this is that I don't get a golden handshake and I have to stay and work even harder as a result of fewer people remaining in the organisation . . . this is totally unfair!' Again, morale and performance can be adversely affected in such cases. Some companies have risk-managed these situations successfully by granting loyalty bonuses to key staff after restructuring when the organisation re-fires and attains new target levels of performance.

In one case, I was called in to provide career counselling to an employee who, after six months of being told his request for voluntary redundancy would likely be accepted, at the eleventh hour found his request was rejected. His reaction was to go on stress leave for two weeks and a resolve, on returning to work, to do the barest minimum 9am to 5pm, with the objective of triggering an involuntary redundancy at best, or a better work and home-life balance at the very least! Even a small loyalty bonus might have eased this situation, and of course, he should never have been led to believe his request for voluntary redundancy would be granted in the first place.

However, voluntary redundancy certainly has its place if carefully and sensitively planned and implemented, and has many advantages in the contexts of dismissal avoidance and enhancing sought-after employer status in the community.

In summary, and as addressed in the book *Coping with Job Loss* by Carrie R Leana and David C Feldman, because of the devastation layoffs create, there are a range of alternatives corporations should consider. When layoffs are unavoidable, the authors have found, advance notification, severance pay, extended benefits, retraining programs and outplacement counselling help employees most, and also benefit the company.

Alternatives to Dismissals for Reasons of Capability, Motivation and 'Not Fitting In'

There are a broad range of such alternatives, and these include: *internal redeployment, allowing resignation rather than dismissal, term contracts, proper use of performance appraisal processes, performance improvement programs, 'square-peg-in-round-hole' counselling,* and *mid-career counselling.*

Internal redeployment

Internal redeployment is a humane and sensitive approach, and for a broad range of reasons may be very appropriate to consider in many instances, and invariably are preferable to dismissal. These instances can include:

- when the 'atmospherics' in a certain part of the organisation do not attend to the motivational needs of the individual, be they material needs, structural needs, behavioural needs or emotional needs

- when the individual exhibits leadership traits considered more desirable and relevant to other parts of the organisation
- when the individual possesses a style which is considered to add greater value to a team elsewhere in the organisation, the individual perhaps being too much of a clone in the existing team, or, too diametrically opposed to the current team leader in terms of operating style
- where current job fit is poor — in other words, the interests, values and motivational capabilities of the individual are not represented in the current job
- where career alignment is poor — in other words, where an individual's career path aspirations are better met by the individual working elsewhere in the organisation
- where the individual operates in a staff management capacity, whereas a more functional or technical capacity may better suit the individual's strengths, or vice versa.

However, in reality, there may be limited opportunities for internal redeployment, as comparable-level jobs may simply not be available (comparability means within 95 per cent of the salary of the former job, at a reasonably nearby location, and requiring a comparable skill-set), meaning that the potential internal redeployee may well claim a separation package instead of being redeployed.

Also, a major danger inherent in internal redeployment may be the 'dead-wood transfer' syndrome, where an individual who is perceived to have very poor capability, motivation or ability to fit in, is transferred across to another area of the organisation as a problem for someone else to manage!

Resignation rather than dismissal

Allowing an individual to resign rather than be dismissed may enhance self-esteem and dignity on the part of the departee, albeit somewhat superficially. For some departees, it is what others perceive which is important to them, and they may feel far better if they can be perceived as having resigned rather than as having been dismissed. From a re-employment perspective, a credible resignation is also better than a dismissal, but the emphasis has to be on the word 'credible'.

However, encouraging someone to resign rather than be dismissed may be fraught with legal dangers and can lead to cases of constructive dismissal and large payouts. A strategy to offset these risks is first to communicate to the individual at the termination interview that it is 'all over' and that the individual has to move on, career-wise. Then, when the dismissal message has really sunk in, ask how the individual would like this information communicated to other parties within and outside the organisation. Invariably the conversation comes around to the concept of the departure being communicated as a resignation to other people, although the departee needs to understand clearly that this option is offered purely on the basis of meeting the best interests of the individual, and that the official behind-the-scenes 'line' remains that of the organisation terminating the individual's employment.

It might be unwise to offer this option, however, if the performance of the individual has been very poor and is recognised by employees or customers as such.

Under these circumstances, and if a 'resignation' is allowed, there is a danger that management may be seen as lacking intestinal fortitude and as going for the soft option.

Term contracts

Term contracts are becoming more popular in both public and private sectors, the term usually being between one and five years, although three years is often used. Such contracts offer the potential for non-renewal if the employing organisation is less than inspired by the performance of the contractee, and thus provide a cost-effective exit route and an incentive for the individual to perform if seeking contract renewal.

However, term contracts may not always seem attractive to new potential hires who perhaps favour the permanent employment option. The length of their terms can pose problems if they under-perform. Finally, payout arrangements can prove costly, if the organisation needs to effect a termination prior to contract expiry.

Performance appraisal

Formal performance appraisal processes are rarely correctly used. First, the paperwork associated with them is often used subjectively and becomes no more than a 'happy sheet' to be completed every year. Secondly, when performance is assessed at being below satisfactory, this is often inadequately communicated to the appraisee, who does not always 'hear' bad news anyway. Thirdly, individual development needs often are poorly identified and development plans inadequately defined or implemented. Finally, if unsatisfactory performance is the case, formal warnings and supporting information are rarely adequately communicated or documented.

Yet the more objective use of performance appraisals and the real identification of, and attention to, development needs — let alone the correct application of formal warnings in extreme and adverse cases — offers a real alternative to dismissals, through rectification of performance problems before it becomes too late. The advantages of using these processes correctly include:

- The individual being appraised knows exactly what is expected.
- They have time and organisational support to develop their personal performance.
- There is early warning of potential outcomes if they are unable or unwilling to develop.
- In fact, they can 'shape up' or 'ship out' — shipping out more often than not on a voluntary basis, usually knowing when the time is coming for this to happen, and with time to seek alternative employment.

However, until the executives and managers involved in the performance appraisal process buy ownership of the need for, are adequately trained in performance improvement counselling and coaching, and are prepared to invest the time, then it is unlikely that the full benefits of performance appraisal will be realised.

Performance improvement programs

Such is the case with performance improvement programs, which can usefully be applied following an unsatisfactory performance appraisal or at other times when an individual's performance is perceived as being below satisfactory or deteriorating. Such programs are often given a timeframe, anything from three to six months, and indeed, have a start and end date with specific objectives, action plans and review dates which often are monthly.

In addition to such ongoing reviews, regular discussion is needed regarding all key incidents — good and bad — between the individual and their manager. The human resources function can also usefully be involved, with a human relations executive present at pre-, interim- and post-reviews. The goals, of course, are to improve personal performance and to prevent the situation deteriorating into a dismissal.

If, however, they do not result in improved performance to the extent required, then the process can be extended, or the individual may be transferred to another job position, demoted (and what has happened to the demotion option? It is rarely seen these days.) or dismissed. The key is that all concerned in the process understand and agree on the goals and the alternatives at the very outset of the program.

Additional key elements of such programs include:

* regular feedback regarding progress and regular coaching sessions
* specific written objectives which spell out the results to be achieved, the extent of the desired achievements and the timeframe
* the results being sought, not just effort
* mutual acceptance of objectives, attained by their joint establishment and agreement
* a mutual understanding of what non-achievement may result in — for example, demotion or relocation (internal or external)
* fewer objectives rather than too many — 'less is more' (too many objectives may be received negatively by the incumbent, reducing their tolerance for the whole exercise or negative feedback)
* opportunities for the individual to have progress recognised, and to receive help with any required corrective action
* written records regarding progress
* a supportive approach throughout
* when progress is not being realised, the restatement of possible outcomes and benefits of making progress, and possibly the establishment of new interim objectives.

'Square-peg-in-round-hole' counselling

'Square-peg-in-round-hole' counselling applies to those individuals who seem, for one reason or another, to be in the wrong job or somehow misaligned, adversely impacting on attitude, morale or performance. Such counselling can be undertaken by external specialists such as Davidson & Associates. It is also used when internal efforts to improve performance or fit issues have been exhausted and dismissal is a real possibility. The orientation for such counselling can be 'career management', when an individual's career is perceived to be in crisis and when there is a need to rekindle the person's motivational fires to optimise their contribution to the organisation.

Mid-career counselling

Mid-career counselling by an external specialist can also be useful applied at that critical mid-career period for people in their early or mid-forties. Such individuals may have been promoted beyond their capabilities, be in a performance 'plateau', be experiencing chemistry and fit problems, or indeed be in mid-life crisis.

Whatever the cause, the notion of saving a valuable asset, where up to $1 million may have been invested in the development and training, say, of a 25-year service employee, simply makes sound business sense. Such counselling can be difficult to accomplish purely internally, however, as both performance and fit issues can be very difficult to discuss, particularly with senior, long service mature executives or managers, exacerbated by underdeveloped communication and counselling skills or insufficient available time on the part of the senior executive having to conduct the counselling.

Such externally conducted 'career management' exercises, whether with a square peg or mid-career orientation, usually commence with a consultant undertaking familiarisation and a preliminary assessment with the line manager responsible for the problem individual, with a human resources executive also present. Symptoms and problems are addressed, the individual's career is reviewed, and the strategy for introducing the external third party is jointly developed, in the context that the problem person needs to be in agreement and buy ownership of the career management program.

Once the program has been initiated, the early elements include self-assessment by the individual, with a personal, job and career focus. This can be complemented by confidential interviews with the individual's superior, peers, direct reports and sometimes customers, all with a job performance and future career options orientation. Fit issues, if indeed they exist, are usually uncovered in this interview process, as indeed are any other problems.

The desired outcome is to attain agreement with the individual regarding perceived problems and potential solutions which may entail clarifying any ambiguities or uncertainties, improving understanding of, and communication with, others in the organisation, and identification of other development needs and appropriate resources, whether this be for technical, functional, management or personal development.

Career management programs of this nature culminate in action planning and implementation. Action planning involves a mutually agreed development program using the organisation's internal development and training resources wherever possible. Implementation of this is the responsibility of the individual, the line manager and the human resources representative — in other words, it is shared, with the external consultant appearing periodically for progress reviews and always available for hot-line advice. At senior levels, the consultant can continue to be used effectively for ongoing coaching in the key development areas ascribed.

The bottom line of such career management programs is to achieve some sort of outcome, whether it be improved performance or fit in the present job, modifications to the present job or reporting relationships, or successful redeployment within or outside the organisation — the latter via resignation or joint agreement, rather than straight dismissal.

Outcomes and Implications

Apart from all these potential courses of action helping organisations to avoid dismissals, there are direct financial benefits. For example, in the case of the $100 000 total cost per year poorly performing individual who shapes up and stays, rather than is dismissed, direct savings can easily be in the order of $160 000 when one takes into account the costs associated with the separation package, the outplacement service, possibly lower morale and productivity by others at the time of the dismissal, the costs of recruitment to find a suitable replacement, and lost performance and productivity during the induction of the new recruit.

Another example is the case of the poorly performing individual who resigns rather than having to be dismissed. Savings in the order of $65 000 can easily be realised. Similarly, if some of the strategies mentioned in this chapter — internal redeployment or a career management program — are applied to talent at risk of leaving the organisation, and if the talented individual stays rather than leaves, direct savings can easily amount to upwards of $65 000, plus the benefits of retaining a human asset of increasing value which is usually worth many times this sum of money.

However, the main opportunity for executives and managers deploying dismissal avoidance strategies is high levels of morale and performance, the further development of sought-after employer status by the organisation, and the attraction, retention and development of talented employees. There is absolutely no reason why executives and managers cannot, and should not, prioritise dismissal avoidance principles and practices in their business operations. For those that do, the benefits are enormous.

The acid test is to ask yourself the following question. Who are more important, customers or employees? Your answer initially may be customers, but without motivated, productive staff, how can customer needs be fully met? The answer has to be both customers and employees — equal in importance.

Would you ever dream of dismissing customers, particularly bearing in mind the costs associated with securing their custom in the first place? You would only allow this to happen if they were heavily in arrears or trading with you at unacceptably low margins, and even then the average company would think twice about terminating their custom. Every effort would be taken to seek to retain them at acceptable levels of cash flow or profitability. Every effort also needs to be taken to retain employees at acceptable levels of morale and performance. This is the first principle of management and needs to replace the hire-and-fire mentality that is prevalent today.

SUMMARY

Chapter 9 raises the following key issues:

- Leaders of change need to ensure they retain, motivate and develop staff at all levels, if they wish success for themselves and their organisations. Executives, managers and organisations are only as good as their people.
- The reasons for dismissal can be economic, capability, motivation or not fitting in, and in each case there is a range of potential alternatives to dismissal, including:
  — natural attrition, early retirement, part-time work, job sharing, leave of absence, study leave, secondments to other organisations and voluntary redundancy
  — proper use of performance appraisal processes
  — coaching and training; performance improvement programs
  — 'square-peg-in-round-hole' counselling
  — mid-career counselling; retirement counselling
  — internal redeployment, term contracts and resignation (rather than dismissal).
- There can be huge direct financial benefits in deploying such alternatives, the costs associated with separation packages, rehiring, induction of new recruits and so forth, easily running into six figures at senior levels.
- The main benefit of alternatives to dismissals is high levels of morale, productivity and job performance of staff, and the further development of the public image of the organisation as a 'sought-after employer', along with a steady stream of talent seeking to join as employees. Further benefits include:
  — Top-quality new recruits are always available, enhancing succession planning in the organisation.
  — Top-quality staff become committed to the organisation and tend to develop their careers within it, rather than leave.
  — Staff are given every process, support and encouragement to enable them to perform well and to be successful.

10

Nurturing Talent In This Era Of 'Hire And Fire'

'I believe we do a far better job than our principal competitors at selecting and developing high-calibre staff. Our staff turnover is lower — we rarely lose good people — and we always seem to have a choice of talent when seeking to fill those key vacant senior positions. Clearly, we are deriving huge benefits and competitive advantages from the changes we have made to our whole approach to selection and development.'

Leaders of change not only have to retain, motivate and develop their staff — in the context that managers and organisations are only as good as their employees — but they also have to be able to select and develop committed, high-calibre employees, utilising essential techniques which are so often given too low a priority.

'Managers get results through people. The better the quality of the talent you attract and retain, the better your own results,' remarks Ron Hopwood, director of human resources, 3M Australia Pty Ltd. 'Most employers would like to be recognised as an "employer of choice". Nurturing talent is a critical element,' says Bob Paterson, director human resources, Unisys Australia Limited, previously chief manager, card services, Westpac Banking Corporation.

Nurturing talent is 'fundamental to success,' says Tony Harbour, independent management consultant and formerly group personnel director of the Ocean Group PLC in the UK. 'Creating a culture which believes in "people" rather than "labour" is the key to future success.' However, nurturing employees can go too far. Says John Walmsley, production and engineering manager Masport Pty Ltd: 'Supporting a subordinate who is not performing because of poor skill levels can lead to the distrust of senior management, overwork of the manager and poor team performance.'

Selection of Talent

Over the years recruitment and selection approaches have polarised into three main 'clusters': *recruitment agency or executive search, unstructured approaches* and *behaviourally-based selection*.

Recruitment agency or executive search-type approaches usually entail candidates being sought and selected on the basis of having demonstrated a capacity to generate excellent results in job settings and organisational environments relevant to the needs of the hiring organisation. Unstructured approaches are where the interviewers and selectors have had little if any formal training in effective selection principles and practices. Behaviourally based selection approaches are those which concentrate on defining the critical requirements of the job in the form of a range of sought-after competencies relating to skills, knowledge, behaviours and self-motivation. By examining past behaviours in these competency areas, those involved in the selection process are then better able to predict future behaviours by the candidate in the new role.

Whatever approach is undertaken in selection, my experience indicates that insufficient understanding and priority attention in the selection of individuals is given to such success factors as those described in this book. Your *Executive Armoury* lists the factors which should be addressed, and in some cases relevant questions which can be used to derive appropriate information from senior-level candidates.

In summary, the key factors to be addressed in senior-level interviews include:

- matching an individual's major occupational interests, motivational capabilities and values to the job
- selecting and developing major leadership of change competencies
- ensuring an appropriate organisational 'atmosphere' exists, according to the needs of the individual
- clearly specifying and pursuing desirable leadership and related traits
- targeting the ideal make-up of teams
- focusing on management capabilities (particularly motivation and delegation), primary business drivers, and external futures when selecting new executives and managers
- taking into account the need for personal selling and group presentation capabilities.

Career Alignment of Talent

I will start off by recapping what is happening in the career environment and why executives and managers should be considering career alignment as one of the main planks in their human resources development processes. In the career environment today, we see many smaller flatter organisations, fewer middle management positions, apparently fewer promotional opportunities, and continuing organisational change. It is no small wonder that staff view their future careers with uncertainty. In many cases their commitment to the organisation, let alone trust, has eroded, with a significant impact on their job performance.

However, help is now at hand. Not only can career planning and ownership provide more clarity about an individual's future, a greater sense of control over one's own destiny, and thereby improved morale, but it should also be a fundamental element of performance management, and is often the 'missing link', as shown in Figure 10.1 overleaf.

Conventional performance management systems start with what the organisation seeks in terms of skills, competencies, aptitudes and so forth, which through

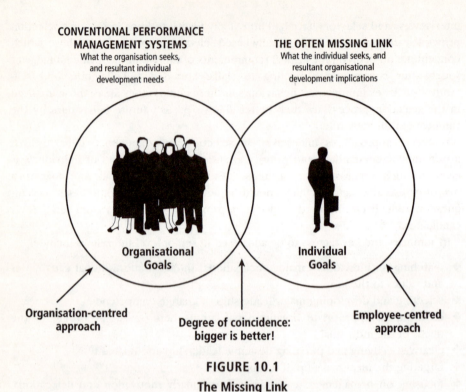

FIGURE 10.1
The Missing Link

performance appraisal leads to the identification of individual training and development needs. This is primarily an organisation-centred approach to performance management — so often seen in organisations today — but usually failing to take full account of the interests, values, capabilities and preferences of the individual. In fact, the *employee-centred approach*, often the missing link in performance management systems, takes great account of what the individual seeks, leading to implications for organisational development, training, management succession and so forth.

The 'bottom line' is that when both approaches are applied in an organisation, there becomes a greater degree of 'coincidence' between organisational and individual goals, leading to enhanced organisational and individual performance. Naturally, the greater the degree of coincidence the better. As executives and managers, therefore, what are we trying to achieve through greater career alignment?

First, we are trying to attain improved morale and a sense of personal control and destiny by each individual. Secondly, we are seeking improved job performance and individual 'value' to the organisation in the case of each employee. Next, we are trying to redefine career progress: central (expanding the existing job) and horizontal progress (job rotation at the same level), as well as vertical progress (promotion), the potential for the last of these being much reduced in many organisations.

Finally, by concentrating on individuals and their careers, we are trying to develop a sense of personal security in lieu of job security, or an ethos of lifetime 'employability' possibly with *several* employers, rather than 'life employment' with *one* employer. In fact, we are trying to help individuals attain personal commitment to an outcome, which can include staying and progressing within the organisation (for most employees), or leaving the organisation voluntarily and developing one's career elsewhere (perhaps for a small number of employees who cannot see their own futures coinciding with the future of the organisation).

Tim Hessell, human resources director of Frito-lay Australia, provides these insightful remarks: 'As knowledge work becomes a critical source of sustainable competitive advantage, demand will exceed supply for highest-calibre knowledge workers. Business success [will be] highly dependent on growth and reflective of this talent. Executives will need to create a "voluntary organisation" concept, where employees in demand choose to stay with the business because it can better satisfy the intrinsic and extrinsic needs of the individual, more so than competing alternatives.'

In endeavouring to maximise career alignment for their staff, executives and managers need to help their employees understand and apply relevant areas of Bulletproof Executive thinking, as follows:

- *Job fit*. Staff need to be able to identify their main occupational interests, motivational capabilities and values, and ensure they are represented in current and future jobs. If they are not, then the job parameters need to be changed, or the individual needs to change to a job offering a better match with these criteria, in order to maximise self-motivation and personal effectiveness.
- *Career consulting*. Few of us have ever had any career guidance, and career ownership starts with employees being given the tools and techniques for developing career focus and job targets. This is best facilitated by external experts who are objective and are seen to be detached from organisational politics. There are several specific areas where external consulting input can add particular value:
  — Where talented individuals are perceived to be at risk of leaving the organisation, and where there may be an opportunity for greater career alignment between individual goals and organisational goals. With the problems and costs associated with finding and hiring talent, far better to retain and further develop this talent than experience costly, and often unnecessary turnover.
  — Where new hires need to assimilate themselves into the organisation quickly and effectively — the critical induction period! Coaching programs which address cultural issues, chemistry and fit, as well as a broad range of other career success factors, can really assist in the assimilation process, helping the new hire get up to speed quickly and produce!
  — For mature executives, managers and staff perhaps in their early fifties, needing to think through next steps and consider their 'second careers' which may include retirement, and/or a portfolio of business and other interests (for example, consulting, contracting, directorships, volunteer work and so forth). Some assistance with structured thinking here can turn a threat into an opportunity for those in the last phase of their full-time corporate careers.

— For virtually any executive, manager or employee who is trying to come to terms with the changes in organisational life and work practices, as well as the apparent 'demise' of the job, and who needs to develop a greater sense of personal career focus — which in itself substantially uplifts self-confidence, self-motivation and performance in the job.

The advantages of external career consulting in these and related areas are threefold. First, such instances as described above can be turned into successful outcomes for both the individual and the organisation. Secondly, such programs need not consume too much time nor create difficulties for the senior line manager to whom the potentially 'at risk' individual reports. The time invested is mainly between the individual and the consultant, whose particular expertise complements the normal ongoing line management relationship. And finally, in the worst case scenario, such processes prevent unnecessary separations which can be costly and damaging to both the organisation and the individual.

- *Strategic directions of the organisation.* Employees need to be clear about the future directions of the organisation, to maximise the alignment of organisational and personal goals. These future directions need to be specific enough to be converted into the outlook for organisational structure, roles and required competencies. However, in most cases, such specification may be difficult to attain, so individuals need to be encouraged to sell themselves, network and develop informal alliances within the organisation and find out for themselves where, when and how organisational developments may coincide with their own plans for their career development.
- *Chemistry and fit.* Whether it relates to the team setting, to desirable leadership traits, to atmospherics, or to politics, power and influence, the organisation needs to monitor individual chemistry and fit, and where difficulties are perceived to exist, assist individuals in this vital area, which may require helping them to modify their behaviour, reporting relationships or team composition.
- *Performance appraisal and improvement programs.* Such programs need to give an equal emphasis to the goals of the organisation and the goals of the individual in order to optimise career alignment, job performance and the value of individuals to the organisation.

If all these areas are prioritised, and appropriate development initiatives undertaken as the need arises, the career alignment of individuals and the organisation will be enhanced substantially. The benefits of this include:

- individuals feeling more in control of their careers and less vulnerable to the vagaries of organisational life
- talented individuals being less likely to leave the organisation for 'pastures greener' and more likely to stay, contribute and develop
- helping those who may feel themselves or be perceived as being on a 'performance plateau' — uplifting their performance levels
- helping staff become more emotionally aligned to the organisation (particularly at times of organisational change and restructuring)

❖ becoming more aligned to the organisation in terms of job fit, organisational fit, career goals, commitment and personal chemistry.

In achieving these outcomes, the role of the line manager to whom the individual reports must not be underestimated or avoided. By providing them with the language and thinking behind the Bulletproof Executive they will be able to enter into constructive dialogue with their direct reports, maximising their alignment and minimising the chances of bail-outs or bullets!

'It is absolutely vital for staff working with you to understand your commitment to their professional development. This leads to them wanting to achieve, rather than feeling that they have no choice,' concludes Michael T Duffy, senior manager group human resources at the Commonwealth Bank of Australia.

SUMMARY

Chapter 10 raises the following key issues:
- At times of senior-level hiring, selection strategies which executives and managers need to consider include:
  — matching an individual's major occupational interests, motivational capabilities and values to the job
  — selecting and developing major leadership of change competencies
  — ensuring an appropriate organisational 'atmosphere' exists, according to the needs of the individual
  — clearly specifying and pursuing desirable leadership and related traits
  — targeting the ideal make-up of teams
  — focusing on management capabilities (particularly motivation and delegation), primary business drivers, and external futures when selecting new executives and managers
  — taking into account the need for personal selling and group presentation capabilities in senior-level hires.
- A critical and often missing element in performance management systems is 'career alignment', which is about maximising commitment, job performance and an individual's value to the organisation, by aligning personal and organisational goals.
- For improved career alignment, executives and managers need to assist their staff in the areas of job fit, career planning, their understanding of the strategic directions of the organisation, how to network internally to uncover career development opportunities, personal chemistry, and performance appraisal and improvement programs.
- Career alignment enables executives and managers to better ensure that their staff align themselves to the organisation, and perform and develop, to the mutual benefit of the organisation and the individual.

Further Resources

In Section 10 of your *Executive Armoury* you will find a list of factors and questions to be used in selection interviews.

PART FOUR

Creating And Controlling Your Own Career Destiny

Destiny — Includes both what is destined to happen and the power which pre-ordains the future. People with destiny usually get there.

11

Focusing On Your Future And Targeting Your Ideal Career

'I run a medium-sized packaging equipment company. I don't know about you, but I really never had any career guidance. At school, I remember the local bank manager must have visited our career counsellor, because the flavour of the month suddenly became "working for the bank". As I was leaving school my Yorkshireman father told me to "get stuck into industry, lad", and so I did! The strong work ethic in my family and the theme of "getting on in life" probably got me to where I am today. I wonder what might have happened had I engaged in some systematic career planning, and if I'd established and pursued my own career goals? Just where might I be today . . . or tomorrow?'

This chapter addresses the need to create and control your destiny during these times of uncertainty and turbulence in organisational life, and assists executives and managers to accomplish this through planning, revitalising and succeeding in their careers — by 'career ownership', rather than by assuming the organisation will always provide a job and career. In the words of Robert H Waterman Jr, author of *What America Does Right*, the focus now needs to be on continuing employability, 'career resilience' and self-reliance.

'Who controls your career — you or the organisation?' asks Rob McPaul, human resources director Australasia, Reckitt and Colman. 'Organisations come and go. Manage your employability and direct it in the way you want, into the area you love. And if you love it, it shows, and the rewards will follow.'

Alan Popham, human resources director of Rothman International BV, London, notes: 'This is an area ignored or not understood by many "dependent" executives, who look to the organisation to manage their careers and come unstuck or go stale as a result.' Vic Betteridge puts it this way: 'In the final analysis, the only person with a vested interest in your career is yourself. Self-interest is a powerful motivation force.' Betteridge is general manager corporate services of GIO Australia Ltd, and stresses that these are his personal views.

Michael T Duffy, senior manager group human resources at the Commonwealth Bank of Australia, agrees: 'A must — you cannot rely on someone else (sponsor, etc) to manage your career. A proactive stance is essential.'

Career destiny and ownership is 'increasingly important for the modern executive,' says Tony Harbour, independent management consultant and formerly group personnel director of the Ocean Group PLC in the UK. This results in 'personal freedom and control to make things happen, rather than having things happen to you'.

'If one does not take ownership of one's own career, it is certain that no-one else will! The days of companies accepting this responsibility are gone — if indeed they ever existed,' says Ron Hopwood, director of human resources, 3M Australia Pty Ltd.

Robert C Stephenson, local divisional manager of SCA Molnlycke AB in the UK, has a different point of view. 'A nice concept, but in the final analysis, comes last in my ranking. Maybe influenced by a lifetime in one company!' But how many executives and managers have had, and will have ahead, a lifetime in one company?

Taking Stock of Your Career

Whatever way you look at it, career planning and management into and through the turn of the century is going to require far more knowledge, skills, courage and determination than has ever been demanded of individuals before. We are living in extraordinary times, and this demands extraordinary methods of dealing with the career situations executives and managers find themselves in. Taking stock of your career is the first step and in so doing, you need to undertake some self and career assessment covering a range of elements of the career mix. These include:

- *Your atmospheric needs*. Be very clear about your material, structural, behavioural and emotional needs and how your existing or future employing organisation meets your needs, in order to maximise your self-motivation and personal effectiveness.
- *Your management capabilities and leadership traits*. Address the requirements and expectations of your employer regarding (i) management capabilities and (ii) desirable leadership traits to help propel the organisation into the future. In this context, leadership traits include: Production controller, Paternalistic autocrat, Inspirational leader and Visionary strategist. Be very clear about what your existing or future employer seeks.
- *Your operating style*. The possibilities include the Commander/Doer, Responder/Initiator, Empathiser/Humanist, Evaluator/Detailer, Idea generator or All-rounder. What this means in terms of existing or future team make-up needs to be assessed.
- *Your interests, motivational capabilities and values*. Don't work in a job or career environment which neither fully accommodates your interests, motivational capabilities or values. Job fit now and ahead is essential in order to maximise job satisfaction, self-motivation and personal performance.
- *Your track record*. Here your career assessment needs to include your qualifications, experience, competencies in the world of work (be they technical, functional or managerial) and your achievements — the results you have been able to attain and the actions you have taken to accomplish them, which in themselves tell you and others a lot about your skills and other personal traits.

These are the ingredients of taking stock of your career, and in fact represent your career self-image which is the focal point on which further career planning is based.

However, many people focus on what they want in their careers, where they want to be and how much money they want to make, without taking the time to really look at where they are now, and what they have to work with. What's the point of planning a journey, checking the road-map, knowing where you are headed and when you expect to arrive, if you neglect to tune up your engine and make sure you have enough petrol, oil, or air in the tyres to get you there? All the enthusiasm in the world won't get you to your destination, without first taking stock of where you are now, and what you will need, to get you to where you want to be. This is actually a unique opportunity for you. We seldom take the time and make the effort to examine ourselves in such depth, and the experience and self-knowledge gained in so doing is well worthwhile.

Key Elements of the Career Environment

Having taken stock, the next step is to assess certain elements of the career environment within which you operate, and this can be described by examining four main areas: *information, technology and telecommunications ('IT & T'); the economy and business; government and politics;* and *social demography*.

Information, technology and telecommunications

The rapid growth of technology is having, and will continue to have, a dramatic impact on career development. In fact, it has been predicted that some 50 per cent of the jobs that will exist 15 years from now have not yet been invented.

Here are some questions to consider:

- What new kinds of businesses and executive and managerial jobs will the new technologies create?
- Where will future career opportunities relating to technology lie?
- Which jobs will experience technology-driven growth in the years ahead?
- Which jobs will experience technology-driven decline?

The economy and business

Economic and business variables in the environment can certainly affect career development. Some questions to ask here are:

- Which parts of the economy and business are likely to expand or contract over the next decade?
- What will be the impact of globalisation in this context — local business investing overseas and overseas business investing here or elsewhere?
- What kinds of skills, abilities and personal characteristics are in demand today, and what kinds will be in demand in the years ahead?
- Will they remain in demand over the short or long term?
- Which areas of the economy or business are likely to use your capabilities the most?
- Is the demand for your capabilities cyclical or fairly consistent?
- What are the costs of upgrading your capabilities or developing new ones?
- What are the potential returns on time and money used in such upgrading and development?

In looking at the economic and business environment, you are basically looking at those factors which influence the demand for your own capabilities, the supply of these capabilities from yourself and others, and the competition for jobs requiring these capabilities in the economy. The relationship between supply and demand drives price, and in this case salary levels!

Also, keep in mind that people with highly specialised expertise in one area may find the market for their capabilities more limited, than for those with expertise which is more generally applicable. However, don't underestimate the potential of selecting a specialisation for which you believe there will be demand well into the future, and then becoming one of the best at it.

The caveat here, however, and by way of example, is an individual with a high degree of expertise in, say, aerospace engineering. That person will not have the same range of career options as someone with accounting, legal or general management expertise, which is more easily transferable among different organisations and industries. On the other hand, there are a lot of unemployed general managers.

Too many people ignore the fact of economic and business cycles when planning a career. In good times the tendency is to reap the benefits of one's sought-after capabilities with little concern for the future. Then, if the hard times hit, and the demand for these capabilities falls off, there is a struggle to develop new capabilities which should have been developed earlier in anticipation of a downturn or change in the cycle. This all takes its toll, in time, money and frustration. Economic and business cycles, and variation in demand for certain skills and capabilities, are a fact of life. Prepare yourself accordingly.

Government and politics

In developing a career plan, it is becoming more necessary to take into account governmental, political and legal implications. The various levels of government are affecting our lives to an ever-increasing degree. For example, tax legislation has a great influence on personal lifestyles. It also can affect such career decisions as whether or not to start up your own business. Also, individuals are now seeking satisfaction and self-fulfilment in their careers, rather than just financial security. These aspirations decrease somewhat in a recession, but the underlying need for job satisfaction is still there, and can affect the morale and productivity of employees who are forced to remain in jobs they dislike.

Social demography

Environmental shifts in social demographic attitudes, behaviours and values must be taken into account in career planning. Understanding these trends puts us in a far better position to take advantage of potential career opportunities. For example, increasing career opportunities for women and minority groups can affect the career strategies of people outside these groups. Increasing competition for executive and managerial positions is a reality, and no longer limited to the 'chosen few' in any organisation. Organisations today are just as likely to bring in talent from outside to fill these positions, as they are to promote from within.

Also, individuals no longer feel an obligation to remain with one organisation for most of their careers. There is a growing restlessness, as people switch employers and even careers, if their needs are not being met. Concern for self-development encompassing all aspects of one's life, means that people no longer are willing to sacrifice everything for the demands of the job. Mid-life career switches, allowing individuals to develop a new set of talents and interests, are becoming common, and the coming trend may be towards a complete career change every ten years or so.

The aging population, along with smaller families, also offers opportunities and threats — opportunities, given time, for the continuing employment of mature executives, although not necessarily in top positions; threats, as many individuals in the ranks of the baby boomers currently experience when being cast out of organisations to make way for younger, more up-to-date and less expensive human resources. All of these social trends affect your career, but can be seen as opportunities, rather than threats, with careful career planning.

Compass
Land and sea explorers need to know where they are headed, the compass being the basic navigational instrument for this. Transitioning through your career can be just as precarious: always follow your true interests, values, motivational capabilities and 'atmospheric' needs. Let them guide you to your next destination.

Transitioning Through Today's Employment Market

So you are considering, for whatever reason, looking for another job, whether within your existing employer organisation or in another organisation. Or you are considering self-employment. Whether you begin your research while still employed, or take your job search on full-time, you must look upon this process as a job in itself, and treat it as such. Anything less than full commitment will not get you very far.

The current employment period is the most unpredictable since the Second World War. With executive and management unemployment rates still so high, the competition for available jobs is fierce. This applies just as much to higher-level executives as it does to blue-collar workers and lower-level support staff. In fact, the job market for some executives and managers has gone from bad to worse, as organisations cut costs across the board, including the jobs of higher salaried employees. The danger is that once eliminated, these top-level jobs may never be fully reinstated, as companies learn that by utilising remaining staff more efficiently, they can do without the extra people on the payroll.

Where does all of this apparent doom and gloom leave the executive and management job-seeker? While the current outlook for some may be bleak, there are still many great jobs available. Finding them, however, demands hard work and perseverance, along with careful research and planning. Here are some practical tips to help the executive or manager confront today's job market:

- *Exit your current job position smoothly.* Many people do not realise how an abrupt or acrimonious departure can damage their chances when seeking another position.
- *Develop a good personal profile or resume — no more than two to four pages long.* This is your door-opener and should present you in your best light, while omitting things which could limit you, such as salary requirements and job objectives which are too narrow.
- *Maximise the use of your personal and professional contacts.* Enlist the help of family, friends, business acquaintances, former customers and other contacts, and give them a resume they can potentially pass on or which will prompt them to refer you to a prospective employer.
- *Manage your time efficiently and effectively.* Treat the job search as a serious job and aim to make at least five direct contacts a day, in person or by telephone, preferably to people with decision-making authority in organisations.
- *The process may take far longer than you initially think it will.* Landing an executive or management job these days can take anywhere from one month to a year, and the average timeframe is between three and six months, so you need to be tenacious and stay on track.
- *Make twice as many applications as you initially think you need to.* In making job applications, try to use the direct or indirect referral approach as much as possible, rather than mailing out hundreds of application letters 'cold' — this simply does not work and is a waste of time and money.
- *Expect some initial negative reactions.* 'Cutbacks' and 'hiring freezes' may be the formal responses to your initial enquiries, but openings still become available through the need for new skill-sets, organisational change, retirement and resignations, so endeavour to arrange meetings anyway, and match and promote your capabilities to the current or future needs of the organisation you are targeting.
- *Are you unrealistic in your demands?* The executive and management market is highly competitive, so be prepared if necessary to lower your sights accordingly with respect to job targets, salary requirements, job location and other criteria. But *do not* lower your sights too soon, as you never know what might be waiting for you, just around the corner!
- *Don't throw in the towel!* Maintain your momentum throughout your job search — it will help if you regard the process as a regular job — taking frequent, short breaks rather than doing nothing for weeks on end and thereby losing touch with possible opportunities.

❖ *Remain in touch with prospective referrers and employers*. An executive or management job opening can come up at any time, so make sure you stay on the 'active list', by telephoning back once in a while and getting an update on the organisation's status and outlook.

Creating Your Own Opportunity

For those who have acquired excellent business and management capabilities throughout their careers there is another solution to the career search or unemployment problem: why not create your own opportunity? This can involve setting up your own independent business, as many are now doing, or entering into association, partnership, a joint venture or a strategic alliance with others.

Think back through your career and decide which of your capabilities could be put to use right now — do you have marketing or financial expertise which can help to get you going in a new venture? Do you know others in your situation who have the necessary complementary expertise, and who may be pleased to join you?

Creating your own opportunity may require that you lower your sights somewhat, in terms of income and career aspirations. But it beats unemployment, keeps you productive, and may eventually turn out to be more satisfying and profitable than your previous position.

Sometimes creating your own opportunity means a complete career change into an area where there is a sufficient or growing demand. In such cases, you may have to take some time out to upgrade certain skills and gain the required knowledge.

Make sure the potential benefits outweigh the costs, in money, time and effort, before embarking on a major career change. You don't want to end up back at square one again, if you find you still cannot put your skills to work — the key is to try to identify the growth areas, and aim your new career efforts there.

The Self-employment Option

Self-employment is one response to the realities of today's executive and management job market. Making the transition from employee to entrepreneur, or to the independent business person is not an easy one, but there are many outside resources available. These range from scores of books on the subject, to government departments and professional advisers (check their credentials!) who can provide both financial and counselling assistance to new and established entrepreneurs. Don't underestimate the potential for franchise or licence arrangements in this regard, which are invariably offered with plenty of back-up expertise — but again, this needs to be checked out with due diligence!

Before setting out on your own, however, you should ask yourself the following questions:

❖ To what extent do you really want to 'go out on your own'?
❖ How willing are you to build up your business solidly, one step at a time?
❖ Do you really want to take the risks, and commit the necessary, often significant resources of time, effort and money?

- Is your family fully supportive in this?
- Does a market really exist for your service or product?
- How open is this market, and how easy is it to enter the market and get established quickly?
- Do you have adequate capital to get you going properly? (Don't underestimate the need for capital.)
- Who is your competition, and can you really compete effectively against them?
- Why should prospective customers purchase your products or services compared to those of your competitors?
- What are your differentiators and unique marketing advantages compared to your competitors — price, value-adds, availability, breadth of range, etc?
- Are you sufficiently persistent, determined, independent and energetic to cope with the inevitable ups and downs?
- Do you have sufficient initiative and capability to think 'outside the square', in order to overcome the inevitable obstacles along the way?

Self-employment is one way to achieve your goals in a tough job market, but it is certainly not for everyone. As a further screening device to help decide whether or not the self-employment option in the context of starting or buying a business is really viable for you, the following checklists describe the main reasons for business failure.

The person:
- incompetent in business
- lack of business management experience
- lack of experience in the area of business activity
- lack of experience in functional aspects of business— for example, sales, finance, marketing and accounting.

The problems:
- operating expenses too high
- sales too low
- run out of cash as a result of the above and receivables problems/excessive inventory
- under-capitalised — too dependent on the bank
- inadequate attention to, or expertise in, the sales effort
- inability to attract, retain and motivate staff of adequate calibre
- poor accounting and financial control
- poor awareness of business financing options
- inadequate attention to profit performance
- poor marketing — lack of understanding or application of the function
- poor staff management and organisation
- lack of awareness of tax considerations and availability of business advice
- purchase price of business too high
- franchise or industrial licence royalties too high.

The challenges:

❖ It usually costs far more to get a business operating in terms of time, talent and dollars than anticipated.
❖ Twenty-four hours a day can be the norm. Time out for golf is a rarity!
❖ As an employee, one believes one is owed a living — as an independent business person, no-one owes you a living.
❖ The joy of freedom can become the threat of isolation — you are on your own.
❖ Usually the independent small business person would earn more being employed by someone else!

If you are convinced the reasons for business failure do not and will not apply in your own case, and if you are prepared to accept the challenges, then you may be on to a winning proposition — your own business. Good luck!

SUMMARY

Chapter 11 raises the following key issues:

- The first step in focusing on your future is to take stock of your career in terms of your atmospheric needs, leadership traits, operating style, interests, motivational capabilities and values, and your track record — in other words, who are you *really* and what is your self-image?
- You need to consider the career environment in terms of information technology and telecommunications, the economy and business, government and politics, and social demography — which all will impact on your future.
- If you are considering changing your job, you need to be aware of the vagaries of today's employment market at the executive and management level, and how to transition through it successfully.
- Exiting your current job position smoothly, maximising the use of your personal and professional contacts, and keeping up your activity levels and confidence are all key in this.
- Creating your own opportunity or the self-employment option also needs to be considered, but in this you need to ask yourself a range of probing questions to reality-check such alternatives, and to ensure you are aware of the very considerable risks and challenges relating to going out on your own.

Further Resources

In Section 11 of your *Executive Armoury* you will find a complete career planning process which will help move your thinking from your own self-image to realistic career objectives and strategies. Section 12 addresses the financial planning and related aspects of changing your job. In Section 13 you will find self-help checklists regarding the independent business option: further self-evaluation, business feasibility checks, buying a business and the business plan.

12

Marketing Yourself Successfully And Winning That Ideal New Job

> 'When I think about my career and how I have won new career development positions, invariably it's come down to target marketing, listening and attending to the needs and interests of the hirer at the interview, and above all, uncovering those hidden job opportunities in the invisible job market. When I think about it, in 30 years this formula has served me well, and now it's time to share it with others.'

In this chapter I will address the vital elements of how to track down that next ideal job opportunity, be this within your existing employer organisation or elsewhere. The chapter starts by suggesting how you should go about changing your current position and moves on to preparing your 'personal profile' or resume, as well as covering letters, and the critical components of these documents. Also addressed is how and why you should concentrate on using your contact network, and how to perform well at interviews.

Playing and winning the career game requires preparation, rehearsal and perseverance, and this chapter arms you with the top, proven techniques which will enhance your self-confidence and your effectiveness on this challenging journey.

Changing Your Current Position

The very first step in any career change should be to make a point of changing your present job position with goodwill in the case of all parties, as far as possible. If you must begin your search while still employed in a particular job, carry on in your role as normally as you can and don't make any lack of interest too obvious. However great the temptation, don't vent your pent-up frustrations as you move on.

In fact, moving on within your existing organisation or leaving gracefully really makes sense, as it will leave a lasting, positive impression. Make no mistake, this last impression of you will be remembered if your future boss calls your last to check you out, as will likely be the case. Try to stay on good terms with everyone, and increase your chances of leaving with your reputation intact and with a good reference later on when it is needed.

Preparing Your Personal Profile or Resume

For internal use — in other words, for use within your existing organisation — the document you need to prepare is called and headed 'Personal Profile'. For external use, use the term 'Resume'. They are very similar documents both in content and format. When I refer to 'profile' from now on, I am referring to both types of document.

Your profile is the foundation of your job search, and will save you time and effort later if you do a superior job compiling it well the first time around. Dragging out an old resume and adding a few lines is not good enough.

Beware, also, of professional resume writers. They will never know you as well as you know yourself and you will have to make running adjustments to the document as your campaign progresses anyway. For example, you may recall something in your background which you neglected to include but which is extremely relevant to your next prospective job position or employer. Also, professional resume writers have their own particular style and no matter how good that style is, it is not your style and this becomes apparent at the interview. Those people who are used to reading resumes can recognise the characteristics of many professional resume writers.

What might this say about you? It might indicate that you lack ability or confidence in written communication. So take the time to develop the profile *yourself* — it will be well worth the effort, and the process of compilation will prepare you for discussing your background coherently over the phone or at interviews. The money you might spend on professional resume services would be better spent elsewhere.

Before you sit down to develop your profile, remember that its sole purpose is to obtain an interview by presenting some of your credentials in a way which gains the reader's attention, interest and curiosity — enough curiosity to invite you to a face-to-face meeting. No-one hires on the basis of a written profile alone — you will be hired on the basis of the face-to-face interview, and so gear your profile towards attracting enough interest to 'get your foot in the door'.

Although the final product should be no longer than four pages in length, profile preparation is a very lengthy and detailed process. It will take you several hours to complete but will ensure that all the important information required for your search is recorded, organised and instantly available as required. Having this information on hand will not only increase your self-confidence but it will also save you a lot of time later.

There are basically two types of profile, a career-oriented version and a capability-oriented version, as shown in Section 14 of your *Executive Armoury*. I suggest you have a look at them now.

The career-oriented profile is particularly useful for line management or operational jobs, or where your most recent experience, say over the last five to ten years, is highly relevant to the job position you are considering.

The capability-oriented resume is more relevant for technical, specialist, functional, advisory or consulting-type jobs, or where your earlier — rather than more recent — experience is more relevant to the job position you are considering. This type of resume is also useful if you have had a long career with just one employer, or where taking the career-oriented approach may emphasise a skill-set other than the one you are trying to portray. For example, 25 years in banking and using the career-oriented version may well cast Tom Smith as a 'banker', whereas by using the capability-oriented version Tom can cast himself as a 'general manager', 'operations manager', or whatever his skill-set and career objective dictates. I refer to this as 'repackaging' and it is most useful where career moves entail changes in business sector or job function and when you need to promote yourself in this new idiom, rather than historically.

Always commence the profile development process by completing a career-oriented version first, even if you actually need a capability-oriented version. By completing them in this order, you will develop a better capability-oriented version, since the achievement statements, more easily derived by assessing your chronological career experience, can then be transferred verbatim across to the capability-oriented version of your profile.

The following are some of the 'do's' and 'don'ts' of profile writing.

Do:

- make sure it is easy to read
- use short sentences and remember that 'less is more' — less has more impact
- leave adequate space between lines — space is almost as important as text!
- make it no longer than three to four pages
- attract interest with your achievement statements, as described later
- be very specific and quantify results achieved
- focus only on information relevant to the future employer, and in the case of a specific job opportunity, on information that is 100 per cent geared to the needs of that job and future employer organisation.

Don't:

- include a photograph or written references, or contact details for referees
- use odd-size paper — only use A4 size
- use bright-coloured paper — white is best
- use cheap-quality paper — the paper should be crisp and have a nice feel
- list salary history or expectations
- list job or career objectives unless you are clear they relate to the specific vacancy for which you are applying
- list reasons for leaving past positions
- list age, nationality, marital status or children
- list referees.

Achievements are the most important statements in your profile, covering letter and, indeed, even at interviews. Using well-developed achievement statements is akin to selling the 'benefits' of a proposition, rather than the 'features' — one of the rules of professional selling which transfers directly across to personal selling — features in your own case being statements about your responsibilities and duties.

Salespeople are always told to sell the benefits; executives and managers in career transition need to sell their achievements. Here is a two-way formula for working out what your achievements have been, and then for writing them up. I call the formula 'SWOPTIO'. First, in *thinking* about any one job position in your career:

- **S** — what *s*trengths in terms of human, financial or physical resources, or products, services, technology, processes, customers or suppliers, did you perceive to exist in any particular job position?
- **W** — similarly, *w*eaknesses?
- **O** — similarly, *o*pportunities?
- **P** — similarly, *p*roblems?
- **T** — similarly, *t*hreats?
- **I** — What did you *i*mplement — in other words, what action did you take to further exploit, in a positive sense, the SWOPTs?
- **O** — What was the *o*utcome or results which flowed from the actions you implemented? Quantify these results in dollars, percentages, or in units of output, increase, reduction or other form of improvement.

The second part of the formula is then to *write up* your achievement statements, starting each statement with the outcome (O) and finishing with how you implemented it (I). Examples of this are:

- Increased sales by 22 per cent and market share by 7 per cent within 12 months through the development of innovative selling techniques.
- Reduced costs by 12 per cent within 18 months through head-count and overhead cost reductions.
- Freed up $1.2 million cash through stock reduction, which increased stock turns from three to five times per year, and through improved collections, which reduced debtor days from 65 to 45.
- Reduced absenteeism from an average of six days per year to three, and reduced labour turnover from 38 per cent to 18 per cent, over a three-year period, by introducing enlightened management principles and practices, as well as by progressively moving the culture to self-empowered teams.
- Doubled return on total assets from 12 per cent to 24 per cent over a three-year period by selling off non-productive assets and improving sales and margin performance.

If you are unable to *quantify* your achievements, then you may be able to *qualify* them by adding such comments to the statement as:

- '... considered by the Executive Committee to be the most improved performance ... '
- '... as verified by industry analysts ... '
- '... as acknowledged by my CEO ... '
- '... as verified by customer surveys ... '
- '... as verified by our employee climate survey ... '

The Covering Letter

Never send out a profile to a new prospective chairperson, CEO or other senior executive without a covering letter. Personalise your approach by addressing your letter to the key person within the organisation who has the power to hire you, and gear both letter and profile to the organisation's needs, as far as possible.

As emphasised by Harvey Mackay in his book *Sharkproof*, first assess your skills and talents and where you want to go in your career, and then understand what companies look for in job candidates and how you can differentiate yourself from the pack.

Avoid writing to personnel or human resources directors if possible — you will merely be one of a crowd, and your chances of getting an interview may be very slim. Aim for the top decision-making person, invariably the CEO if you are seeking a senior executive position, or the chairperson if you are seeking a CEO position.

Don't be afraid to approach these top people by phone first, and try to arrange a brief meeting to drop off your profile in person. You have nothing to lose, and they may be impressed with your proactiveness enough to want to see you. If they don't, then ask if you can mail them your profile and letter.

Make the most of your covering letter. It can be a very effective tool for marketing yourself, as it is more personal than the profile and, if developed correctly, can make the person reading it really interested in meeting you — this is what you are aiming for!

Some tips on writing covering letters:

- Your letter should be no longer than two pages.
- Always use good-quality white or ivory paper, matching your profile.
- Follow standard business letter format.
- Always submit word processed originals.
- Don't try to use gimmicks, or way-out statements to grab attention, but do start the letter by identifying some of the key needs of the reader (based on your research) and show how you believe you can meet those needs.
- Take a business-like approach, but let your individuality come through.
- State why you are interested in that particular organisation.
- Note the area or position in which you are interested.
- State how your capabilities and past achievements relate to that area or position.
- Insert one or two of your main achievements which will grab the reader's interest, early in the letter, even if they are repeated in your profile.
- Refer to your enclosed profile, if indeed you are enclosing it. It is better not to enclose it if less than 75 per cent of it relates directly to the needs of the hiring organisation. In this case simply expand your letter to three pages, making it 100 per cent relevant to the other party's needs.
- Request a personal meeting.
- Include your contact information.
- Proofread your letter carefully for spelling, punctation or typographical errors.

As noted, an alternative approach is not to send your profile at all, but to send a three-page letter entirely geared to your perception of the needs of the other party, and how you believe you can meet those needs, again by noting some of your relevant past achievements. This is a highly potent form of direct target marketing, and its needs-orientation makes it particularly effective. However, before sending out 'cold' letters and profiles, try to get introductions to your target audience by using your contacts, and mention them in your letter. (Seek your contact's permission to do this first.)

Using Your Contacts

Most people find jobs either within their existing employer organisation or externally, through personal, family or business contacts. For this you need to develop your 'contact network' and use it effectively. Here are the steps to follow:

1. Getting ready

- Set up a card file to keep track of each phone call, letter, interview and follow-up; alternatively, use a PC database and tracking system.
- Have a supply of updated profiles on hand.
- Decide what kind of help you need from each contact — for example, information on a division or subsidiary company, referrals, or advice on your campaign.
- Be very clear about your career focus and objectives — in other words, what you want to do in terms of the next job, and where you want to do it, which should include a preliminary list of target business sectors and companies (your 'target list').

2. Identifying your network

- Make a list of everyone you know who might help you to track down a new position.
- Include immediate friends, family, past acquaintances, past line managers, colleagues and employers, previous clients, customers and suppliers, your doctor, dentist, accountant, lawyer, partner's contacts, and fellow members of clubs and associations. The list can go on and on — the important point to remember is that all your contacts have other contacts, and referring them to you creates your network.
- This is your 'direct approach' list — people who know you, either well or casually, but whom you feel you can approach directly.
- They can rarely offer you a job and should *not* be approached on this basis, but they may be able to introduce you to those who may know about job opportunities.
- Those others to whom you are referred form your 'indirect approach' list, and some of them will eventually be people who are in a decision-making capacity within your target organisations. Such people are often in a position to be aware of job openings coming up, long before they are advertised.
- Gaining entrance to a new CEO or chairperson in this way is far more effective than writing letters or telephoning 'cold'.

3. Tapping into your network

- Complete your contact list, and then begin phoning. Start by contacting those whom you feel most comfortable about approaching — ease yourself into networking!
- Don't put anyone on the spot by asking for a job.
- Don't beat around the bush with a busy contact.
- Explain that you are undertaking some market research relative to possible new career opportunities and that you would appreciate information or advice.

- Describe your career objective and areas of interest.
- Show them your profile and target list in order to trigger ideas.
- Ask for names of and introductions to key people within your target area or to others who may have contacts within your target area, and ask if you can use the referrer's name by way of introduction.
- Tell them you will keep in touch, to let them know how you are doing.
- Arrange to meet with them for coffee or lunch, if possible, to strengthen the personal tie, and explain your situation further.
- Record the result of the conversation and the leads and referrals it has generated on your card file or PC database.

4. Following up

- Touch base with all your established contacts every three to four weeks.
- Don't 'pester' them every second day, or lose touch completely for months.
- Keep your card file or database active and working for you.
- Write thank you notes and letters to contacts who go out of their way for you, and let them know when you find a job.

5. Keeping the network alive

- When you are in that new job, keep your network alive — you never know when you may need to use it again!

More Than Meets the Eye

Surprisingly, advertised jobs comprise only 20 per cent or less of all jobs available at a particular time. This means that at least 80 per cent of available positions are not advertised, whether this is within your existing employer organisation or in the external job market. Whether internal or external, we call this the 'invisible job market', and this is where you should be directing most of your efforts.

Despite the slump in some areas of executive employment, there is 'more out there than meets the eye', and you will greatly increase your chances of success by tapping into this fertile area. The fact is, most employers fill job openings with people they know through personal contact, or with people who are recommended to them by someone they know. This makes sense to many employers. It reduces their risk of hiring someone who turns out to be completely unsuitable, and it also saves them the time and cost involved in putting the position out to an executive search firm or management recruiter, although for many employers this is also a sensible strategy in order to help track down the very best candidate available.

You can increase your exposure to this invisible job market by using your contact network effectively, and by approaching key people within your target organisations through introductions and word-of-mouth referral. By staying in touch with your contact network on a regular basis, you are using the law of averages to increase the probability of being in the right place at the right time — being available just when a CEO or chairperson needs someone with your capabilities.

Many openings are found and secured this way — by direct and continued contact with prospective employers — regardless of whether or not any positions are initially available. Direct most of your efforts to this 'invisible job market' and learn to play the career game!

Your Game Plan

Winning the career game requires a game plan. Staying in control of the game requires that you sit down and plan your time and effort for maximum efficiency and effectiveness. You need also to check up on yourself from time to time, to make sure you are staying on course and not getting bogged down in unproductive activities.

Make yourself a game plan or course of action, and stick to it. There are several alternative courses of action open to you in your job search campaign. Your best move is to cover all these bases, but apportion your efforts according to the probability of success with each alternative. Taking into account which alternatives yield the best results, your game plan could look something like that shown in Table 12.1.

Table 12.1 — Game Plan

Possible Strategy	Per cent of Effort
Personal or business, referral contacts, ie your developing contact network	67%
Direct approach to employer organisations (only if you cannot be introduced or referred into them); job advertisements; executive search firms and management recruiters	33%

You can adjust these percentages once you find out how each alternative works for you specifically. Allocate your time and financial resources accordingly. Set up a daily plan of action with a goal of so many contacts a day or so many letters written, and update your card file or database continuously. This is the only way to keep track of where you are in the game as you will be covering quite a large volume of contacts and a missed follow-up call, or a letter not sent in time, could cost you a job.

It is important to get on the database of executive search firms, which rarely advertise. Management recruiters usually reveal themselves when they advertise for specific positions. Try to get introductions to the key players in search firms through your network contacts, with a view to meeting them and discussing your career objectives. Make sure they have your resume on file and your full details on their database.

The Interview

So you have learned to play the game, made a game plan, and made all the right moves. Sooner or later you are going to score a goal, this being the interview. In fact, to win the game — in other words, to land the ideal job or career position — you will probably need to score several goals — interviews — and prove your superiority over your competition.

So how can you sail confidently through what many consider to be the most nerve-racking stage of job-hunting? Nothing is insurmountable if taken in a logical sequence, and this applies to job interviews as much as anything else. The trick is to be well-informed and well-prepared.

Winning the interview

Up to this point, all of your efforts have been aimed towards getting interviews. In the highly competitive senior-level job market, you will need to be creative and persistent without being obnoxious. Some interviews will come more easily than others, but keep trying and land as many as you can which relate to your target areas.

Getting ready

The two main forms of interviews are 'screening' and 'in-depth'. The screening interview is usually conducted by an executive search consultant, management recruiter or human resources director, who tries to find out your strengths and weaknesses, and how you compare with other candidates. If you pass this stage, or if there is no screening stage, you will undergo an in-depth interview by the senior executive, perhaps the CEO or chairperson, for whom you will work if hired.

The interviewer will try to see how you fit the specific requirements of the job, the extent and nature of your expertise, and how well you get along with people. From your point of view, the objective of the interview is to convince the interviewer that you can offer whatever is needed. In short, you must sell yourself. Therefore, you must present yourself in the best possible light, from a neat, businesslike appearance to a confident, responsive manner.

A good interviewer will evaluate you on all the criteria addressed in Bulletproof Executive thinking, namely:

- *Past performance*. How has the candidate performed in the past in terms of job performance, change management, personal performance, chemistry and fit? What achievements in terms of results, and actions to accomplish such results, can the candidate verify which demonstrate performance excellence in these critical areas?
- *Atmospherics*. Do we as an employer meet the motivational needs of the candidate — material, structural, behavioural and emotional?
- *Management capabilities and leadership traits*. Does the candidate display appropriate management capabilities and leadership traits — the traits we seek to propel our organisation into the future?
- *Team make-up*. Does the candidate's operating style add value to the make-up of the team the candidate will be joining, and more generally, does the candidate's operating style coincide with what we are seeking and provide good chemistry and fit?
- *Politics, power and influence*. Does the candidate give the impression of being able to sell themselves assertively, build a strong network of support and negotiate successfully, rather than indulge proactively in the darker side of political struggles and power plays?
- *Leadership of change*. Does the candidate display appropriate change leadership competencies?

- *Group presentations*. Can the candidate demonstrate capabilities in group presentations, particularly in the process of delivery?
- *Job fit*. Does the job for which the candidate is being considered match the candidate's interests, motivational capabilities and values?
- *Career ownership*. Is the candidate in control of their career destiny, and does this destiny fit in with the future directions and goals of the organisation?
- *Job performance*. Has past performance been of a high order, particularly in emphasising and deriving benefits from prioritising primary business drivers, futures and staff management practices?
- *Attraction, retention and development of talent*. Generally, is this the calibre of executive talent we wish to attract into the organisation, retain and develop; and can we ensure maximum career alignment between individual and organisational goals?
- *Dismissal avoidance*. Is this the type of candidate who will respond well to performance appraisal and improvement programs, coaching and counselling?

In the absence of Bulletproof Executive thinking, interviewers evaluate candidates in the following main areas:

- *Capabilities*: qualifications, experience, skills, aptitudes and competencies.
- *Motivation*: achievements in the past and the degree to which and how the individual has been self-motivated to achieve these results.
- *Personality*: ability to fit in with superiors and peers, and to get results through subordinates and other people.
- *Chronology*: early family life and schooling, university achievements (academic and other), track record in career, progress in terms of promotions, perceptions of strengths and weaknesses, non-work interests and how time is spent, career aspirations and, particularly, reasons for leaving jobs.

During the Interview

Handling the interview successfully requires that you are well-informed about the employing organisation and the position, and well-prepared for the questions you will likely be asked. It also requires that you project a professional, confident and relaxed image.

As well as answering questions, you will be expected to ask some of your own. Some questions you might want to ask are:

- How has this job position been handled in the past?
- What are the current responsibilities and expectations regarding performance?
- How does this position fit into the overall organisation?
- What are the future plans for the organisation?
- Is there a potential for growth in this position?
- Where might I move from here?
- Where is the person who held this job before?

Now for the three golden rules on how to win at interviews. First, the interviewee needs to answer all questions and provide all commentary from the interviewer's perspective — in other words, responses should be geared 100 per cent towards the needs of the employing organisation. Indeed, the candidate really has to enact the role of the professional consultative salesperson, and in this be very clear about the other party's needs and respond entirely to these needs. Many executives and managers fail to realise this, and answer questions and make their responses 'according to the story of their own lives' rather than 'according to the story of the other party's life — *their* needs'.

To establish what those needs are, the candidate should undertake extensive research on the organisation and at the interview, and use pre- and post-check questions and responses. For example, in response to the question 'Tell me about your strengths', the candidate should pre-check by saying, 'I'm told I have quite a broad range of strengths — in which business or functional areas are you particularly interested?' Another example: 'Tell me about your career/yourself' could be pre-checked with 'I've had a long, varied and successful career — which parts interest you most?' Or, 'I'm not sure where to start — what, particularly, would you like to know about my career?'

Post-checking phrases, after responding to questions, include: 'Was that what you were seeking?' 'Does that answer your question adequately?' 'Have I demonstrated that adequately?'

Using pre- and post-checking techniques ensures that you are responding to the needs of the other party, that you have adequately overcome any possible hidden doubts or objections, and that you are engaging in discussion rather than simply answering questions. Remember, good interviews are a *two-way* exchange of information.

Secondly, always proliferate your answers and responses with examples of your achievements, including results attained and your actions taken to attain them. This type of response provides verification and coincides with behaviourally oriented selection procedures which seek to gain a clear understanding of the candidate's past behaviour in critical areas relevant to the new job. The thinking behind this is that past behaviour is a predictor of future behaviour. You are therefore advised to spend a great deal of time on developing your achievement statements and memorising them.

Finally, attend to the start and end of the interview. 'The sale is lost or won in the first 30 seconds' is the salesperson's first rule, and you have to try and win the interview from the outset! Think through all the possible questions you might be asked, and rehearse your responses. The particularly difficult ones are 'Tell me about yourself?', 'Why do you think you are the right person for this job?' and 'What do you think we are looking for?' Plan for these and rehearse!

Similarly, plan and rehearse your closing statements. 'The order is not placed until you have closed' is the final rule for the salesperson, and this is just the same for the interview candidate. Closing statements generally need to summarise your interest in the job and why you believe you are well qualified to win it — restating your key relevant achievements in brief, for closing impact.

Here are some other general interview tips:

❖ Be confident, but not overbearing.
❖ Smile and shake hands firmly with good eye contact.

- Talk clearly and concisely.
- Stick to the point and stop when you have answered the question.
- Endeavour to get a feel for the interviewer's operating style, language and degree of formality, and fit in with it as much as possible, while remaining natural.
- Use positive language, rather than negative: 'challenge', 'opportunity', 'experience', rather than 'problem' or 'mistake'.
- Find out all you can about the job, its responsibilities, and its performance and results expectations.
- Don't undersell yourself, but be truthful about your achievements.
- Delay all mention of the salary package, particularly during the early interviews. If asked, back off, or counter the question with a question such as: 'I'm sure you are offering a competitive package. What salary range do you have in mind?'
- Only engage in final salary negotiations after you have asked for and received your job offer in writing — once this has been achieved, roles have been reversed and you are now the buyer and they are the seller: your negotiation position is much stronger!
- Be realistic in your salary expectations, it *is* a competitive market, but know what salary range you should fall into and what your minimum requirements are.
- Be ready to supply references, but speak to your referees about the position before contact is made by those conducting the reference checks.

After every interview, write a follow-up letter to the person who interviewed you thanking them for the interview and restating your interest in the position. Also remind them how your background experience and achievements fit the position requirements and needs of the employing organisation.

Closing the Deal

The waiting period between the final interview and a possible job offer can be nerve-racking. Protect your best interests, in preparation for possible negotiations later, by keeping the following tips in mind:

- By all means follow-up if you have heard nothing after ten days, but no earlier than this and not too frequently, as you may weaken your position if you appear too anxious.
- Keep the details of any other ongoing negotiations to yourself — don't mention other companies or prospective job positions or salary levels.
- No matter how close you feel you are to a good job offer, keep going full steam ahead with your other leads and lines of enquiry.
- Don't commit yourself too quickly to an offer, without thinking it over and weighing it against other possibilities.
- Do use the Bulletproof Executive interview and selection criteria mentioned earlier to make sure that the job opportunity and organisation you select really fit *you*.
- Revisit your career objective — does the job opportunity fit this objective really well? If not, what are the trade-offs and the opportunity costs?

SUMMARY

Chapter 12 raises the following key issues:

- A personal profile or resume is an essential self-marketing tool. Career-oriented profiles are best for permanent positions where your career chronology is of direct relevance. Capability-oriented profiles are more suitable for specialist or consulting roles where your functional capabilities are more important than your career chronology.
- Developing and using your contact network is the best way to uncover jobs which are otherwise 'invisible' — neither yet being advertised nor in the hands of the head-hunter. Two-thirds of your job search efforts should be directed through your network.
- Interviews represent your opportunity to 'close the sale' — namely, your being selected and offered the job.
- To win the offer, you have to behave like a professional consultative salesperson in the interview. This means identifying and responding to the needs of the other party, the person interviewing you, rather than simply telling them the story of your life.
- The interviewer (the customer) must come first. Focus on *their* needs at all times.

Further Resources

Examples of career- and capability-oriented resumes or profiles are provided in Section 14 of your *Executive Armoury*. A Bulletproof networking system is provided in Section 15.

13

Surviving The Pressures Of Your New Work Environment And Succeeding In Your Career

> 'My problem is that I'm stress-prone anyway, and so living with me is challenging enough, let alone at times when I have changed jobs or when my current job is particularly demanding! Fortunately, I preach and practise a range of stress avoidance and career risk management techniques which really work. More busy executives and managers should try them, least of all for the sake of their families!'

The inevitable periodic conflict experienced in the new job — whether physical, emotional, interpersonal or professional in origin — causes stress. In terms of your ability to succeed and progress, you may have to deal with it some day, somehow. When you encounter a stressful situation on the job which is not going to go away, you have basically seven courses of action open to you:

1. *Attack it.* Dig in your heels and hold your ground until something works out.
2. *Ignore it.* Pretend the conflict doesn't exist, and keep up outward appearances.
3. *Develop resilience through imagery.* The way I do this is to imagine I am wearing a suit of medieval armour. When the slings and arrows come my way, I don't let them through my defences. 'Ping!' — they bounce off! You really can develop resilience through imagery— try it!
4. *Change it.* Change the situation by persuading others to change or get your role or responsibilities revised.
5. *Change your behaviour.* Speak up more or listen more, learn to say 'no' or 'yes' to demands, or work at a different pace.
6. *Change your attitude.* View the problem positively as a challenge or an opportunity to remain alert.
7. *Retreat.* Remove yourself from the conflict by transferring or resigning.

Of these seven possible reactions, the first two should be avoided as non-productive — they don't get rid of the stress, which will continue to eat away at you. Each of the other five reactions will be appropriate in different situations.

There will be times, however, when you should change your own behaviour, and other times when the only sensible thing to do to preserve your career and your sanity is to quit. Before leaving, however, examine the other alternative responses, to see whether or not the conflict can be effectively handled in a less dramatic way.

Stress and Burnout

We all experience stress to greater or lesser degrees, and there is a tendency to regard stress as a negative force since it seems to be the cause of many problems, both personal and professional. If not handled properly, stress can stunt career growth and development, but it can also be a very positive force in our lives— spurring us on to greater achievements.

The problem arises when the stress becomes excessive, or our ability to deal with it is limited. People differ in their opinion of what might be a stressful situation, as what produces stress in one person may not affect another at all. Stress is a very subjective thing, depending on the individual's capacity to 'roll with the punches', the work load taken on, the tendency to worry about things in general, or how much is expected of you.

Some people are able to cope with a great amount of stress and use it in a positive way as a motivator to achievement at a very high level. However, prolonged exposure to stress in the work situation, coupled with an inability to deal with it, produces the occupational condition commonly known as 'burnout'.

Burnout has been described as an exhaustion and cynicism, which often develops after repeated exposure to people, in an intense, involved, stress-producing way, for a prolonged period of time.

How can you recognise whether you, a partner, a friend or co-executive is suffering from burnout? Symptoms will vary depending on the person's individual response to stress and the extent or degree of burnout being experienced. Common symptoms include:

- irritability with others at home or at work
- often feeling tired or lacking in energy
- feeling a lack of purpose or direction in one's life, or a longing to escape
- a loss of, or low confidence
- indifference to one's work
- easily becoming impatient with family and friends
- increased usage of alcohol or drugs.

These symptoms brought on by work stress illustrate a sense of 'uncaring'. Advanced burnout victims literally stop caring about the work they do or the lives they live. They stop caring about themselves and everyone around them.

In its most advanced stages burnout causes executives to stop even going through the motions of work — they stop working altogether. This is when, if nothing has been done to solve the problem up to this point, employers are forced to take action — all too often by firing the victim. Fortunately, most burnout cases do not get to this point. The victim seeks help in time, or is forced into seeking help by a worried partner or concerned employer. Obviously, the earlier the symptoms are recognised and dealt with, the better for all concerned.

Your Idiosyncrasies

What about your idiosyncracies? Do they suggest you are stress-prone or stress-avoiding? Read over the following statements:

- ❖ I believe 'If you miss the plane, there will be another one soon — no need to worry about it'.
- ❖ It doesn't worry me being late for a meeting.
- ❖ I like talking about matters other than the successes I have enjoyed.
- ❖ I really relax with a game of tennis, handball, by swimming or by participating in other sports.
- ❖ I really enjoy taking a holiday and just doing nothing.
- ❖ I couldn't care less if I lose in a game, even if I'm really good at it.
- ❖ I enjoy working steadily without making any fuss about it.
- ❖ I never seem to feel hostile or angry with the world.
- ❖ I lead my life so that I'm hardly ever rushed.
- ❖ I never feel impatient.

Now read the following statements:

- ❖ My schedule is usually crowded and I find it hard to refuse people.
- ❖ I enjoy being ahead of others, especially others who are competitive.
- ❖ When I'm doing something else, such as playing squash or cards, some of the best solutions to problems at work come to me.
- ❖ I usually feel guilty if I don't make good use of my time. It's hard for me to relax and do nothing.
- ❖ I like to talk about things that are important to me; small talk bores me.
- ❖ Rather than wade through a whole book, I prefer reading book summaries.
- ❖ What really irritates me, is a slow driver ahead.
- ❖ I am a fast eater.
- ❖ When I'm talking, I tend to accent key words.
- ❖ I always walk and move rapidly.

Which group of statements sound more like you? If the first group, then you tend to have stress-avoiding idiosyncrasies; if the second group, you have stress-prone idiosyncracies. It has been determined that stress-prone idiosyncracies are much more likely to cause heart disease, regardless of diet, weight, and even smoking patterns. Stress-avoiding idiosyncracies enable people to handle stress better, and are more conducive to good health. So check your idiosyncracies and see where you can perhaps modify them.

Stress Management

Since burnout is the result of prolonged exposure to stress, it follows that burnout can be prevented or controlled by learning how to handle stress more effectively. Even those who have not reached the burnout stage will benefit from an effective stress management program, of which there are five basic elements:

1. *The supportive element:* being able to talk about it with a partner or close friend and developing a support structure.
2. *The physical element:* taking exercise regularly, reviewing diet, ensuring periods of relaxation, having a health check-up annually.
3. *The behavioural element:* resolving conflicts, reviewing your behaviour, reordering your values.

4. *The spiritual element:* prayer or meditation, confronting aging of self or family members, and in some cases illness or even death, developing a philosophy of life — 'What's it all about? Why am I here? What's my reason for being?'
5. *The organisational element:* identifying causes of stress, using group problem-solving, improving work and home environment, managing time more effectively, allowing time for leisure pursuits.

One of the greatest ways of ensuring that your stress levels are kept at manageable proportions in the world of work is to think like a Bulletproof Executive!

Career Stages

Stress management and career success need different pointers at different stages. I will now briefly trace through the career journey from the 20-year-old to the 60-year-old, to see how young, middle-aged and senior executives regard their jobs, their careers, and the people they work with.

Many young people today, unlike the 'flower children' of the 1960s, are highly ambitious and career-oriented. They are pursuing undergraduate and graduate degrees in droves. Many are holding down jobs during the day and taking courses at night to upgrade their knowledge and skills and thus further their careers. More than any other age group, people in their early twenties are anxious to get a job which will allow them to use their talents and educational background. Unfortunately, they must sometimes lower their expectations, at least to start out.

People in their twenties tend to be impatient with incompetence and are disappointed with what appears to them to be a lack of professionalism and a rigid outlook displayed by some older people at work, which may or may not be a valid opinion.

Here is some advice for people in this age group: learn your job thoroughly, particularly the base (and sometimes more boring) elements, and get to understand the organisation structure in your work environment. Do your share of the dirty work, work hard, but seek help when needed. Communicate, get feedback, and develop career focus and goals. Be prepared to bide your time, as it may take a while to get to where you want to be. Don't job-hop, but be prepared to move on in order to gain experience elsewhere.

People in their late twenties and early thirties are on the move more than any other age group. They are determined to find positions which will propel them to success. As a result, it is not unusual to find people in this age group making two or three job changes within a ten-year period. This involves a certain degree of risk, but they can afford to take such risks, at least until they hit the really heavy financial responsibilities in their forties or fifties. They are, however, more careful and deliberate about job changes than people in their twenties.

People in their late twenties and early thirties become impatient with a job which does not allow them to get ahead fast enough. This period is also characterised by complete career shifts as values and goals are re-examined. Many people continue or complete their formal education at this age through full-time or part-time study. Concurrent with this, if they manage to find a satisfying and well-paying position they tend to settle down for the long haul, at least until their market worth changes drastically.

People in their late twenties and early thirties like to be creative, utilise their talents, influence the organisation's direction and work with other motivated people. The main causes of job dissatisfaction at this age are lack of support from top management, lack of direction, poor communication, organisational politics and interpersonal problems. Many in this group switch jobs if they don't like or respect their manager or top management, or if they can find a position elsewhere offering a better chance for growth and success.

Some tips for people in their late twenties or early thirties include: understand the informal network in organisations and build relationships. Delegate properly and develop yourself to be able to fill the job above yours. Develop your direct reports also. Keep your sense of humour and stay physically fit, up to date, decisive and honest. Make contributions and, above all, be seen to get results.

Many people in their late thirties and early forties are restless and looking for a chance to move up or on in their careers. They realise that there will be fewer and fewer opportunities later. Their approach to changing jobs is more cautious, as they can no longer afford to take great risks, but they still often seek positions with more money or prestige. However, people in this age group feel that they can no longer switch jobs as often as before, as potential employers may look suspiciously at job-hoppers of this age group. They realise that their work record and reputation will be on the line more than when they were younger.

Many in this group feel that it is impossible for them to move, perhaps because they lack a formal education or fear a loss of financial security. Some may have been with the same organisation for 20 years or so in a speciality field, and feel trapped. Most have become fairly competent at their work, however, and have learned how to utilise the political network to get ahead. They value good communication skills, good health, a competent staff, teamwork, and the ability to give praise and recognition where it is due.

Some tips for the late thirties and early forties include: develop a sense of personal security by ensuring that your skills and capabilities will remain in demand. If necessary, retrain or acquire new skills. Don't lie, double-deal, stagnate or become self-centred at work. Don't be opinionated or a part of the rumour mill. Don't be ruled by money. Don't spend all your time in meetings. Ensure that sufficient quality time is spent with your partner, family and close friends, watch your health and weight, and get enough exercise.

Now we come to one of the most critical periods in anyone's career, the mid-forties through early fifties age group. This is the time when all your past mistakes can catch up with you, and there is little time to rectify them. If you can survive this period, you will sail through to retirement, but sometimes the decade of the late forties through early fifties is when, in terms of a person's career, the roof seems to be falling in.

What do people in this age group have to worry about? There is an increased chance of sudden death— through a heart attack, cancer and so forth, whether this be themself or their partner. There is also the fear of finding oneself out on the street owing to a merger, acquisition, restructuring or divestment. The 50-year-old finds this much more devastating than the 20-, 30- or 40-year-old, because of their perception (often inaccurate) of the reduced chances of their being re-employed. Unemployment hits this age group especially hard, since they are used to a certain comfortable standard of living and cannot believe that their job is not there anymore.

Their job-search skills are rusty and even if they find a position, they often find it difficult to adjust and start all over again. Fifty-year-olds who have allowed themselves to stagnate in their jobs, who have poor performance records or problems in the areas of chemistry and fit, will obviously feel the pressure of the axe more than those who are more successful performers. But sometimes in today's economic turbulence, the good must leave along with the bad.

Fortunately, most organisations are willing to help the displaced executive or manager find another job through the provision of outplacement services. But executives and managers in their mid-forties through early fifties can survive this period with a little 'contingency planning', a lot of alertness to what is happening around them, a commitment to keeping up to date, and competent work performance and fit.

Some tips for the mid-forties through early fifties age group include: further develop a sense of personal security by contingency planning. Develop and promote 'UMDs' — unique marketing differentiators relating to your competencies and capabilities — in other words, your unique and marketable strengths which differentiate you from your competition. Your UMDs need to coincide with demands within and outside your existing organisation and they really represent your point of differentiation and competitive advantage compared to others. Remain aware of the political climate in your organisation and adapt to changing conditions. Keep abreast of developments in your field. Develop supportive social contacts and maintain a code of ethical behaviour, not blaming others for your mistakes and not taking all the credit for successes. Plan to continue working effectively until retirement, but be prepared with a plan of action, should the axe fall anyway. Finally, consider and plan 'second career' options of consulting, contracting, non-executive directorships and so forth, and in this regard be clear about, and further develop, your UMDs!

In spite of the myths about older workers, there is no real evidence that productivity decreases with increasing age. Many people remain active and productive throughout their later years. Although executives and managers in the mid-fifties through sixties age group may be more prone to health problems, they usually take better care of themselves than do younger individuals.

As a group, executives and managers of this age group have an excellent record. If they have made it this far, they have usually proved their competence. The ability to adapt and change does not depend on age, as mature people are often quite flexible, while many younger people can be more set in their ways and in their expectations. Thus there is no adverse correlation between age and work performance, and often a positive consideration.

Issues of concern to executives and managers in this age group are time management, obsolescence, fatigue, and the speed of technological change. Many are bewildered by the developments in computing and telecommunications technology, and envy younger people who seem to cope better.

Some advice for people in their mid-fifties through sixties includes: discuss your career and retirement intentions with your employer and ask for input or advice when needed. In fact, start planning retirement or 'second career' options if you have not already done so, and consider the alternatives for part-time work. Make decisions and be ready to say 'no'. Become involved in the community. Be honest, considerate and accessible, and keep a sense of humour. Above all, stay up to date, train your direct reports, delegate, and check your performance and fit continuously.

Through the Year 2000

What will be some of the work trends over the next decade?

- *Information technology and telecommunications*. IT & T will have a greater and greater impact upon our personal and work lives. There is no stemming the tide, and people who are serious about future career growth and opportunities will do well to learn how IT & T can and will affect their careers and adjust accordingly.
- *Aging workforce, fewer younger executives*. As the baby boomers age, there will be a shortage of younger people coming through, creating employment opportunities for older executives and managers who wish to keep working, although not necessarily in senior positions.
- *Regular job changes*. Executive mobility among jobs and organisations is increasing as people look not only for more money but also for opportunities to learn and grow in their careers.
- *Greater utilisation of talent*. Executive, managerial and professional talent existing within an organisation is often greatly underutilised. As we move through 2000, every individual has to count in these leaner, keener organisations.
- *End of life-long employment with and loyalty to one employer*. Individuals will stay only as long as they are meeting their personal career goals. This doesn't mean they don't commit themselves fully to the job at hand while they are there.
- *High level of restructures, mergers, acquisitions and divestments*. The search for increased profits by these means will continue, with their resulting shuffle in executive and management ranks.
- *Dual-career marriages*. As more and more women enter the executive world it can no longer be assumed that either partner will give up a lucrative career to follow the other. Offers of promotion and transfer will increasingly be evaluated in terms of each career, and decisions to accept or refuse made on this basis.
- *Higher educated executives*. Higher education will be appreciated and rewarded even more, with master's and doctorate degrees becoming more common in executive suites. Psychologists and others interested in the utilisation of human resources, will be more in evidence.
- *Flexible work arrangements*. Today's fairly rigid work schedules will increasingly be replaced by part-time, project and contract arrangements to take advantage of high-level skills and know-how as and when needed.
- *Leisure time*. The time demands of work may or may not decrease owing to technological innovation and more efficient work methods, leaving more or less time for non-work pursuits. The jury is divided!

❖ *Continuing emphasis on productivity*. Executives and managers are even now having to be more efficient and productive than before, for less money. This is in response to the need to keep costs down and efficiency up, ensuring individual job security and advancement.

A Final Word of Encouragement

Some executives and managers are discouraged by the rate and acceleration of the changes taking place around us. Is there any point in planning ahead very far, they ask, and why invest time and effort in a career if it will not even exist five or ten years from now? The answer is 'Yes'— it is worth the planning and effort. We all need to feel productive in a job we enjoy and to feel that we have a future. So we must know ourselves well, plan for what we want and go after it with enthusiasm.

But the real key as we build our careers is to keep a wary eye on what is happening around us and expect to be making continual adjustments to keep pace with new developments in our fields and to take advantage of the vast range of opportunities as they arise.

SUMMARY

Chapter 13 raises the following key issues:

- When confronted with stress in your new work environment, the courses of action open to you are: attack it, ignore it, develop resilience through imagery, change it, change your behaviour, change your attitude, or retreat.
- Job stress and work burnout are common problems today, and burnout — emotional and even physical exhaustion — is particularly prevalent in high-pressure jobs with intense exposure to people.
- Stress management requires attention to five basic elements: supportive, physical, behavioural, spiritual and organisational. It is within your power to be in control of each of these elements.
- Additionally, in order to continue to succeed in your career, you need to understand and manage the risks applicable at different stages. For example, 28-year-olds may need to concentrate on developing their networks within the organisation; 42-year-olds may need to start a contingency plan and ensure their skills remain in demand; 51-year-olds may need contingency plans to be well in place, and to have developed and promote personal unique marketing differentiators about their capabilities, for which they have ensured there is continuing demand.
- Executives and managers of all ages need to prepare for the work trends over the next decade: information technology and telecommunications; aging workforce; fewer younger executives; regular job changes; greater utilisation of talent; end of life-long employment with, and loyalty to, one employer; continuing high level of restructures; dual-career marriages; higher educated people; flexible work arrangements; more, or perhaps less, leisure time; and continuing emphasis on productivity.

PART FIVE

Selling Yourself, Networking Allies And Negotiating Your Way To Success

Network of allies — A complex system of mutually supportive contacts which are linked together. Enables the accessor to progress from one contact to another — previously known or unknown — with speed, ease and effect.

14

Winning Hands Down At Power, Politics And Influence

'I'm really impressed with Tom Jackson, my neighbour, now CEO of a transportation group. Not only does he perform well as an executive, but he seems to understand and survive the politics and power struggles in his organisation — he always seems to come out on top. He has developed an amazing range of allies over the years and I know he's found this network supportive when there's a problem or need for advice. He can sell himself, too, both one-on-one and in front of audiences, and seems to be able to influence others in his industry, particularly when making presentations at those industry forums. No wonder he's so successful.'

This chapter provides guidance to executives and managers on how to deal with and succeed at power, politics and influence. This is by selling yourself assertively, individually and with groups, by building a strong network of supporters — allies — and by negotiating successfully, rather than by indulging proactively in the darker side of political struggles and power plays. Comments Brian Armour, employment development manager of ADI Technology Group: 'A *healthy* focus on this reality needs to be encouraged.'

Christopher Conybeare, independent consultant and associate director of Davidson & Associates, provides a different spin on the subject of politics, power and influence, claiming this area to be: 'An important machinery aspect of success or failure — it should be automatic, like car-driving skills and not an end in itself.' But car-driving has to be taught and learned!

'On the way up, or at middle management level, you need people above you who are comfortable with your style, ideas and the way you work — if they are uncomfortable or uncertain, then it is difficult to move on,' remarks Michael Rowan, formerly chief manager commercial and agribusiness banking, NSW Country and ACT, Westpac, who ranked politics, power and influence at the top of the list of career success factors for executives and managers.

Robert C Stephenson, local divisional manager of SCA Molnlycke AB in the UK, agrees: 'Having spent my life in a major multinational, latterly under the leadership of the infamous Al Dunlap, this has to be top of my list!'

Jay Lowrey, human resources director of AMP and previously senior vice president of Chase Manhattan Bank, agrees: 'Sad but true . . . these factors (politics, power and influence) may or may not be ones you utilise per se, but others might, and therefore affect you. Says more about "failure" than success!'

Power

Every organisation has its networks and we are not talking here about the formal lines of power and authority, but the ones which operate 'behind the scenes'. The sooner you become aware of these networks, the sooner you can begin to use them for the further development of your image and for your own career success.

This doesn't mean fighting or clawing at other people's expense — such an attitude will backfire on you eventually. What it does mean is that you do *not* stick your head in the sand as to how the organisation really operates and who the real decision-makers are. Take the time to look around and ask yourself the following questions:

- Whose advice is sought and followed?
- Whose criticism counts?
- Whose ideas carry weight?
- Whose opinion causes others to change theirs?
- At whom do people look when they make a recommendation?
- Who confides in whom?
- Who backs whose suggestions?

Endeavouring to answer these questions is not just an exercise in people-watching, but a necessary requirement for your own ongoing success, career protection and advancement. Once you have identified the power plays and networks, you will be in a better position to use them to your own advantage and to enhance your own influence. To do this effectively you will also need feedback on how you are seen, in terms of your work performance and your relationships with others. This feedback can come from the senior executive to whom you report, your peers and even your subordinates.

Be aware of how people respond to you in terms of tone of voice, their desire to know your opinion, and unspoken signals. Don't neglect to ask for feedback directly on how you are doing and where you may need improvement. In this way you can set up a channel for communication and feedback which will prevent potential problems and keep you informed, rather than isolated. 'Image, profile and network come in handy when needed,' remarks Graeme Duhs, managing director, Davidson & Associates Limited New Zealand.

However, the biggest potential obstacle in the context of 'power' — and also the most significant opportunity — is to work out where the power *really* resides in your organisation. Take the case of the newly appointed CEO of a major division of a large group. He was appointed to follow through on some recommendations he had made earlier while acting as a management consultant and advising on divisional strategy and operations improvement. This newly appointed divisional CEO had been told by his boss — the CEO of the overall group — to watch out for one of his direct reports, an older-style general manager who managed, in a highly autocratic fashion, one of the companies in the division. It went further than this. The division needed rationalising and part of that rationalisation might include the early retirement of the 'difficult' general manager, who had been a thorn in the side of the group CEO for years. However, the group CEO had lacked sufficient intestinal fortitude to do anything about it.

The new divisional CEO went about his task and found, indeed, that rationalisation and the phasing out of the general manager in question made sense. Pressure was applied in the context of the need for change and improved bottom-line performance. Just a few short months into the job, the divisional CEO was called into a meeting with the group chairman, who had flown in from the overseas group head office. The meeting was a fight from start to finish. The chairman challenged the divisional CEO from the outset and it became clear that he was in real trouble, although the reason for this was unclear at the time. The group CEO watched the confrontation like a salamander, watery-eyed and licking his lips, but making no comment and certainly not leaping to the defence of his new divisional CEO, who up to that point had made an excellent start in his new role. Shortly after this disastrous meeting the divisional CEO received the bullet — several actually, over a period of a couple of weeks, until the *coup de grâce* finally came. He never knew what hit him.

Now for the bitter truth! The group CEO did not, after all, hold the power. The power — and in this case the forces of darkness — actually resided with the general manager. It turned out that he had a strong personal relationship with the group chairman because they had worked together closely, earlier in their careers. The exiting divisional CEO learned a lot about power, politics and influence from this episode, although it took him quite a long time to recover from the experience. I should know — he was me!

I should have sought the advice earlier of Ron Enestrom, senior adviser, AIG Financial Products Ltd and associate director of Davidson & Associates, previously senior vice president and regional head of The First National Bank of Chicago, who proclaims: 'Maybe I am cynical, but I believe that in any organisation, with more than a handful of people, corporate politicking is the most important factor.'

Paul Lilley, general manager human resources, (Australian Banking Group) Westpac also sees this area as important. 'I have always said that in organisational terms, it is best to always have one more friend than enemy! Perception is critical to success. It is important to be able to manage the politics of your organisation, and the internal network will often provide useful information as well as a good support network. This can be overplayed, however, and an individual who is seen as being over-political can also limit their career. A difficult balance to maintain sometimes!'

Stuart Hamilton, executive director of the Australian Vice-Chancellors Committee, previously secretary (CEO) of the Commonwealth Department of the Environment, sums it up this way: 'You can know your business, have a first-rate team, know your environment, be a good leader and planner, and be undone by factors outside your control, unless you manage the "politics" of your organisation.'

'Many, if not most of our outplacement candidates are with us because of political naivety — just can't read the signs,' says Geoff Wright, former state director Western Australia, Davidson & Associates. 'It should not be such an important factor, but it is.'

Influence

I have been involved, directly or indirectly, in executive and management development for some 25 years, and over that time I have advised countless numbers of executives and other people on how to become successful in organisational and business life, through winning at power, politics and influence. One of the key success ingredients in this area is perhaps best described by the phrase 'It's not *what* you know, but *who* you know!' Indeed, it is clear that personal selling — selling your views, ideas and yourself to others, networking to expand your contact base of allies, and effectively negotiating with others within and outside your immediate work environment — is a critical success factor in this.

Paul Martin, state director Western Australia, Davidson & Associates, comments: 'Many of those I deal with rarely see themselves as being in the driver's seat. Few of them feel they actually have a choice about who they work with, what they have a say in, or how the place is managed. Many executives in large organisations have become institutionalised and lose their individuality and differentiators. They must realise that they don't need to subjugate their skills and abilities. Obviously there are many ways of preventing this, and many may have been let go because they haven't worked out the best way to "sell" an issue or themselves internally, before launching their initiative on the world at large. Diplomacy, strategy and tactics need to be worked out first and not on the run.'

I have found that executives and managers can accomplish this by developing an understanding of professional consultative selling techniques, adapting them to their own unique circumstances and honing such skills to an advanced level. In a word, what the executive or manager is trying to achieve here is greater 'influence' and this can only be accomplished through effective personal selling and the development of informal 'alliances'.

The Business of Personal Selling

Here are two examples of personal selling. The first relates to Eugene Graff who was human resources director of a major food group. He used to spend core office hours circulating and meeting with senior executives and others in the company, to the extent that they took him into their confidence and depended on him for advice. They saw him as their 'ally'. He became the one person in the company with his finger on the pulse of the organisation's climate and employee morale. He also developed a strong external network of allies by working with the local chapter of the Human Resources Institute and serving on its national committee. In addition to excelling at personal selling, he was a strong delegator and relied heavily on the functional expertise of his team. He eventually became CEO and was an outstanding success in this role also.

The second example relates to David Johns, who was also a human resources director of a major resources group. He attained this role because he was acknowledged as an authority on most, if not all of the key human resources functions. Indeed, he spent much of his time in keeping up to date through reading (even during office hours) and attending, participating in and sometimes leading human resources seminars. Unfortunately, he did not last in this role because executives and line managers within his own company found him to be inaccessible and 'above them' — too theoretical and concerned with perfection rather than Pareto. (In this context, Pareto means getting the top 20 per cent right and thereby reaping the 80 per cent beneficial impact.) Clearly, personal selling was not his forte and it may never have occurred to him that, in effect, this oversight cost him his job.

The first step in making a success of personal selling is to acquire the attitude of an entrepreneur — the executive or manager seeking greater influence has the responsibility to run their business of personal selling efficiently and profitably.

Goal-setting is the starting point of achievement — we have to know where we are headed and what we hope to achieve, before we can take the steps necessary to get us there and effectively monitor our progress so that we stay on course. Goal-setting in personal selling involves the following principles: *the setting of realistic, specific achievement goals*; and *monitoring your goals regularly.*

Setting realistic, specific achievement goals

In order to be effective, goals must be realistic. They should be attainable, but set a little higher than would be required for easy achievement — you should have to work hard to achieve them. Setting them way out of reach, however, will only result in discouragement and eventually work against you.

Your goals should also be specific, so that you can easily tell whether or not you are achieving them. To set a goal of 'improving personal selling performance' or 'making more contacts' is so general as to be meaningless. Some examples of specific personal selling goals might be:

- liaise with each member of the board of directors, monthly
- touch base with each senior executive in the organisation or division at least once a week
- make four presentations a year to external groups
- develop four new external contacts and two supporters or allies per quarter
- phone two former external contacts and one ally per week for an update.

Monitor your goals regularly

Make sure your goals remain realistic in the light of current developments and changing circumstances. Don't be tempted, however, to revise your goals downward at the slightest excuse. Your goals should stand, regardless of your current performance, unless there have been major positive or negative factors beyond your control. Continuous monitoring will keep you on track and help keep your personal goals and objectives in sight and attainable.

Knowledge, and the Psychology of Personal Selling

The increasing need for expertise and knowledge relating to market and industry developments is making unprecedented demands on today's professional executive and manager. The human mind can only absorb so much.

Eugene Graff through his association with the Human Resources Institute kept pretty well up to date. He was also a good delegator and relied on the experts in his team. David Johns, on the other hand, went overboard with knowledge acquisition to the point of failing to develop an internal following through personal selling. Fortunately he had a strong external presence and so when he lost his job he was able to find another within six months. I lost contact with him, however. Had he learned his lesson? Did the next job last?

Rather than try to take in everything, the trick is to try to pick out what is essential and to concentrate on absorbing as much of that information as possible, while ignoring the rest, or relying on your subordinates.

Phillip Hart, executive director, Red Cross, New South Wales, sees this as an important area: 'Ability to analyse information from diverse sources is now imperative as organisations make large changes in methods, eg off-shore production, outsourcing, contracting staff, etc.'

Now the focus of selling yourself is the person with whom you wish to develop some form of informal alliance, and all the knowledge in the world will not be of much use if that knowledge cannot be related somehow to genuine interests, needs and wants of other people.

The psychology of selling yourself attempts to understand the behaviour of other people, and what motivates them potentially to develop an alliance with you. Understanding behaviour patterns may help to determine how influential they are; it may also help to predict how they will react to your personal selling efforts. This knowledge of behaviour and motivation will be useful to you in tailoring your personal selling approaches to individual contacts. Flexibility is the key — the 'canned approach' is out. Remember initially to focus on the interests and needs of your contact, not on your underlying reason for wishing to develop some type of alliance.

In selling yourself at the executive and managerial levels you are not always dealing with independent contacts. You are often dealing instead with 'organisational' contacts, who may be in some way involved, directly or indirectly, in helping you to gain greater influence. These contacts may include executives in your own or other businesses, manufacturers, wholesalers, retailers, agricultural and resource companies, government agencies, associations and so forth.

In attempting to focus on organisational characteristics, you should realise that there are some major differences between independent and organisational contacts. For example, organisational contacts:

- normally associate with others, particularly those outside their employer organisations, for fewer *personal* reasons than do independent contacts
- are sometimes restricted by well-defined company policies and practices, as well as the inevitable time pressures
- typically distribute liaison with external contacts among several other people.

Thus, in trying to understand behaviour and motivation, you must consider not only the individual with whom you wish to develop an alliance, but also the organisational characteristics which will impact on this alliance. For example:

- What are the policies of the organisation?
- Apart from the contact I am targeting, how many other people are likely to be involved in developing this alliance?

- Who is the main influencer?
- Is it one individual or a group?
- If it is a group, who are the key people who tend to sway group opinion?
- What kind of individual operating style (or styles) am I likely to encounter, and to which I must adapt and respond, in order to get desired results?

Being able to answer such questions, as they relate to each of your organisational contacts, obviously takes some preparation.

If you want to be effective in developing alliances and generating greater influence with organisational contacts, you need to understand the process — the 'how' of a decision, whether or not to develop an alliance with you, will throw some light on the 'way'. Remember that all decisions take time and generally speaking, taking the harder case of the *external* organisational contact, they will follow four steps.

1. Need recognition

The identification or recognition of a need sets the decision process in motion of whether or not to develop some form of relationship or alliance with you. Once begun, the process continues until the alliance is cemented or rejected. But in order to get the process started, the individual or individuals with whom you are liaising must be motivated to form such an alliance.

Thus the first task in selling yourself is ideally to identify and appeal to an unsatisfied interest, need or want on the part of your target contact, as this will serve as the motivating force. Before an unsatisfied need can motivate behaviour, however, it must be recognised and acknowledged by the contact — some people have needs of which they are unaware until they are pointed out to them.

There are two ways in which contacts become aware of their needs: by receiving new information and by re-evaluating their current situation. You can be instrumental in either case. Contacts generally need to be reminded or told about your experience and capabilities and how they can satisfy their particular interests or needs. They also have to be appraised of the need itself, because sometimes the need is latent and it is up to you to convert the latent need into an obvious need, and into a 'want' which you can satisfy!

2. Search for information

Once the need has been recognised and acknowledged, the contact will then require a certain amount of information.

All contacts, whether independent or organisational, have two major sources of information: internal and external. Internal sources of information are those facts which are already known to the contact, whether through reading, discussions with others or actual experience. Organisational contacts may have extensive databases, files and records at their disposal, catalogues, trade journals, company brochures, correspondence records and so on, to help with information gathering.

Even with all of these internal sources, however, most contacts look to external sources, perhaps to you to supplement their information needs. This is why one of the most important characteristics in selling yourself is credibility. Less than honest claims and approaches are easily exposed and you need to be a knowledgeable, believable source of information for your contacts.

3. Selection among alternatives

Once the contact feels that enough information has been gathered, there must be a selection. This selection may be between similar external contacts, or between associating or not associating with a specific contact — perhaps you!

You need to realise that in this stage of the decision-making process the outcome will depend upon two things: which factors the contact will consider in making the decision to develop an alliance, and the relative weight or importance attached to each factor. Identifying these factors, and their relative importance to the contact, is not as difficult as it sounds. A little preliminary investigation, coupled with some careful questioning, should bring these out. This is an area in which selling yourself usually improves dramatically with experience.

4. Ongoing alliance

You can and should seek to have some influence over the strength or longevity of the ongoing alliance — and remember, we are talking about an informal alliance here based on mutual support — by following through to ensure that your contact is satisfied with the alliance to date, and if not, why not. Any problems can thus be put right, or minimised as soon as possible. Thus direct and continuous follow-up during your alliance is an essential part of successfully selling yourself.

Although the steps described above relate to external organisational contacts, they also apply to internal contacts and you can modify them to meet the needs of your personal selling objectives within your own organisation.

Time Management and Prioritisation

One of the toughest challenges facing executives and managers today is to make every hour of the day count for more. Challenging economic conditions and a highly competitive commercial environment have made efficient and profitable use of time essential for survival.

Working harder and longer is not necessarily the answer. What is needed is a good hard look at where you are spending your time and whether or not you are getting maximum pay-back for your efforts. It may be that too much of your time is spent on associating with marginal or non-productive allies, time that could be spent developing and maintaining the more profitable allies. This is just good business sense. Remember that in selling yourself and developing your influence you are managing your own business and you must keep one eye on the results, without rushing, pressuring or alienating any of your allies.

By far the best way of ensuring that your time is spent efficiently and profitably, while interacting with your allies properly, is to plan. Time management and planning is essential to your personal success, but is often ignored in favour of the 'hit and miss' approach. Planning takes time, but if undertaken in the evening or at weekends it need not eat into your personal selling and business time. How and where do you get started?

A common pitfall in selling yourself is to devote far too much time to low-potential allies and insufficient time to high-potential allies. If all of this time can be recouped, it often improves personal selling efficiency by one-third or more. A close analysis of how you spend your time should point out where your plan may need some restructuring. In order to do this, you will need to complete a classification of your existing and prospective allies, and one way to do this is by a 'I, II, III Analysis'.

In this analysis 'Is' are the high-yield/high-potential allies (existing and potential allies) and you may find they represent 20 per cent of your allies, yet 80 per cent of your alliance and influence potential. Devote maximum time and attention to each 'I' ally. 'IIs' are the mid-yield/mid-potential allies. You may find they represent 30 per cent of your contacts and 15 per cent of your alliance and influence potential. Devote some time and attention to each 'II' ally. 'IIIs' are the low-yield/low-potential allies. You may find that they represent as many as 50 per cent of your allies, yet only offer alliance and influence potential of 5 per cent. Devote minimal time and attention to each 'III' ally and consider referring them to someone else in your organisation or dropping them altogether.

The first step should be to gradually discontinue your low-yield/low-potential allies. The time saved can be used to increase the results from your existing, high-yield allies, as well as to cultivate those prospective allies with a high-yield potential.

In submitting your existing and prospective contacts to the I, II, III Analysis, don't be too hasty in rejecting current low-yield allies, particularly if you have some reason to believe that the yield will improve dramatically in the future. But as the manager of your own personal selling and influence development business, you should dedicate the major portion of your time and effort to those allies who yield the greatest return on your time, efforts and expense.

The Importance of Selling Yourself Externally

Generating new allies within the organisation is a prerequisite for developing your internal influence and network of support. However, in today's turbulent economic and organisational environment, it is just as important to develop external influence and allies. Whatever the position you occupy, you are a representative of your organisation. If you have a strong network of allies externally who think well of you, this will enhance your organisation's reputation. It will also enhance your own reputation, which will be fed back to those who matter in your own organisation. This in turn strengthens your position and future. A strong external network of allies also balances your perspective in terms of preventing you from becoming too introspective. A strong external network of allies can tap you into a cadre of external experts and advisers who will not charge you a cent in fees! I know of one major company which makes it a policy to use management consultants on a professional fee-paying basis only in extreme cases, yet whose senior executive team has developed the finest and largest informal 'Board of Management Advice' in the land — and it doesn't cost them a cent, other than the odd lunch. They have even been able to implement Total Quality Management without using external consultants, but by using advice, tools and techniques sourced from other companies through their network of external allies. Neither do they use executive search consultants. They have such an expansive external network that when a senior vacancy arises it is always filled by the best and most relevant executive talent available, through word-of-mouth referral.

Generating new external contacts is the very first step in extending your external network of allies and influence. Indeed, your success in this is directly proportional to the number of people you contact (everything else being equal). As such, the importance of generating new external contacts cannot be overemphasised.

First, let me define exactly what I mean by some terms: 'contacts', 'leads', 'alliance' and 'prospects'. A 'contact' is just about anyone you know or seek to know, or who may seek to know you! A 'lead' is a contact who *may* have an interest or need to develop an alliance with you. The term 'alliance' means ongoing informal liaison and mutual support. Leads can come from many sources, such as existing allies, newspaper announcements, social contacts, family and friends, and so forth. Keep in mind that since most leads will have neither a definite interest in nor a desire to develop an alliance with you, you may have to generate many leads to get the few who actually do have a need or interest.

Once a lead has demonstrated or acknowledged a definite interest or need to develop an alliance with you, the lead becomes a 'prospect'. However, before expending considerable time and effort in trying to form an alliance with a prospect, you should first *qualify* the prospect, for which there are three main steps:

1. *Determine which factors you feel are important and should be used in your qualification.* Some typical factors for analysing organisational prospects might be: the type of business and area of expertise of the prospect; the level of seniority and influence of the prospect; range of contacts accessible through the prospect.
2. *Determine whether or not the prospect possesses these qualifications.* It may be that the prospect doesn't need to pass every test — some factors will be more important than others, and you must decide if the prospect possesses enough of the important variables to qualify.
3. *Decide whether or not it will be worthwhile pursuing the prospect.* This should really be an economic decision. Some prospects may qualify very well, but should not be pursued because to do so would be unprofitable. The main example is the marginal prospect who requires a high proportion of time in relation to the benefits derived. Your decision not to pursue such a prospect should be balanced by a consideration of whether or not the benefits will be likely to increase sufficiently in the future.

By effectively qualifying prospects, you can save a lot of time and frustration chasing after people who, for one reason or another, are not worth forming an alliance with. Once a prospect has been qualified, effective personal selling skills will hopefully result in an alliance being formed, and turn the qualified prospect into an 'ally' — someone with whom you will continue to liaise and with whom there is some form of mutual support.

Forming the alliance is not the final step. Appropriate follow-up and a satisfied ally produces an ongoing profitable alliance, and this should be the final goal of all your prospecting efforts. Systematic, well-planned prospecting will allow you to get the jump on other business networkers, by aiming your efforts at individuals and organisations who will produce the best results for your efforts. Very often, effective continuous prospecting is what separates the high performers from the low performers in external personal selling, forming alliances and generating greater external influence, support and advice.

Indeed, all executives and managers will need to become increasingly involved in customer contact and revenue generation in the future. According to Richard Koch and Ian Godden, the authors of *Managing Without Management: A post-management manifesto for business simplicity* (Nicholas Brealey Publishing, London, 1996), the 'post-management' corporation will be aiming for a doubling of profitable sales in ten years, and in this context executives and managers will need to spend half their time dealing with customers, compared with only 5 per cent currently. Get ready for the post-management era — step up your external personal selling efforts and effect!

How to Source New External Leads

There are numerous sources of external leads available. I will address several of these sources here, but no list is ever complete. To be good at selling yourself, you should be flexible and experiment with a wide variety of potential sources. Some of these will be exhausted in a short space of time, while others may continue to be fruitful for years. We will now consider some of the more common sources of leads.

Your existing prospects

Your own current list of prospects can be a good source of leads. This source can be tapped by asking a few simple questions during your liaison with prospects — for example: 'Do you know of anyone else who may be interested in discussing this?' or 'Is anyone else in your company experiencing similar problems?'

Some people in personal selling make it a common practice to try to get one or two leads for every person with whom they are in contact. This is known as the 'endless chain' method of generating leads, and if handled tactfully, it can be very effective.

Allies for referrals

Satisfied allies provide the best single source of leads. If they are pleased with their alliance with you, they may tend to mention your name to others in casual conversation. This gives you a personal endorsement which increases your credibility and makes your networking job that much easier.

You can also ask your allies directly if they know of anyone who may be interested in what you would like to discuss or if they will introduce or recommend you to new prospects. This is known as the 'direct referral' method and is very productive since it reduces the time spent on prospecting and qualifying. It also increases the possibility of receiving a positive response to the subsequent contact made.

In seeking leads from allies, try using the following system. The best time is when you have just concluded a fruitful discussion or meeting with them. Give them a focus — 'Do you belong to any professional associations?' 'Is there anyone you know of with expertise in this area . . . ?' Based on the above focus, ask them for the names of people who might be interested in meeting you. Then ask qualifying questions, and the contact details. Even ask your ally to make a call on your behalf and introduce you or help you to arrange an appointment. If your ally's reaction is not too positive in this, ask if you can use their name, when you make contact yourself.

Internal sources
Other people and areas within your own organisation can be a valuable source of leads.

Social contacts
Because of their close association with you, family, friends and social acquaintances can also be helpful in providing leads. Here the 'direct referral' method can be used.

Another method is to use your social contacts to reach the 'centres of influence' in the community — people who, because of their positions within business and professional groups, exert a lot of influence with certain types of prospects.

Clubs and organisations
Professional clubs and service organisations can provide an excellent source of leads, but be careful not to join for this sole purpose. Avoid obnoxious 'lead chasing' and make sure you believe in the philosophy and goals of the organisation, and that you can contribute something to it — keeping things relaxed and in perspective will usually result in some prospects materialising anyway.

Public records, newspapers and magazines
Publications such as newspapers, magazines, trade journals and related publications should be scanned regularly for leads. Professional appointments, new business and office openings are just some examples of potential prospects to be followed up.

Conventions, conferences and trade shows
Participation in professional conferences, conventions, trade shows and exhibitions is a very good way to identify prospects. In fact, in the professional selling idiom, prospecting is very often the main reason for taking part in such shows and get-togethers.

One-on-One Communication

Selling yourself, finding allies and negotiating your way to success comprise basically a communication process. Selling yourself successfully depends on your communication skills. These skills can be learned and improved upon, so as to upgrade the quality of communication and all subsequent contacts with your target audience.

What do we mean by communication? According to the dictionary definition: 'Communication is a process by which meanings are exchanged between individuals, through a common set of symbols.' The symbols take the form of speech, written messages, facial expressions, gestures and actions. Effective communication requires both a transmitter and a receiver. Simply 'explaining something' to a contact does not guarantee that communication has taken place.

In moving from you (the transmitter) to your contact (the receiver), or vice versa, there may be interference, or 'noise', which prevents the message from being properly understood. Some examples of 'noise' are:

- ambiguous words and phrases (such as 'We'll meet as soon as possible' — be more specific, such as 'We'll try to meet next Friday')
- speaking too quickly, or mumbling words
- failing to clarify. You may know what you are talking about, but your contact may not understand you.
- failing to use terms which are easily understood, and trying to impress with 'jargon'
- not taking into account the mood, attitude and corresponding attention span of the receiver, your contact, in delivering your information.

Effective communication implies the correct usage of language and grammar, as well as tone of voice and volume. But it also implies the effective use and reading of body language (such as posture, facial expressions and gestures). Finally, effective communication implies 'active listening', since communication is a two-way process. Here are some rules for active listening:

- Be committed to *concentrating* on what your contacts are saying, rather than on formulating what you will say next.
- Take an active *interest* in what they are saying and express your interest through your responses, facial expressions and body language.
- Be willing to hear your contacts out fully. *Never interrupt* or try to take the words out of their mouths, as the complete story may throw more light on the situation.
- Try to prevent *distraction*, by shutting out background noise and movement as much as possible. Focus on the contact's face and voice.
- As you listen, rather than interjecting your own thoughts, *summarise* what the contact is saying, and pick out the key points.
- *Practise* your active listening skills at every opportunity. As with most skills, practice makes perfect!

The bottom line in active listening is that God gave us two ears and one mouth, and we should use them in that proportion!

Group Communication

It is interesting how far we have developed in communications. We can speak to people around the world and in space, and we can receive and project images over huge distances. We all treat long distance telephone calls as a natural part of business and our personal life.

However, what happens when you have to stand up in front of an audience and make a speech or presentation? Do you get a knot in your stomach? Does your voice rise an octave? Do you forget your words? How do you start? How do you perform as you get under way? How do you end your presentation? Here are some speaker traits you need to try to avoid!

- *Rambling on and on and going off in many different directions.* This speaker is not usually prepared and often loses himself, as well as the audience, by moving from one subject to another without apparently noticing. The effect is disastrous as he fails to make his point successfully and the audience turns off completely.

- *Pacing backwards and forwards,* like a lion in a cage. This trait gives the speaker a thoroughly bored appearance. It is almost as though he thinks the time will pass more quickly if he walks to and fro.
- *'I...I...I...'. Focus on the self.* This speaker is constantly saying '*I* did this, and *I* believe in that and *I* must tell you about the other thing that happened...'. She is pompous, sometimes arrogant and certainly has a good opinion of herself. She puts the audience off quite early in her speech.
- *Lack of animation.* This presenter is expressionless, statuesque, blank-faced — and has a remarkable ability to put people to sleep after a good lunch.
- *Lack of sincerity.* This speaker is too contrived and too much of an actor to be convincing. She goes to the other extreme and tries to appeal to the audience's emotions, but without sincerity. She assumes that the audience will be fully behind her as she play-acts her role. The only trouble is, the audience senses that this is a well-rehearsed sham and they switch off.
- *Forced funniness.* How many funny presenters really are funny? One in 20 perhaps. The funny presenter often assumes he has to make his audience laugh and so he tells a joke, often resulting in laughter out of sympathy. Forced funniness can turn an audience off.
- *Difficult to hear.* The presenter who cannot be heard fails to realise she is speaking to an audience, and she rambles on with her dissertation in a one-to-one affair with the lectern!

Most executives and managers suffer from some or all of these symptoms, some or every time they make a presentation to a group. Such apprehension and traits are often caused by concerns about not being able to remember your lines, or making a fool of yourself, or making a poor presentation, or failing to meet your objectives, but mainly from inadequate training and preparation.

Stand back from all this for a moment, and do some 'imagineering'. Dream a little! Suppose you were flying across the Pacific and the pilot asked you to take over the controls, how would you react? Suppose you attended a symphony concert and the conductor handed you the baton, how would you react? Suppose you were in the operating theatre and the surgeon asked you to take over an operation, how would you react?

You would likely get a knot in your stomach, you would get that tight sensation around your collar, and you would not know how or where to start. You would definitely portray some strange and atypical traits as you tried to grasp the fundamentals of your new and strange role! This is because you are neither trained nor prepared to fly a plane, conduct an orchestra, or perform surgery. If you had been trained or prepared, how would you have reacted? No problems: hand me the controls; music, maestro, please; hand me the scalpel, nurse!

Yes, the secret to making successful speeches or presentations is to be both *trained* and *prepared*, particularly in the art of delivery which is 80 per cent of the group communication success formula.

Most executives and managers, on the other hand, can find group presentations quite difficult, as did Demosthenes in ancient Greece, who was afflicted with a terrible speech impediment which caused him great difficulty early in his career.

However, he persevered to overcome his impediment and practised his speeches by shouting at the surf and talking with small stones in his mouth; in this way, he coached himself to become the greatest orator of his time. His presentation 'delivery' became outstanding!

Speaker Styles

In developing your delivery to maestro standards, you first need to be clear about speaker styles — in fact, your own speaking style. By way of reminder, your operating style is likely to be one or more of the following:

- *Commander/Doer:* usually directs other people and works energetically to get results.
- *Responder/Initiator:* seeks to understand others, communicates very well and leads enthusiastically.
- *Empathiser/Humanist:* the people- rather than production-oriented individual, with an amicable style.
- *Evaluator/Detailer:* the analytical, logical and meticulous planner and organiser.
- *Idea generator:* the conceptual and creative thinker who can see endless possibilities and show extremes in behaviour.
- *All-rounder:* the balanced individual who has a flexible style, yet doesn't show extremes in behaviour.

The *Commander/Doer* often delivers speeches rapidly and enthusiastically and usually exudes an air of confidence and a down-to-earth attitude. However, when overutilising these positive attributes, *Commander/Doers* can speak or progress too quickly, and can appear to be somewhat short-sighted and too keen on action, rather than on taking longer-term or bigger picture scenarios into consideration. They can also at times be overly blunt and disinterested in social niceties.

If you are a *Responder/Initiator* or *All-rounder*, this suggests you have behavioural flexibility and that you should find it quite easy to adapt your speech or presentation to meet the needs of most audiences. The only caveat here is that *All-rounders* may come across as being a little flat or uninspiring at times.

The *Empathiser/Humanist* probably reads the audience well and empathises with them. Such speakers usually come across in a friendly and courteous manner and often seek audience involvement through their use of questions, comments and examples. However, when overutilising these positive attributes, *Empathiser/Humanists* may become swayed by the mood and views of the audience and even lose control. They also may harp too long on the historical perspective — 'the way we used to do things' — and appear not to come to the point too quickly. They may also be too anxious to please.

Evaluator/Detailers often deliver speeches with accuracy and clarity and achieve their objectives in the time allocated. However, an overutilisation of these positive attributes may include a preference for reading from a script (which I do not advise) and a failure to empathise with the audience. The delivery can sometimes be dull and monotonous, and preoccupied with content rather than *how* the speech is delivered.

Idea generators can often deliver very interesting speeches with plenty of creativity and bright ideas. However, when overutilising these positive attributes they can be hard to follow or understand and may be too theoretical. They can also be poor time managers, and have difficulty in emphasising the main point or ending their speeches with impact. They may also fail to read the audience accurately, being more concerned with their own presentation content.

First Impressions Count

What happens to the audience when the speaker stands up or goes to the speaker's lectern? They stop, look, listen and form first impressions.

Here are some examples of first impressions. The first speaker immediately searches for a glass of water and gulps it down while eyeing the audience nervously. He coughs and loosens his collar. He has trouble getting out his notes and overheads, and drops something on the floor. His hands are shaking, and as if to stop them he grasps the lectern with both hands and stares at the back of the room. He is obviously so *nervous* that the audience feels embarrassed or turns off completely.

The second speaker starts by not being sure where she should position herself for the speech — where she is sitting, at the table, or at the overhead projector. She scratches her head and looks blank or somewhat baffled. She 'ums' and 'ahs' and starts her speech by saying that she really cannot add much to the previous speakers. She is obviously *unprepared* and can turn the audience against her. Why should they bother to listen if she is unprepared? She is wasting their time.

The third speaker walks very slowly, even slinks up to the lectern, looking very serious indeed, and very *unhappy*. He scowls at the audience and starts off by saying they will have to bear with him as he does not normally speak in public. He seems as though he is about to take on a task he would far rather avoid. The audience can react by being reluctant, too — reluctant to listen to him!

The fourth speaker has problems getting up off her chair — it is too close to the table. As she rises, she staggers forward as she catches her thigh against the table. Her glass of water rocks perilously and she makes a lunge to save it! A *shaky start* like this does not bode well for the rest of the speech, and the audience knows it.

The correct way to start and to create a good impression is to slide back your chair from the table and walk over to the lectern (if there is one) as though you are walking over to greet an ally whom you have not seen for a while. Then pause, look at the audience, smile and then start your presentation. Your audience is there to hear your speech. Make sure that your first impressions count and help them concentrate on your speech.

SUMMARY

Chapter 14 raises the following key issues:

- Power in organisations does not always reside solely in the senior executive ranks. Once you have identified the 'behind the scenes' power plays and networks, you are better placed to use them to your advantage and to enhance your own influence.
- It's not just *what* you know, but *who* you know, that will determine your success.
- Any executive or manager therefore needs to engage in the business of personal selling, networking and negotiating, based on professional consultative selling techniques in order to excel.
- Organisational contacts, be they internal or external need to be sought out, qualified in terms of their relevance to your cause, and nurtured.
- Qualified external contacts, converted to ongoing 'allies', in addition to enhancing your external influence, can represent your personal 'Board of Management Advice'.
- The essence of effective personal selling is one-on-one and group communication. Whether it be active listening, good first impressions, or other positive speaking traits, successful communication techniques can be learned and used effectively, with practice.

Further Resources

In Section 16 of your *Executive Armoury* you will find the Convincing Communications Clinic — 39 steps (self-examination questions) helping you diagnose problems and opportunities, along with prescriptions for success!

15

Selling Yourself Outside The Organisation And Motivating Audiences

'John Bassett heads up our northern operations as general manager, and over the past two years he has really made a difference — sales have doubled and we have moved from a substantial loss to more than 20 per cent net sales margin. The sales team just love working with him! Although he probably doesn't realise it, he's quite exceptional at business development, be it one-on-one or hosting and presenting at functions. Even though the market is quite tight, he is able to get those important meetings, and when making group presentations, he inspires his audiences. His capacity to close is excellent. Without him there is a danger we could lapse back into the old ways of too much of a preoccupation with production.'

Getting meetings, convincing individuals and audiences to think your way, and 'closing' — getting the results you want from people — are increasingly important skills for executives and managers.

Approach Planning

In professional selling, approach planning is the preparation for sales calls on specific prospects or clients. In personal selling, approach planning is the preparation for meeting with specific prospects or ongoing allies. The approach itself is actually opening the discussion and setting the stage for the meeting. How you handle these steps, and their main purpose, will depend on the current status of the other party.

When you are calling on qualified prospects (and they really should be qualified prospects if you are going to take the time to call on them), your approach will be crucial in building confidence and respect. We all know the importance of first impressions. Make this work for you rather than against you, by becoming familiar with these initial steps of the personal selling sequence.

The main elements in approach planning are: *meeting content*, *focus on the other party*, *discussion technique* and *obtaining the meeting*.

Meeting content

In deciding the actual content of the meeting, or what you are going to say, keep in mind that all the other party really wants to hear is how you can satisfy and discuss their particular interests, needs or wants.

Obviously in order to do this effectively, you must do some preparation by learning something about the other party's organisation, processes, products and problems. Once this has been done, the next step is to translate the features of what you want to discuss into benefits which will coincide with their interests or needs.

Focus on the other party

Once you have reviewed the content of your upcoming meeting, you will need to focus on the other party in order to decide on the most appropriate technique to use in this particular situation. Who you are calling on will affect what you are going to say, and how you will say it, as well as the topics and benefits which you will focus on at your meeting. For example, a meeting to discuss computer systems with a senior executive (who may have little 'hands-on' contact with such systems, but who may be concerned with how such systems can increase company efficiency and profitability) will differ from a meeting with the company's information technology managers and staff.

Discussion technique

Achieving success in personal selling depends just as much on the technique you use, as on your knowledge and extent of preparation. You should tailor your technique and behaviour to fit the other party, not expect them to adjust to your own particular operating style. This is the concept of 'flexible behaviour'. The operating style you plan to use is best decided before you approach the other person, from information obtained during your preparation.

However, this style may have to be adjusted, depending on the other person's mood at the time of the meeting, or on whether other key people are present. Commonsense and flexibility should be the rule, which is why you should steer clear of 'canned presentations'.

Tailoring your degree of 'proactiveness' and 'receptiveness' to the other party, and to the situation at hand, will increase your chances of success. Of course, if in doubt about the other person's operating style, observe them carefully and adapt to — or even 'mirror' — their style.

Obtaining the meeting

Make sure the person you are going after is the most appropriate person, unless you want to waste a lot of time. A little checking ahead of time should help you to establish this. Once established, there are several techniques for obtaining the meeting: *cold calling in person*; *cold calling by telephone*; *third party introductions*; and *letter writing*.

When cold calling on people in person, it is essential that you identify yourself and state the purpose of your call. Don't try to deceive or trick your prospects just to get a meeting, as it will inevitably backfire on you. The main problem in using this method is that it can waste a lot of your time if the other party is unavailable for a while.

Cold calling by telephone can save you a lot of time, but remember the purpose of such phone calls is ideally to obtain an appointment, not just to conduct a phone discussion, if you seek to develop a close alliance with the prospect. Again, identify yourself immediately to the prospect and state why you are calling.

Be flexible in arranging appointments — let prospects fit you into their schedules, not the other way around. Keep the initial phone call brief, positive and general, so that there is no opportunity for a turndown at this stage — concentrate solely on getting in to see the prospect.

When being introduced by a third party, ideally you will need something tangible, such as a letter of introduction, a phone call to the prospect by the third party, or even a business card with a note scribbled on it. This is usually very effective in getting an appointment, as it gives you some credibility.

Writing letters to prospects asking for appointments can save you time, if done well. You don't have to compose each letter individually — have one or two standard letter formats which you need to personalise by name and opening statements. This method has the advantage of getting through to the prospect directly, but needs to be followed up with a phone call anyway.

Only you can decide which methods work best for you. If you are just starting out in proactive personal selling, try them all, and then evaluate the response you get in relation to the time and effort spent.

The Meeting

Meetings are really the meat and message of developing your alliances. These are where — as with the professional salesperson — all your careful preparation, experience and training should come together eventually to convince the prospect to form an alliance with you. The main advantage of the face-to-face meeting is that it can be tailored to the prospect. It provides you with instant feedback on the other party's response, so that immediate adjustments can be made if necessary.

Since the communication process is two-way, you are not only giving information, but receiving it. In fact, the most effective people at personal selling act more as receivers rather than transmitters in the meeting by 'tuning in' to the prospect and by practising active listening skills. Without a certain amount of empathy (where you sense reactions and respond to them), it will be difficult to establish a relationship of trust, which is essential in building a close alliance.

There are six steps in conducting an effective meeting:

1. Gaining attention.
2. Arousing interest.
3. Building desire.
4. Winning conviction.
5. Getting action.
6. Writing notes of appreciation.

Gaining attention

Your opening statements should be such that you gain the prospect's attention immediately. This doesn't mean that you should turn somersaults or make wild, impossible claims! What it *does* mean is that you should have prepared an opening statement which introduces you and your organisation and then launches into a benefit of the topics you wish to discuss which will grab the prospect's attention right away, since you know this to be a very high priority for that particular individual.

Arousing interest

Once you have gained the prospect's attention, you should maintain it by arousing interest in what you are saying. This can be done by introducing a little touch of drama into your discussion. You don't let everything out of the bag at once — try to encourage the prospect to become involved by holding back some aspects of the topic you wish to discuss, which you know will be of interest and thus encourage questions.

Unless you can get the prospect to talk, you won't get very far. Encourage a two-way dialogue, where both you and the prospect ask and answer questions. This will maintain their interest throughout the presentation and discourage mind-wandering or 'tuning out'. If at any time you sense the prospect's attention is wandering, you can bring them back by asking an open question which needs some thought to answer, rather than just a 'yes' or 'no' response.

Building desire

Psychologically, before your prospect can make a positive decision to accommodate what you seek, they must actually want to do this. Once they reach this stage, they have a definite desire to follow through.

You can build them up to this desire by making frequent reference to how accommodating what you seek will benefit them, how their interests or needs will be satisfied, their problems solved and so forth. This should be explained in language they can understand — jargon and overly technical terms will turn them off, rather than build desire.

Winning conviction

This is where someone, or something other than you and the content of the discussion, convinces the prospect to accommodate what you seek. This can be a personal endorsement from another satisfied ally, a visit to your facilities, or a practical demonstration which gets the prospect more involved in what you seek. In other words, at this stage you must provide the prospect with proof that what you have been saying is true.

Getting action

The final step of the meeting should focus on getting the prospect to act, by signalling agreement to accommodate what you seek. There are several effective ways of doing this, often referred to as 'closing', which will be addressed later.

Writing notes of appreciation

'Thank you' is one of the most important phrases in personal selling and by sending notes which say 'Thank you', you will be leaving your mark or impression on the prospect. Thank you's should be sent:

- after first and all subsequent meetings with prospects and allies
- after the prospect or ally has helped you in some way
- to referrers
- whenever you have had a positive telephone conversation with a contact, prospect or ally, or after an encounter with anybody who can potentially refer other prospects to you.

Structured Versus Personalised Approach

There has been a lot of controversy over the best type of approach to use in personal selling meetings — *structured*, *personalised* or *balanced*.

In the *structured*, or 'canned' approach, you have total control, since the whole meeting has been worked out ahead of time, right down to the exact wording to use. All possible objections which may be raised are anticipated and responses are prepared. With this approach, you know that all key points will be covered, and nothing will be missed. The advantage of this type of approach is that it can provide the new, inexperienced personal salesperson with confidence. It also simplifies personal selling self-development efforts, since one basic approach is developed, potentially to be used in all meetings.

The obvious disadvantage is that it doesn't allow for the differing needs, interests or behaviour of the other party. Also, it can sound very stilted and unnatural and the other party may resent being treated 'just like the others'. We all like to think we are special, and this goes for prospects, too. The totally structured meeting can also be a problem if the same person is visited several times. On the other hand, the problem with the completely *personalised* approach is that a different one must be prepared for each situation, and this can get pretty unwieldy and time-consuming. It can also be confusing if you handle more than one or two personal sales meetings a day.

It has generally been found that a *balanced* approach is best, where some kind of framework or meeting outline is prepared which ensures that nothing important is overlooked — sample statements and questions can be written down. In this way, you can retain some control over the meeting. However, there is some flexibility, in that decisions on the exact wording to use, information to add, or what to omit, are left to your discretion at the time of the meeting. This leaves room for questions from the other party, as well as interaction in the process — essential ingredients in most successful meetings.

This brings us to an effective way to elicit participation by the other party — the use of visuals.

Use of Visuals in Personal Selling

Visuals can help you develop a better discussion, and are often used by the more experienced personal salesperson. They include brochures, presentation manuals, slides, overheads, videos and testimonials. In using visuals, you can often present more in a crisp and timely fashion (bearing in mind you have only 15-20 minutes to retain the other party's attention and interest).

Visuals can be used in 'structured', 'personalised' or 'balanced' meetings — you can either stick rigidly to them, or orientate the main benefits in the visual to the specific needs of the other person. In using visuals, make sure your prospect or associate is seated in a way that they can see the visuals, and you can see their reactions.

Whether you use presentation manuals, slides or overheads, it is recommended that you have one set relating to each topic you wish to address. Topics they might address can include an introduction to yourself and to your organisation, information relating to what you or the organisation have accomplished or undertaken in the past and which is relevant to the meeting, and information relating to what you or your organisation can do for the other party — all related in the form of benefits.

In using such visuals you need to be fully conversant with their contents. Point with a pen for emphasis, and look at the visuals yourself and then at the other party for reactions — this will keep them looking at your visuals, and then at you, intermittently.

With regards to brochures, underline or circle key points, and leave the material with the other person.

Closing

'Closing' is the ultimate goal of your meeting — it assists your prospect or ally in making the right decision — in other words, to accommodate what you are seeking. If you cannot close, then you cannot accomplish this, no matter how good you are at planning, prospecting, approaching, questioning, and overcoming concerns or objections. A football team might have all the moves, speed and techniques needed to get the ball near the goal, but it won't win if it doesn't score! Over the long term, success in closing determines the extent of your network of allies and influence, the achievement of your goals, and even your level of income.

In spite of the importance of closing, many executives and managers engaged in personal selling fail to learn and practise closing techniques, and thus limit themselves to a network of allies, influence and income level much smaller than they could attain with a little extra knowledge and skill in closing.

There are certain times during the meeting when attempting to close may be appropriate — the trick is to learn how to recognise these opportunities. Closing doesn't have to wait until the end of the meeting; if the other party is ready, it can come very early in the personal selling process — sometimes right after the approach. Take the case of the football team where goals can be scored in the last and *first* few minutes of play.

How do you recognise when the other party is ready to accommodate what you seek? There are certain 'closing signals' which you must watch for. Those who learn to identify these signals will be more successful in closing than those who try to close indiscriminately throughout the personal selling process. Closing signals can be classified as either *verbal* or *physical*. Some examples:

- *Verbal:*
  'Yes, I guess that would solve our problem.'
  'Did you say you would consider providing some ongoing input?'
  'How soon can you get involved?'
  Verbal closing signals are also when the other party asks more questions about the topic being addressed, or when they apparently start to slow down — both may indicate a high level of interest.
- *Physical:*
  The other person nods in agreement. They re-examine the visuals more closely. They check something in the files or on their computer.

Verbal and physical clues are numerous — you can probably come up with many more from your own experience. Practice will improve your ability to recognise these signals of interest and readiness to form an alliance with you or accommodate your other needs.

Closing Techniques

Once you have determined an opportune moment for closing, there are several methods which may be used and they can be built into the following sequence:

- Display a full understanding of the other party's requirements, motives, preferences and any objections (which should have been overcome).
- Portray sincerity, empathy and a confidence that you are able to address their interests or meet their precise needs.
- Recognise closing signals.
- Apply a test close.
- Apply one or more closing techniques.
- Be silent after you have asked the closing question. Don't say another word until the other person has responded.

Two popular closing techniques are *assuming a close* and *direct close*.

Assuming a close

Here you proceed as if the other party is ready to accommodate what you seek, whether or not they have indicated as such. With this type of close, the onus is on the other person to stop you if they aren't ready. The sequence is to pause, smile and ask such questions as:

'Incidentally, which is the best date for our next meeting?'

'Incidentally, which of your colleagues should I meet at our next meeting?'

Direct close

Here, you ask the other person directly — for example, whether they would like to continue to meet. Obviously, the risk is that they will decline, so don't use this method unless they have somehow indicated a definite readiness to accommodate what you seek.

A powerful analogy to this is the fly fisherman. Such people go to great lengths to equip themselves and to venture forth to cast and hopefully make a catch. In the final analysis, however, unless they get within range of the fish, and unless they cast the right type of fly across a patch of water the size of a small table-top, they will fail to attain their objective. Closing is like this. You have to be equipped and prepared. You have to have tracked down leads to find prospects. And you have to find the right moment and place to cast that all-important fly with accuracy — the close — in order to attain your objectives.

How to Develop Successful Speeches and Group Presentations

So far in this chapter we have concentrated on the one-on-one type of meeting. We now need to review group meetings and the development of group presentations.

There are several elements to be reviewed, including *administration*, *objectives*, *fact-finding*, *assembling content*, and *format*.

Administration

Review the following:

- date, time and location of speech
- duration of speech and whether there will be time for audience questions
- room size, shape and layout, and whether it allows the use of visual aids
- availability of visual aid equipment
- speech subject and orientation — you may know the subject, but are you aware of any preferred orientation — for example, theory versus practice or personal experience versus secondhand experience
- the make-up of the audience in terms of age, sex, background, interests and reasons for attending the presentation
- who the other speakers are and why you were chosen.

Objectives

Review the following:

- What information is to be imparted to the audience, and how can it best be imparted? Through a straight lecture? Using a 'Socratic' approach (questioning the audience)? Through stories or anecdotes? Through audience involvement in case study, group discussion, individual exercise or simulation?
- How are you to excite the audience and provoke thought and possibly action? By being enthusiastic yourself? By demonstrating a knowledge of relevant facts and figures? By demonstrating conviction? By being short and to the point? By asking the audience for response or action?
- How are you going to amuse the audience? Through limited use of humour? By keeping the speech short and easy-going? By appealing to their specific interests? By orientating your presentation to the specific event?
- How are you going to be convincing? By being logical? By appealing to their emotions? By quoting facts and figures authoritatively? By being precise? By quoting with accuracy? By articulating audience advantages?

Delivering information, exciting the audience, amusing them and being convincing are all important ingredients for successful speech-making.

Fact-finding

Being asked to speak on a selected subject or subjects requires the acquisition of information or facts. Fact-finding can be conducted in many ways:

- *Through desk research:* use of publications, books, periodicals and files at the office or at home.
- *Through library research:* similarly, at the public library. Main branches can provide information on virtually any topic.
- *Through computer databases:* you can access a wide variety of information on the Internet and other databases. By using key words you can source abstracts and summaries from wide-ranging data sources.

- *By contacting people with the necessary knowledge:* informal or formal interviews, either over the telephone or in person, can provide very useful judgemental information which may be able to amplify some of the bare bones or facts derived from other forms of non-personal research.
- *Through careful analysis of all acquired information:* the 'raw' information derived from all these sources needs to be 'refined' through careful analysis in the context of audience needs and appeal.

Assembling content

Once the fact-finding is refined and oriented towards the audience, the material has to be assembled in an order and format that can be presented. In terms of order, the following is offered as a guide and is somewhat similar to the steps for successful one-on-one meetings:

- How shall I start in a way which grasps audience *attention*?
- How shall I continue in a way which develops their *curiosity*?
- How can I continue in a way which enhances their *trust* of me and my presentation?
- How can I develop the *main thrust* of my speech?
- How can I end with *impact*?

Format

Some of the key points here are:

- The information provided must be to the point and relevant to the audience.
- The speech must progress logically from one part of the speech to the next.
- Time must be allocated suitably to each part of the presentation — for example, 'attention' 10 per cent, 'curiosity' 10 per cent, 'trust' 10 per cent, 'main thrust' 35 per cent and 'ending impact' 10 per cent.

However, in planning your time allocation, remember to allow five minutes for setting up. Also allow for questions, which, depending on the length and style of your presentation, may account for 10 to 20 minutes.

How to Grasp the Audience's Attention

You may have heard the expression: 'You win or lose the sale in the first 30 seconds!' The same can be the case with making a speech or presentation — you can win or lose your audience in the first 30 seconds. In order to improve the chances of successfully winning your audience in the first 30 seconds, you *must*, as stressed earlier, have done your homework and know who comprises your audience and what they are expecting, both as a group and as individuals. Also, in order to attain and retain audience attention, the way in which you 'open' the speech is vital. Some of the do's and don'ts are:

Don't:

- waiver — once you have taken your place at the lectern, taken a few seconds to get yourself organised and to allow the audience to become quiet, move forward boldly to your opening.

❖ start negatively by using such phrases as 'Public speaking is not my forte', 'I have not had time to prepare', 'Please bear with me', 'I am not very knowledgeable about this subject', 'I have been asked to speak against my will' or 'I am afraid you will find this topic unpalatable'.

Do:

❖ breathe deeply before beginning your speech
❖ move your chair away from the table before being introduced
❖ make sure you have approached the lectern or stood up at the table in a positive, business-like fashion (like when meeting an ally!)
❖ organise your notes, visual aids and microphone before you start speaking.

How to Build Curiosity and Trust

Having grasped the audience's attention, the speaker's job is now to develop the audience's curiosity and trust. As noted before:

❖ *'Attention'* will only last so long, and relates to the audience's subconscious question, 'Is this interesting?'
❖ *'Curiosity'* is the next phase in the sequence and relates to the audience's subconscious question, 'Might I learn something here? What has the speaker got up their sleeve?'
❖ *'Trust'* is the next phase in the sequence and is likened to the audience's subconscious question, 'Can I trust what the speaker says? Are they someone of integrity?'

The sequence of the speech can be likened to the ebb and flow of surf on the beach as the tide comes in. That tide has got to work its way up the beach, but in so doing the surf comes and goes, always moving higher up the beach. This is similar to audience interest: as the sequence of the speech unfolds, their interest ebbs and flows, but it must progress not only through the opening, curiosity and trust phases, but also through the key issue and ending phases.

It is your job as speaker to control the audience's interest, just as it is the job of some divine right or power to control the tides of the ocean! You have to get them up the beach. To do this, we will now concentrate on the 'curiosity' phase — the phase immediately following the opening of the speech, when the audience's attention has been grasped by your wonderful approach and opening statement. Here are some techniques:

❖ *Positive reactions*. It is often said that closing the sale is the culmination of a series of 'yes' responses from buyers. Get them and keep them in a positive frame of mind and they will close! This also applies to speakers and audiences, particularly during the early portion of the speech — you simply cannot afford to turn the audience off by provoking negative reactions.
❖ *'Confidential' information*. So-called 'confidential information — don't quote me' has an excellent effect on the audience and arouses considerable curiosity. Watch what information you give the audience, however. They are almost certain to quote you!

- *Visual aids*. We will review these later, but they are useful tools for arousing curiosity and for use later in the speech.
- *Audience interests*. Whenever possible, relate to the personal interests of your audience, be this social, domestic, business or career. Work out in advance how your subject matter can relate to the personal interests of the audience — leaving your own interests until last, if you include them at all. 'You' followed by 'we' appeal is the name of the game.

In order for your audience to develop trust in you as a speaker and in what you are saying, the following aspects need careful consideration:

- You must appear to be sincere and to be telling the truth.
- You must not appear to over-exaggerate; whatever you say must be believable.
- You must appear to show respect for the audience, by being punctual, by dressing suitably for the occasion, and by making an effort in terms of content, delivery and manner.
- Verify your presentation with quantifiable evidence or support, such as statistics and factual accounts, wherever possible.
- Try to demonstrate your own expertise and experience, whether this be qualification, career, research studies, other speaking engagements or practical experience. This is best managed by the person introducing you, detailing your relevant experience in their introduction. You should then enlarge on certain aspects of your background which enhance the credibility of your presentation, as and when applicable. Keep these brief and to the point.
- Talk at the audience's level — never over the top of them, and never down to them.
- Incorporate all the positive elements of voice, word, breath and eye control.

How to Deliver the Main Thrust of Your Speech and Gain Audience Acceptance

Speech-making and presentations are a communication process — presenting effectively very often depends on the communication skills of the presenter, just as it is the case with professional and personal selling. These skills can be learned and improved upon, so as to upgrade the quality of personal presentations and communicating with groups.

Effective presenters know that they must vary their approach and operating style, depending on their audience. This is quite natural. We don't act the same way with different kinds of people we meet or different family members; we are constantly adjusting our style, depending on the response we get. By understanding different operating styles, professional presenters adjust their presentations and overall style to elicit the most positive response. Audiences tend to prefer professional presenters whom they perceive to be most like themselves.

We all have enough facets to our personalities to downplay some traits and emphasise others in a particular situation, without appearing phoney. By identifying the operating styles of the majority or main members of the audience, you can adapt your own style in order to gain the most favourable reaction and response. The research for this is best undertaken in advance.

As a group, there can and will be differences — for example, a group of business directors will be a very different audience to a group of supervisors or shop floor workers. As individuals, you need to assess who the key people are in the audience and their individual operating styles.

- *The Responder/Initiator*. These people are assertive, responsive, enthusiastic, expressive and make quick decisions. They listen to you, but also tend to want to have their say. You need to 'engage' in communication with these individuals to be most effective.
- *The Commander/Doer*. These people are assertive, goal-oriented, impatient for results, and decisive. They dislike inaction or beating about the bush and prefer it if you stick to business, talk facts and come to the point quickly.
- *The Humanist/Empathiser*. This type is warm and friendly, but a little hesitant to take risks and makes decisions very carefully. Here you will be more successful if you show interest and support, and provide reassurance rather than pressure in your presentation.
- *The Evaluator/Detailer*. This person is very organised, precise, analytical and cautious. There is a dislike of sloppiness, a failure to provide concrete facts and evidence, or a disregard for rules and regulations. You will increase your chances of success with this person if you are on time, provide guarantees and full details, and allow sufficient time to verify facts and make careful decisions.
- *The All-rounder*. This person has a flexible style and can get on with anyone providing they don't show extremes in behaviour. Showing versatility in your own style, but using moderation throughout your presentation, will have the best impact on the All-rounder.
- *The Idea generator*. This person also has a flexible style but shows extremes and sometimes even inconsistencies in behaviour. Idea generators need to be enthused and excited by both the content and delivery of your presentation to have the greatest effect on how they perceive you as a presenter. They tend to fly off in several directions at once, so need to be kept on track. Summarising your key points at the end of your presentation will be effective with these individuals.

Clearly, a natural question is how to cope with different operating styles in the audience, as some of these styles seem to conflict. First, you need to identify who the key members of the audience are in terms of decision-making, politics, power and influence, and secondly, when developing eye contact with them, engage in an appropriate style of delivery which coincides with their own operating style. If you haven't been able to identify who the key members of the audience are, or their operating styles, then the main thrust of your speech can be enhanced by ensuring, just like the salesperson, that you concentrate on presenting benefits (rather than features) along with verification.

Features are things that are important to you, the presenter. Benefits are things that are important to the audience. For example, in making a case about why the audience — a group of prospective customers — should do business with your firm, features you may consider using may include: oldest firm in the business sector, most experienced staff, or most technologically advanced products and services.

Converting these to benefits, they become: 'We represent your "least risk" purchase decision, as we have been in business for 15 years.' 'Our highly experienced staff have the greatest capacity to understand and meet your precise needs.' 'Our products and services are designed to be cost-effective and quality assured as a result of our state-of-the-art technology in production.'

Verification in the case of your group presentations relates to providing validation, evidence or proof in the form of independent reports, testimonials, competitor comparisons, facts, statistics, case studies, demonstrations, anecdotes and examples. By building in such verifiers during the main thrust of your speech, you will become much more believable in the eyes of your audience.

Ending with Impact

The football team starts the game with style. Their footwork, passing and team coordination is inspirational. They fail to score, however! This is the analogy of ending your speech or presentation with no impact. No matter how good the speech has been up to the end, if you don't end with impact, you won't have won over your audience. The ending needs to leave the audience inspired, motivated and, above all, in full accordance with what you have been saying. Ending with impact can be accomplished with the following techniques:

- *'Act now'*. This technique asks the audience to do something right way, to act. In fact, the audience is likely to act sooner rather than later after your speech if you ask them to do so. If you ask them to do something the following week, they will more than likely forget or procrastinate. 'Act now' creates an excellent climax. Example: ' Register today and be assured of a place on the program!'
- *'Questioning'*. Ending by asking the audience a question can also have excellent impact. The question best relates to the main thrust of your speech, or to your opening statements. The question should be phrased so that the audience focuses on the main issues you have raised. Example: 'What will *you* do about drinking and driving now?'
- *'Saying'*. By quoting a better-known saying as an ending statement, one which directly relates to the main thrust of your speech or important elements of it, some speakers can have good ending impact. Be careful not to use a saying which is neither less than totally relevant to your speech nor which goes over the head of the audience. A better-known saying from an authoritative and well-known source is by far the best. Example: 'All work and no play makes Jack a dull boy.'
- *'Based on my experience'*. This technique summarises a third-party factual experience that directly relates to the main thrust of your speech. Example: 'In England as far back as in the 1930s with their Special Areas Act they attempted to diversify industry away from the major cities. They failed and in the main have continued to do so. It simply does not work.'

   With a factual example, the credibility of your speech and impact at the end are enhanced.
- *The 'accountant's' ending*. You literally develop a balance sheet by summarising the pluses and minuses of your argument — the pluses far exceeding the minuses.

Example: 'On the plus side, you have better prices, greater choice, better parking and higher levels of service. On the minus side, it will take you a few more minutes to get there. Isn't the choice obvious?'

In summary, ending with impact is important if you are to leave the audience in a favourable frame of mind or motivated to follow your advice. The ending must leave them 'on a high'.

SUMMARY

Chapter 15 raises the following key issues:

- Preparation for meetings, or 'approach planning', enhances the chances of successful outcomes and should address: content, focus on the other party, discussion technique and obtaining the meeting.
- For the meeting to be successful, there are six important steps: gaining attention, arousing interest, building desire, winning conviction, getting action and writing notes of appreciation.
- The development of group presentations requires attention to administration, objectives, fact-finding, assembling content and format.
- In delivering group presentations, the ideal sequence grasps the audience's attention, develops their curiosity, enhances their trust, develops the main thrust of the speech and ends with impact.
- Both in personal selling and group presentations you need to 'close' — to get what you seek out of individuals and audiences — or else all the preparation, discussion and delivery are worthless.

Further Resources

In Section 16 of your *Executive Armoury* you will find the Convincing Communications Clinic — 39 steps (self-examination questions) that will help you to diagnose problems and opportunities, along with prescriptions for success! In Section 17 you will find an 11-point plan for preparing group presentations, plus a worksheet.

16

Beating Your Competition With Powerful Self-promotion And Group Presentation Techniques

'Susan Jamieson has been head of public relations for three years and I must say she is an endless source of great ideas, both for use in personal selling and for group presentations. She keeps telling us that with so much competition in the market place, we must deliver maestro performances — and with her coaching and encouragement she makes sure we do! Without her tools and techniques we wouldn't excel in our business development endeavours.'

The list of tools and techniques executives and managers can use for purposes of personal selling and group presentations is virtually endless. This chapter includes those which I have found to have the greatest beneficial effect for both personal and corporate promotion.

Meeting the Needs of Your Allies

Many people consider 'closing' to be the final step in the personal selling sequence. However, personal selling doesn't really have a final step. For the executive or manager who wants to build a solid base of satisfied allies, and wants to constantly expand on that base, personal selling should be viewed as a cycle, without a definite beginning or end.

Closing with a prospect is merely the beginning of an ongoing relationship, which must be maintained with effective follow-up and service where necessary. There are several ways in which new allies can become established ones, and established allies maintained and developed effectively.

Building loyalty

This requires taking care of the interests of your allies. Stay in touch with them by planning and scheduling your calls and visits.

Some executives and managers keep a daily 'reminder' file, so that they call their allies or visit them at predetermined times. There is no 'right' number of times to keep in touch, or 'right' amount of time to wait between making contact again. This will depend on each ally, the types of topics addressed with them, and their importance to you as individuals. The main point to remember is to schedule call-backs and visits into your planning — this will ensure that each ally receives adequate attention.

Meeting the needs of your allies is not just a cliché or an attitude — for the professional executive or manager, it is a blueprint for action. It should be more than winning one-off meetings and ensuring the meeting is successfully concluded. Effective 'servicing' of your allies encompasses every contact point with not only yourself, but with your company or organisation also.

Corporate notifications, mail-outs or invitations, although not necessarily your direct responsibility, should be of concern, in order to ensure that each of your allies is properly serviced. Good service can help to maintain your existing base of allies — your network of supporters.

Handling difficulties

This is one of the most challenging aspects of ensuring ongoing liaison with existing allies. If an ally has a concern about you or your organisation and the concern is serious, it will probably affect your ally's preparedness to continue to liaise with you or to accommodate what you seek in future. Therefore, to build long-term relationships means that any difficulties need to be handled properly.

The best way to do this is obviously to try and reduce the possibility of their occurrence as much as possible. A difficulty represents a failure of some kind — whether in you or your organisation — in meeting your ally's expectations. Your performance, or that of your organisation, may be below par, or their expectations may be too high. In either case, you may not have fulfilled the responsibility of ensuring that your ally understands just how well you or your organisation can match up to their genuine interests, needs and expectations, and where there may be limitations. This illustrates, once again, the importance of acquiring thorough knowledge relating to the reason for your alliance and the topics you wish to address.

If you have done everything possible to avoid difficulties and they still occur, the first thing to find out is whether or not the concern is valid. One way or another, amends must be made. The extra time and effort involved in ensuring that this situation doesn't arise in the first place will be well worth it.

Special requests

Allies sometimes make special requests, over and above the normal networking give-and-take. If a special request is made, this may command extra time or resources — be aware of your organisation's policy here. If your ally expects the organisation to deliver, you have to make a decision — should this be accepted and the costs absorbed, or should you decline the request, and risk losing an ongoing association?

Be very careful to treat all special requests consistently if you want to avoid problems of comparison cropping up later — allies do tend to talk to each other!

Expanding Your Influence

Simply maintaining your current network of allies is not enough if you want to be really successful. It is the consistent growth in the size of your network of support which distinguishes the mediocre executive or manager from the outstanding one. There are basically three ways to increase the potency of your network: *increase dealings with current allies, develop new allies* and *win back lost allies.*

Increase dealings with current allies

Your best chance to develop your influence is to deal more with your existing allies, as they have already been won over to you. How much easier it is to build on this existing goodwill than to search out and win over new ones.

Dealing more with existing allies can mean either developing your relationship more on the current lines, or meeting more of your ally's needs by addressing a wider range of topics. Also, as your know-how is being upgraded and improved constantly, there is a great opportunity to make your allies aware of this increased knowledge and how this can apply to their interests and needs.

Let us take a professional selling example of increasing sales to existing customers. The prospect has been closed on a car insurance quote. The astute insurance agent then asks a raft of questions that supposedly relate to information needed to complete the application process, so that the car insurance policy can be issued. In fact, the insurance agent is certainly doing that, but more besides. They are finding out about potential additional insurance needs. When their new client drops by to collect the policy, the agent will be ready with alternatives for her for home insurance and other forms of cover.

This example, while not conventional personal selling, illustrates clearly a technique for developing your existing allies. Apply it to your own personal selling environment. Adapt it and, in the process, 'buy ownership' of your own adaptation!

Develop new allies

Existing, satisfied allies are an excellent source of leads for new allies. They can usually provide you with several names of good prospects, as well as offer suggestions as to how to meet the prospect's interests or needs. Clues picked up in this way are one of your best methods of developing new allies. Remember, elitist executive and managerial networkers acquire up to half a dozen referrals for every alliance developed. Elitist networkers also dedicate more than 90 per cent of their networking time to referrals.

Win back lost allies

Because personal selling to establish allies forms the basis of successful networking, losing allies can greatly erode your current and future networking scope and potential influence. If you lose an ally other than through them moving away or going out of business, then something has happened to upset the status quo. If you value the ally, it is important to find out what happened. Either their views about you have deteriorated, their interests and needs have changed, the effort entailed in your alliance has become too great, or others have done a better personal selling job. For whatever reason, if the loss of your ally comes as a complete surprise, you haven't been doing your job in staying in touch with your ally, or keeping up to date with developments in this field.

Once allies are lost, you may be able to win them back if you find out the real reasons, and do your best to rectify the situation. Spend as much time and effort on trying to win back the ally as you feel is justified, considering the value of your alliance, and your chances of being successful. Otherwise, you'll have to let the ally go — but learn from the experience, in order to prevent such a loss happening again.

Major Ally Management

Major allies are those, perhaps no more than 20 per cent of your total allies, who represent, or have the propensity to represent, 80 per cent of your potential for developing your influence. This 80/20 rule (Pareto's principle) is found to apply time and time again. But in order to generate that 80 per cent, these major allies have to be 'managed': management often being defined as getting superior results through and from people.

Here is a real life example of major ally management in the professional selling environment, where such allies are known as 'key accounts'. The example relates to a major commercial bank where I undertook some preliminary research and analysis of their key account management capabilities in business banking. I found that their major business customers ('accounts') had fairly wide-ranging needs in terms of bank services, and of their expectations of bank officers, as summarised below from my study:

'I want to deal directly with someone who:
. . . knows what they are talking about in terms of:
— finance and lending
— business management
— the economy
— bank products and services
. . . can make decisions, who can respond rapidly, who can respond positively, and who will make suggestions for alternatives rather than simply turn me down
. . . is on my side, who can recognise and understand my needs, and who can offer a range of financial solutions
. . . has demonstrable expertise in main-line business lending, and who can source and introduce me to the specialists for specialist banking areas
. . . is a peer — a business manager. Not a salesman. Not a bureaucrat
. . . is approachable, professional and trustworthy.'

Based on my initial findings, I felt that at that time there was an excellent opportunity for a business banking operation to differentiate itself against its competition, and at the same time generate superior results, by adopting a 'key account management' orientation with its major business accounts. In fact, this was the orientation these accounts were seeking, and this orientation needed to embrace:

- exceptional customer service
- a consultative approach rather than an obvious 'selling' approach
- less selling of bank products and services and more selling of the impact that the bank and its offerings might have on the key account's business operations and performance
- concern for the profitable growth of the account, generating enhanced bank earnings as a result
- the seeking out of profit-making/cost-reducing opportunities for key accounts
- the development of a 'win–win' and 'partners in profit' relationship
- genuine interest and, as far as possible, immersion in the business interests and affairs of key accounts

- development of account relations and loyalty which make them hard to break by competing banks
- development of service excellence, where cost becomes secondary to service
- effective management of bank expertise and resources on behalf of the key account.

Key account management also requires the development of superior management skills — in other words, getting desired and superior results through people. Such people include the key accounts themselves, and on behalf of such accounts, other bank personnel. Managing people 'in' your own organisation, as well as outside — that is, the key account, or in the personal selling idiom, your major ally — is the cornerstone of any key account management philosophy.

Promotional Techniques for Executives and Managers

There is a wide range of promotional techniques executives and managers can use, some of which relate to personal selling, and others more to the corporate setting.

Publications

Over the years I have developed a wide variety of papers and other forms of publications, and have found that the following considerations are important, in the context of promotional impact:

- Publishing material that is targeted to specific business sectors, rather than general business audiences.
- Taking into consideration the direct mail 'time-bomb' when designing a publication or mail-out. A typical response by the receiver of a mail-out:
  - First few seconds: 'Shall I throw it out or retain it?'
  - Next few seconds: 'Shall I examine it now or later?'
  - Next few seconds: 'Is it pertinent or interesting?'
  - Next few seconds: 'Is there a specific benefit in it for me?'
  - Next few seconds: 'Where shall I start reading?'
  - Next few seconds: 'Shall I continue reading?'
  - Next few seconds: 'Bang! This is interesting' — you have had the desired effect!
- Taking a reader orientation rather than a sender orientation, in both language and content.
- Minimising text and maximising graphics: the busy executive needs all the help available in time management!
- Using quality paper stock and covers.
- Using colour in print and text.
- Publishing quarterly newsletters (one of the fastest growing sectors of periodicals), again on a business sector basis, but calling them something other than a newsletter.
- On a targeted basis, circulating transcripts of professional speaking engagements — try cassette tapes rather than transcripts.

- Developing comprehensive handouts to go with seminar presentations, briefings and conferences in which the executive or manager presents or participates.
- Attaching a compliments slip (bearing an executive's name that is known to the recipient) to all publications that are sent out.

Corporate brochures

Research, as well as trial and error, have shown that the following elements are important, in developing corporate brochures:

- One brochure theme and heading has more impact than a multiple theme/heading: this requires a series of targeted brochures, rather than one general brochure.
- The orientation of the brochure must be the reader's needs, objectives and benefits first, and the sender's capabilities second.
- Use of sub-headings and minimisation of text enhances reading conduciveness.
- Soft 'pledges' from the organisation have impact: 'We will undertake whatever is necessary in an attempt to ensure your complete satisfaction.'
- Starring (*) some of the benefits, and adding this copy line can be very effective: 'Starred services include tested, innovative approaches unavailable from others in our industry.'
- Include a section in which one attempts to quantify the benefits of dealing with the organisation or the costs of not dealing with the organisation.
- In such quantification, use charts and graphics for credibility and substance.
- Encourage feedback from allies and prospects about their reaction to corporate brochures.
- In preparing brochure copy, the following criteria are important:
  — Who is the target audience and why should they listen to us?
  — How will they benefit?
  — Be specific — for example, describe a technique that was developed in August 1996 (rather than 'recently'), which improves productivity by as much as 38 per cent (rather than 'greatly'). Every vague phrase risks losing credibility and readership. Enumerate whenever it makes sense ('The five steps are: 1....., 2....., 3....., etc') as this makes for more logical, easier reading.
  — Use words and phrases rather than lengthy sentences in order to get more descriptive copy in less space, which generates livelier, more compact, faster-to-read material.
  — Stress uniqueness: the different, the startling, the unknown, the new. Avoid the old hat, the stereotype, the obvious.
  — Write in a lively, powerful, exciting style — start by taping an oral presentation of the subject and then typing a transcript (spoken words are often more exciting than written ones).
  — After the first written draft (based on the transcript), edit, rewrite and polish. Test it on colleagues. Read every word, asking: 'Will the average prospect be interested in this?'

— Eliminate 99 per cent of the 'soft' copy: history, introduction, background and so forth. Contacts seek up-to-date, hard-hitting, practical information and solutions to their problems.

Other promotional materials

Other promotional materials which I have found to be successful include:

- using 'tickler' advertisements and mail-outs, which tease and engender curiosity on the part of the reader and are geared to developing responses and leads
- sending out *regular* media releases with industry information and comment on topics of current interest (but these releases have to be newsworthy), in so doing, becoming acknowledged by the media as a source of expertise and knowledge
- developing information packages for media representatives attending seminars and conferences
- writing articles for publication in newspapers and periodicals, always enclosing a photograph of the writer and brief information on the organisation
- becoming known as an authority on a certain subject, with resultant periodic radio and TV interviews, at which brief written information about the organisation is always provided for accurate newscast introduction purposes
- developing low-budget videos, demonstrating capabilities, for use at open houses in the organisation's offices and at other events. Make sure you are in them!
- circulating information packages on the organisation and yourself to prospective allies attending seminars and conferences
- using invitation cards, rather than conventional letters or mail-outs, for invitations to special events sponsored by the organisation, and hosting 'free lunches' or breakfasts at such gatherings (usually generating greater response)
- using telemarketing for a variety of market research and direct mail follow-up purposes
- envelope 'stuffing' — taking the opportunity of introducing or reinforcing specific topics, by appending special write-ups, to normal everyday correspondence.

Developing Writing Effectiveness

Writing has no other goal than to help readers understand and comply with your propositions, requests and ideas. The reader should never experience problems working out what you are trying to say. The first rule of any written information is to assist the reader to follow and understand what you are trying to communicate, and the guidelines below will help you attain this.

Giving your document 'person-appeal'

Check out these two statements:
  'The package will be shipped express courier on Tuesday.'
  'I will send you the package via express courier on Tuesday.'
  The first sentence suggests a production line. The second expresses more person-appeal, as it tells you who will be involved. Include person-appeal wherever you can

in your writing. Compare the following statements to see the effect of the person-appeal approach:

'An error was found when your invoice was compiled.'

'I found an error when I was compiling your invoice.'

Emphasise reader first, sender second

When you write, place yourself in the shoes of your audience. What might their first question be? How might the reader react to the write-up? What extra information might the reader seek? What information might raise doubts in the reader's mind? For example, a marketing manager reviewing a brief for the latest promotional campaign may be less concerned with costs and other financial matters if the writer emphasises the creativity of the promotions.

Be factual

Minimise unnecessary vagaries in your text. Listen to these two statements and assess which might be more effective in persuading you to accept the new approach.

'This latest approach can increase production and enhance your bottom line.'

'This latest approach can increase output by 15 per cent without any extra staff expense, adding $90 000 to your margin in six months, according to our preliminary assessment.'

Write like a 'video camera'

Try to visualise your subject while you write, just as though you were looking through the viewfinder of a video camera. Also help your reader to *see* your ideas, not just read your words. For example, 'Your restaurants are seas of happy faces' creates a graphic and realistic impression. 'You have a lot of customers in your restaurants' is an oblique and easily forgotten statement.

Simplify the reading

'Signpost' statements act as guidelines for your readers. They guide them to where your text is going. These statements are known as signposts because they reveal what is about to follow. They simplify reading, so your readers do not have to work out what you are trying to say. For example, 'Next I will summarise some possible disadvantages to our program and then why I believe you should accept it.'

Effective writing techniques

Some key techniques for communicating written messages effectively are:

- *Anecdotes:* 'Across the board we experienced great savings. For example, the technical division saved 15 per cent against forecast by improved filing systems; dispatch saved 10 per cent by recycling.'
- *Benchmarking:* 'Although personnel expenses increased 8 per cent last year, in our business sector a 12 per cent rise was more often reported.'
- *Metaphysics:* 'Our approach to monitoring operations follows the principle of the temperature gauge. It alerts the need for action if labour costs exceed expectations.'

Structure

Formal correspondence should never deviate from the theme that is being addressed at any one place in the text. For example, in a proposal for public relations, costs relating to investor relations might be addressed. In that same section, don't deviate by introducing an idea for better newsletters, unless this directly relates to the subject of those costs.

Structure relates to the sections of your reports and needs proposals, paragraphs and sentences. All the paragraphs in one particular section should relate directly to the same subject. A paragraph needs to address just one topic. A sentence needs to include one single notion, not a range of concepts.

Establishing certainty

Writers strengthen their cases by establishing certainty in their texts. The best text is assertive and sounds credible. It makes direct assumptions rather than clouds the reader with uncertainties or ambiguities. Compare the following ambiguous statements with the more credible statements:

'Our process may perhaps cause minor irritation.'

'Our process will cause some minor yet tolerable irritation, bearing in mind the benefits.'

Clarification

Probably the most annoying question for the reader to have to ask is: 'What are you referring to?' Here is an anecdote demonstrating this: 'Our parts were sent in different packages without approved labelling and delivered by truck. We did not expect this.' What does 'this' refer to? Was the person writing the report concerned about the packaging, the labelling, the mode of delivery, or all three?

Statements which are unclear give the impression of muddled thinking. Whereas some mistakes are mere hindrances to easily digested communication, failure to be accurate about what you are referring to can cause confusion.

Speech Aids

There are several different kinds of speech aids which can be used in group presentations according to specific requirements. The main ones are *fully-typed scripts* and *prompter cards*.

Fully-typed script

This is best used for formal occasions, or for when you are 'going on record'. It can also be used when you have very tight time constraints — a typed script will allow for an average of double the content, compared to speaking from prompter cards.

When preparing a script, simply follow the sequence suggested earlier: develop the speech, the start of the speech, curiosity and trust, the main thrust and end with impact.

Double-spaced typing and plenty of paragraphs are suggested, along with wide margins for making necessary notes regarding first impressions, speaking style, and voice, eye and word control.

The most important delivery criterion is to regularly eyeball the audience. This will require a slower delivery than if you were simply reading a book out loud. Not only must you regularly eyeball the audience, but you must also animate — use hands, facial expressions and supporting language. The reason for this is that the audience may switch off if they simply see a statue read a text they could have read themselves at home in half the time.

What in fact you are doing, is acting out the text for them. Be animated. Also, don't *turn* pages — *slide* them across from one side of the lectern to the other when you have finished reading them, or slide them under your pad of pages if you are not using a lectern.

The advantages of the fully-typed script relate to confidence that you are not going to forget your lines and that the intended content will be delivered accurately. The disadvantages relate to audience acceptance. You can appear to be too formal, too stilted or too boring, and the audience can react negatively: 'I could have read that — I didn't need him to read it to me.'

Prompter cards

Prompter cards can be used for any speech or presentation, providing you have the necessary notice to be able to develop them. The best prompter cards are of a size that fit comfortably in your hand — approximately 14 cm by 9 cm. They should be postcard weight for durability and ease of handling. Write on only one side of the card, and each card should contain enough information to relate to one important element of your speech. The first step will therefore be to break down your speech into separate elements — each element addressing one idea or topic in full.

At the top of the card, write down the main lead-in sentence that addresses the element. Bold letters are needed to enhance legibility. Lower case often works best, but you can use upper case if you feel this is easier to read. Below this lead-in, note the various sub-elements that support or expand on the lead-in sentence. Again, in bold writing — felt-tip pens are ideal. Each sub-element should be in point or bullet form, to make it stand out from the rest.

On the left-hand margin of the card you can note when you need to show a visual aid, with a letter A, B, C, etc, which is cross-indexed to the visual aids. Also, number the cards in sequence in the top right-hand corner in case you drop them. Use colour for highlighting key points.

For delivery purposes, just glance at your cards from time to time — don't read them. They are prompters only, not full scripts. They can be used at a lectern, or at a table when standing or seated. Either lay them in front of you and slide them across as each one is finished with, or do the same in the palm of your hand, tucking each one behind the last one, when it is finished with.

There is no need to hide the prompter cards — indeed, it would be wrong to do so — but don't rely on them to the extent that you are reading from them. Generally prompter cards are designed to be a brief synopsis of your speech, and are a marvellous prompting device to remind you what to say at any given time. Their advantages are far-reaching:

- They give you confidence that you will not forget your lines and that you will deliver all your intended content.
- They enhance your eye contact with the audience, allowing you to speak to them rather than just read a text.
- They allow you freedom to talk animatedly rather than having to hold a typewritten speech, or to walk about and 'mix it' with the audience.
- They can be carried in a pocket or purse, and handled unobtrusively in the palm of the hand.
- They may be reused often, as they are durable.
- They can be used in front of both large and small audiences.

The disadvantage of prompter cards is that they do take time to prepare and are more effective if you also take time to practise with them.

Use of Visuals in Group Presentations

Visual aids can help you make a better speech or presentation. The most popular alternatives include overhead transparencies and computer graphics, flipcharts and whiteboards. Use of visuals is recommended whenever practicable because they increase audience retention rates — in other words, the amount they remember of your presentation — from 20 per cent to 30 per cent with just words to 40-50 per cent with words and visuals. These retention rates are increased to 60-70 per cent if you use words, visuals and also get the audience involved through discussions, questions, case studies and simulations. Naturally, visuals are not always appropriate — for example, with an after dinner speech.

Visuals provide for greater impact, emphasis, clarity, understanding and interest. They assist the audience to grasp more complex issues, concepts and relationships more readily. They help you, the speaker, stay organised, be more confident and ensure that you don't leave out important items.

Overhead transparencies and computer graphics

There are many commercial firms that produce overhead transparencies — in colour, too, although these can be quite expensive. The alternative is to produce them yourself using a personal computer, graphics software and a colour printer. Transparent overlays can also be used to build up more complex charts and diagrams. For example, you could start with a map of China, then overlay it with the provincial borders, then overlay that with the provincial capitals and so on.

To point with transparencies, use a piece of paper to gradually uncover your transparency revealing an unfolding story, diagram or series of bullet points. Also you can use a pen or pencil to point to particular items on your transparency or you can purchase special arrows for this. *Never* face the screen and talk at the same time, as this detracts from eyeball rapport with the audience.

In developing content for an overhead, make sure the text is bold and large. A standard font is usually too small, as it has to be visible at the back of the room. Keep the overhead simple and precise — don't write too much on each one. Handwritten overheads have to be legible and have a balanced format — using graph paper behind them when you write them up ensures vertical and horizontal consistency. Number the overheads, as this helps to keep them in order and you can reference the number in your speech notes. Turn off the overhead projector when you aren't using it to cut out the glare from the blank screen which can be distracting.

Increasingly, presenters are replacing overhead transparencies with computer graphics which through an adapter, can be projected on to a screen. This makes for a highly professional presentation with great impact, but the impact can be created by the technology rather than by the presenter, which can be the major strength or weakness of computer graphics — you be the judge!

Flip charts and whiteboards

Flip charts are usually large pads of paper on an easel or stand at the speaker's side. They offer a marvellous way to record key points or features of your presentation, or audience comments, questions or replies. They can be written during your speech or presentation, or prepared beforehand.

One useful way to write them during the speech and to remember what to include, is to pencil in the content in the top corner of the flip chart which is closest to you and to copy it when and as appropriate in full size on the flip chart. With complex diagrams you can pre-prepare them in pencil (which will not be visible to the audience), then use a felt-tip pen to trace over the pencil guide — very impressive!

The same rules for content apply here as for overhead transparencies and computer graphics: boldness, clarity, simplicity and not too much verbiage. Use consistent letter styles and sizes, and vary the colour occasionally for effect or emphasis. Felt-tip pens stand out most effectively. When writing on flip charts during your speech or presentation, avoid turning your back to the audience — and don't talk to the chart as you write!

If you decide to prepare your charts before the speech, use a blank sheet to cover the first chart, or intersperse blanks whenever you aren't referring to the flip chart. The height of the letters should be approximately 4 centimetres for every 12 metres of maximum distance from the audience. If it is necessary to refer to more than one flip chart page at a time, you can tear them off the pad and attach them to the walls of the room using masking tape or 'blue-tack'.

An alternative to the flip chart is the wipeable whiteboard with special erasable markers which again provides impact, professionalism and ease of operation. Electronic whiteboards are particularly effective if you need a copy of what you have written.

SUMMARY

Chapter 16 raises the following key issues:

- Meeting the needs of your allies and ensuring their interests continue to be met helps to build and maintain a solid and loyal network of supporters.
- Expanding your influence needs continuous attention also, whether by increasing your dealings with your current allies, developing new allies, or winning back those you have lost.
- The overriding emphasis has to be on maintaining and developing your major allies and for this, major ally management techniques (based on business key account management principles) can be applied successfully.
- There is a vast range of promotional techniques, suitable for use by executives and managers, including publications and corporate brochures.
- Developing writing effectiveness also offers opportunities, and for many, a challenge.
- In the group presentation setting, speech aids enhance the effect and reduce the risks associated with presenting. These include fully-typed scripts, prompter cards and visuals.

Further Resources

In Section 16 of your *Executive Armoury* you will find the Convincing Communications Clinic — 39 steps (self-examination questions) to help you diagnose problems and opportunities, along with prescriptions for success! In Section 18 you will also find guidelines on meeting room layouts. Finally, in Section 19 you will find a process for further developing your group presentation techniques by auditing the speeches of other people.

PART SIX

Your Executive Armoury

A veritable arsenal of tools, techniques and associated weaponry, which when applied consistently, virtually guarantees career success for the Bulletproof Executive and Manager.

17

Focusing These Strategies Into A Winning And Enduring Bulletproof Theme

> 'Our two souls therefore, which are one
>
> Though I must go, endure not yet
>
> A breach, but an expansion,
>
> Like gold to aery thinness beat.'
>
> — John Donne

In the 16th and 17th centuries, John Donne, an English clergyman, was considered one of the greatest writers of love poetry and in my mind, the greatest metaphysical poet. Metaphysics is the practice of using complex metaphors, which compare apparently unrelated ideas or objects.

In 'A Valediction: Forbidding Mourning' of which the first stanza is quoted above, his grief at the parting with his lover is overcome by a metaphysical 'conceit' which assures the lovers of their continuing spiritual union. Indeed, he describes their love as being 'like gold to aery (airy) thinness beat', gold leaf being used in innovative technology at that time, the aneroid barometer. The gold leaf was used to make a small diaphragm — the membrane on a small metal drum partially evacuated of air — which would expand or contract, according to the atmospheric pressure. This would activate a pointer, through a series of levers and springs, for the purpose of predicting weather changes.

It is this delicate, valuable and durable piece of gold leaf which enables the whole power, complexity and unpredictability of the universe to be harnessed, understood and made enduringly predictable — the gold leaf diaphragm, and indeed aneroid barometers seem to endure forever.

John Donne saw his love in similar dimensions — delicate, valuable, powerful, complex, unpredictable and above all enduring — and likened it to the piece of gold leaf.

Executive and managerial life is like this. Executives and managers are operating in their own unpredictable universes, and career success and failure depend on so many interlinked factors, that individuals really do need some form of ongoing barometer to help them understand what to concentrate on at any one time in order to ensure their future career success and longevity with the employer organisation.

In thinking this metaphor through, what I felt was needed was some form of prioritised ranking of all the career success and failure factors addressed in this book. Besides, I needed to verify my findings from my experiences with over 300 executives and managers. I decided I would do this through an Executive Panel of experts — senior line managers and human resources practitioners currently operating, surviving and succeeding in corporate life.

Accordingly, intending to develop an Executive Panel of some 20-30 senior people, I selected and surveyed approximately 200 executives whom I knew or had previously met, assuming that an interest and response rate of about 10-15 per cent would yield my panel of 20-30 experts. More than 85 executives responded — a response rate of some four times my projection, which in itself shows the immense interest in this subject area. Much of this chapter, therefore, is dedicated to the responses and contributions from this Executive Panel.

Ranking of Career Success and Failure Factors

Based on my original assessment and findings, I produced a list of 11 apparent main factors for executive and managerial career success (and failure) for the Executive Panel survey. These can be summarised as follows and are cross-indexed to their respective chapters in this book:

- *Staff management practices:* effective application of staff management practices — for example, planning, organising, monitoring, decision-making, motivating and delegating (particularly the last two practices) (Chapter 3).
- *Primary business drivers:* understanding and prioritising one's primary business objective, and the major drivers of performance towards the accomplishment of this objective, rather than spending a disproportionate amount of time, effort and resources on less essential matters (Chapter 3).
- *External futures:* dedicating adequate time and attention to the assessment of the fast-developing external environment — economy, market place and industry — within which the company/organisation operates (Chapter 3).
- *Nurturing talent:* attracting, retaining and developing staff of the highest calibre available, and helping them to align their own goals with the goals of the organisation, rather than 'hire and fire' (Chapters 9 and 10).
- *Job fit:* ensuring job fit — where one's interests, capabilities and values are accommodated well in the job and work environment, maximising self-motivation (Chapter 4).
- *Organisational fit:* ensuring organisational fit — where one's motivational needs in terms of remuneration and other material benefits, organisation structure and culture, management style, interpersonal relationships and opportunity for personal achievement are all accommodated well within the organisation, maximising self-motivation (Chapter 7).
- *Career destiny and ownership:* developing a sense of control over and personal ownership of one's career destiny, through personal career planning and necessary self-development (Chapters 11, 12 and 13).
- *Leadership of change:* the development and application of leadership of change competencies — for example, managing restructures, adaptability, innovation and

experimentation, risk management, resilience and open, two-way communication (Chapter 8).
- *Other desirable leadership traits:* the demonstration of 'modern' leadership traits — for example, a visionary approach, open-mindedness, a customer service orientation and an emphasis on developing people (Chapter 5).
- *Teamwork:* contributing to one's team, either as member or leader, by ensuring balanced team composition, adding value through one's own operating style, and engaging in mutually supportive teamwork, all generating a powerful synergistic effect (Chapter 6).
- *Politics, power and influence:* survival skills in the area of politics, power and influence which include: selling yourself, networking, developing allies, negotiating, and group presentation capabilities — both within and outside the organisation (Chapters 14, 15 and 16).

Survey Results

In the survey, I asked the Executive Panel to verify and rank these factors. There was virtually unanimous acclaim that these factors were indeed perceived as important for executive and managerial career success. The overall ranking of importance of the individual factors by the panel is as follows:

Table 17.1 — Survey Results

Career Success/Failure Factors	Average Ranked Position (Mean)	Most Often Ranked Position (Median)	Ranking Range	
			Highest-ranked Position	Lowest-ranked Position
Primary business drivers	3	1	1	9
Nurturing talent	5	5	1	11
Leadership of change	5	3	1	11
Teamwork	6	4	1	11
Organisational fit	6	7	1	11
Staff management practices	6	7	1	11
Politics, power and influence	6	11	1	11
External futures	7	6	2	11
Other desirable leadership traits	7	11	1	11
Job fit	7	8	1	11
Career destiny	8	10	1	11

In examining these survey results, a number of important considerations need to be addressed. Although the perceived highest-ranked factor is primary business drivers, based on my *own* assessment this factor, together with staff management practices and external futures, represent less than 20 per cent of the reasons for executive and managerial dismissals (excluding genuine job redundancies), more than 80 per cent being caused by the other factors. This then suggests that for career *success*, primary business drivers is perceived as a top priority, but actually appears to be a lesser priority in the context of the downside risks of *failure*. People tend to fail for reasons other than just job performance or business results.

The fact that the average ranked position (mean) range is a high of 3 and a low of 8 — a spread of five rank positions — suggests that all factors are perceived as important, which was indeed verified by the comments made by members of the Executive Panel, some of which have been included in earlier chapters.

The medians and ranking ranges reveal the very broad spread of responses by the Executive Panel for any one factor. Accordingly, the overall rank order needs to be reviewed with caution, and not read as the definitive result in terms of priority.

Other Career Success and Failure Factors Cited

Some members of the Executive Panel came forward with a broad range of other factors. James Cogan, managing director finance and administration of Credit Suisse First Boston, sees executive career success in this light: 'Ultimately, the executive's success or failure in the job is decided by the "boss" acting on their perception of the executive's performance, relative to the boss's expectations of that executive. Therefore, understanding these expectations is paramount. Then, giving them top priority and accomplishing them equals success. The same applies to the team assisting the executive. Each member of the team must have the understanding of the executive's expectations of the member, so the member can prioritise and accomplish. Then it works for everybody!'

'I wonder where being in the right place at the right time would come in the list?' asks Robert C Stephenson, local divisional manager of SCA Molnlycke AB in the UK. He continues: 'Al Dunlap apart, is anyone bulletproof?'

Ian Moore, general manager human resources of James Hardie Industries Ltd, comments: 'Need to recognise the use of "power" in organisational settings — it still dominates the success agenda. It does not have to be viewed negatively; the issue of values and ethics would be worthy of comment too; certainly as a counteracting influence on power.'

'It goes without saying that success/failure result from a combination of factors working at the right time: sometimes, being in the right place at the right time with the right mentor helps enormously! The skilled executive makes this happen (in a positive way) rather than waiting for it to occur,' says Joe Fischer, manager human resources department and regional staff coordination, Nestlé Australia Ltd.

Peeyush Gupta, chief executive officer of IPAC Securities, talks about 'Clusters of competencies required for success.'

'I have recently been studying the reasons for failed recruitments at senior level within our organisation and I would say that the single common factor has been an inability to operate within terms of reference acceptable to the organisation. Thinking back over other organisations in which I have worked, this 'style fit' has been equally important. Executives often choose to leave or are asked to leave because they cannot come to terms with the 'way things are around here'. If I were advising individuals on their next career move, this would be amongst the most critical factors I would urge them to consider,' concludes Paul Lilley, general manager, (Australian Banking Group) Westpac.

Ken Harris, managing director of ADI Limited, says that a factor ranked equal first in his mind with teamwork is: 'Random events — being there at the right time.'

'A successful career will increasingly be dominated by those who have had a wide range of successful experiences both locally and internationally,' says Brett Haly, general manager customer relations and organisation development, Tower Life.

'In my opinion, a major success factor is managerial courage, ie the ability to handle difficult/sensitive issues in an even-handed up-front way. The world is full of "good news bearers" who duck for cover as soon as difficult decisions are required,' says Michael T Duffy, senior manager group human resources at the Commonwealth Bank of Australia.

'Correct alignment between job description, responsibilities, authority and accountability. If there is a misalignment, then frustration rather than fulfilment will ensue,' says the director of a specialist management consulting practice.

Another success factor cited by Martin Prentice, vice president training and education of a major consumer product manufacturing and marketing organisation in the United States, is: 'Know yourself . . . deeply . . . in the way an objective outsider would know you. Then you can concentrate most of your efforts on using your strengths; a significant time on improving your one or two career-threatening weaknesses; and a little time on improving your other weaknesses.' He continues: 'If you're tough, honest and perceptive about yourself, you'll be realistic and humble about managing and leading others.'

Bruce Coates, general manager employee relations Ampol, agrees: 'I can readily think of at least one other factor, maybe the one I would rate most highly: "Knowing Yourself" — a realistic view of your competencies, attributes, needs etc, and what will give you a satisfying life.'

'Ability to get things done/make things happen. Some executives have this trait and it makes them stand out. In my view, many retrenchees lack this trait,' says R V Matthews, human resources director of Goodman Fielder International.

Another important success factor is: 'Being open, accessible and a real person — someone the team can relate to as a human being. Being more than just an efficient functionary. Being respected and attracted to, because of human qualities,' says Oleh Butchatsky, director of Ward Howell International, and co-author of *Leadership, Australia's Top CEOs: Finding out what makes them best*.

'My overall feeling is that individuals and companies must distinguish between "labour" and "people" and act accordingly — treat people like we'd treat ourselves; learn to recognise and manage "calibre" — invest in calibre, top to bottom; understand customers; make "action" match the "rhetoric" — people listen to what you *do*!' concludes Tony Harbour, independent management consultant and formerly group personnel director of the Ocean Group PLC in the UK.

'Whatever the mix of skills and attributes, long-term success requires understanding, integrity, courage and compassion,' concludes John Matthews, deputy general manager group human resources, Commonwealth Bank.

Two more factors are proposed by David Learmond, personnel director of Unilever Australia: 'Self-confidence and integrity. Ability to stand up for what you believe in — even to the extent of personal risk.' He concludes: 'The ranking is interesting, but you need them all to be really successful!'

Roddy Armstrong, director human resources, Dupont (Australia) Ltd, reminds us of another important factor: 'Simply — hard work — with work objectives focused on company mission and personal objectives.'

'I think we have a conundrum today, in that managers need to give stability to an organisation, while responding to an ever-changing external environment. Not an easy task! Someone who can do this probably has all the attributes of leadership and good management,' concludes Moira Holmes, director human resources, Hitachi Data Systems.

Geoff Wright, former state director Western Australia, Davidson & Associates, adds another success factor: 'Identification. Aside from culture, style and so on, some form of comfort by association is important. Are you "proud" of the company, your job, services/products, or do you positively cringe when asked, "What do you do?".'

Graeme Galt, a leading Sydney businessman and one of Australia's foremost senior-level head-hunters, co-founder of Australia's largest executive search firm, now known as Amrop International, former chairman of Korn/Ferry International in Australia, and former chairman of Sydney Football and the Sydney Dance Company, is quite clear in his mind about the ranking of career success and failure factors for executives: 'The most successful executives that I have ever known, especially entrepreneurial leaders, have a visionary approach and just seem to be doing what they were destined to be doing. Clearly, I'm influenced by my observations of those who are successful at sport and in the arts, who from an early age foresaw their destinies developing in these areas, whereas it may be harder for others to see their destinies, for example, as chief executives manufacturing baby food! In fact, leaders in business need to find that high-level sense of purpose and pursue it at a very early age if they are to be truly successful. The old traditional concept of building your career based on straight loyalty to your employer has flown the coop!'

Lyn Cobley, strategic planning and marketing manager of Citibank and formerly head of securitisation, concludes: 'It is clearly difficult to rank these in strict order of priority. I see three important categories in order of importance: understand yourself and your needs; understand your business and the external market environment; understand how to attract and develop key talent and drive your business objectives in a shared way.'

Ron Hopwood, director of human resources, 3M Australia Pty Ltd, is adamant about two factors: 'If job fit or organisational fit are not right, don't even think of a *career* in that function or organisation.' And he concludes about the 11 factors for career success and failure: 'Rank ordering these traits can be deceptive. Almost all are equally important for executive success in the late 1990s, and will be even more so in the next decade.'

And, sadly perhaps, Michael Nadler, independent consultant and previously chief executive of the Australian Institute of Management New South Wales, concludes: 'I believe that "success" for the individual executive or manager does not always equate to value or benefit for the organisation. There are far too many "successful" executives who have harmed their organisations. While there is much talk today about modern and enlightened leadership, I see little of it in reality.'

Difficulties and Dependencies Regarding the Rankings

The ranking exercise was difficult and the Executive Panel threw some interesting light on other dimensions relating to executive and managerial success. 'I found it very difficult to rank these attributes as each seemed almost essential for managerial career success,' concludes Kerri Burgess, chief of staff, Citibank Ltd.

'My ranking is based on my perception of "what is" rather than "what should be" success and failure factors. For instance, while politics, power and influence probably should be ranked 11, in reality I see it as the second most important factor to primary business drivers,' says J G (John) Koch, chief representative of the Forma Group, formerly a general manager with the Commonwealth Bank of Australia.

Christopher Conybeare, independent consultant and associate director of Davidson & Associates, concludes that the factors and rankings are: 'Highly personal and related to individual experiences in different organisations. The traits which ensure success in one "era" or phase of an organisation's history, may not work well in other phases. This is not just a question of exercising survival skills: a different executive type may be needed for different periods of organisations' cycles.'

Michael Rowan, formerly chief manager commercial and agribusiness banking, NSW country and ACT, Westpac, agrees: 'These success and failure factors apply differently to organisations in various stages of their life cycle — I have marked them for an organisation in equilibrium — but they would be different for Westpac/Goodman Fielder/AWA or a company at a crisis time of its cycle.'

'My rankings are determined by the stage I am at with the Royal Blind Society (eight years as chief executive officer) and would differ from my rankings when I started, or even from three years ago,' says Jon Isaacs.

'Rankings probably depend on the role,' remarks Philip Twyman, finance director of General Accident plc, Scotland.

Peter Herborn, group general manager development, Tower Corporation Holding Limited New Zealand, concludes: 'Firstly, the way I would rank my response would depend on whether I am considering it from the standpoint of: a chief executive; a general manager; a functional or middle manager. Other factors which could have some bearing on the way you rank the factors would include:

❖ *Type of industry.* In an industry like consulting, nurturing talent is almost certainly much more highly ranked than, say, agriculture or mining where you only need a small proportion of your staff to be of the highest calibre. On the other hand, in agriculture and mining, your staff management practices can have considerable ongoing importance, probably much more so than consulting.

❖ *Life stage of the industry.* A start-up business will need different types of people than one which is mature.

❖ Whether you choose to look *long or short term*. There are some things which, if you can get them right quickly, will buy you time to address other factors which may be much more critical in the longer term. For example, some basic level of staff management practices usually need to be in place early in any industry environment, but thereafter other factors will typically become increasingly important.'

How to Develop Your Own Priorities

Coming back to our metaphysical poet, John Donne, I would like to suggest the following sequence of events, in order for you to be able to develop some form of barometer as to where to start and what to concentrate on, to ensure your future career success and longevity with your employer organisation.

First, add to the 11 career success factors any other factors suggested by the Executive Panel, with which you strongly identify. This becomes your master list. Rank this list according to your perceived personal development needs, in other words, the factor representing your greatest personal development need first, the factor representing your greatest strength last.

Secondly, rank the factors again, according to your organisation's perception of their importance. You may need to test the factors on your line manager and other senior people in your organisation, in order to be able to accomplish this.

Finally, rank the factors again according to your own perception of the priorities confronting your organisation, which includes your assessment of the stage of its life cycle and of the universe within which it operates — the external environment and futures. The second and third rankings *ought* to be similar, but are not necessarily so.

Now take these three rankings, and select just two or three of the factors which seem to come forward as being most important in terms of your personal development needs, and concentrate on them, say, for a period of three to six months. After three to six months, go over the ranking exercise again and select two or perhaps three other factors which emerge as priorities.

The important thing to remember here, is that while all the factors are important as verified by the Executive Panel, you need to concentrate on a tight shortlist — your barometer for ongoing career success — at any one time. Trying to make progress across too broad a front simply doesn't work. Just like the concept of primary business drivers, you *have* to prioritise. And by reassessing your rankings every three to six months, just like the barometer, you are responding to the changing circumstances and pressures in *your* universe.

If you do what I have suggested, and if you use the whole of this book as your ongoing 'munitions factory', bulletproof executive and managerial success can be assured.

Good luck!

Focusing These Strategies Into A Winning And Enduring Bulletproof Theme

SUMMARY

Chapter 17 raises the following key issues:
- The subject of career success and failure for executives and managers is a complex one, comprised of many factors.
- There appear to be 11 main factors, supported by a host of others.
- Their rank order of importance varies according to the job, seniority, the organisation and the external environment.
- By developing a master list of factors, the onus is on each executive and manager to rank them by order of:
  — perceived personal development needs
  — organisational perceptions as to their importance
  — the organisation's status, external environment and futures

which together produces an overall ranking.
- Select two or three factors at any given time on which to concentrate for purposes of personal development.
- Revise the rankings and priorities every three to six months.
- In this way, and by using the guidelines in this book, bulletproof executive and managerial success can be assured!

Weapons At Your Disposal

The Executive Armoury now offers you 19 different weapons at your disposal which relate back to the chapter material. Deploy them as you need them to survive and succeed in the battle-zone!

1.

Four Triggers Risk Assessment

This section contains exercises for Chapter 2.

This assessment is designed to help you identify where you may be at risk in your work as an executive or manager. Based on the results of the assessment, suggestions are given on which chapters of this book to read first.

Complete the following checklist using the score guide set out below:

1. Inadequately
2. Less than adequately
3. Adequately
4. Well
5. Very well

NB *Think* about each question before entering a score, and try to avoid patterns of central tendency (such as mainly 3s), low score tendency (mainly 1s) or high score tendency (mainly 5s).

Part A   Circle the relevant score

1. I understand, give sufficient time and priority attention to, and apply the management practices of planning, organising, monitoring, decision-making, motivating and delegating   1   2   3   4   5

2. I know what my single most important business objective is and the primary drivers for attaining that objective, and spend my time prioritising these essential areas, rather than on less essential matters.   1   2   3   4   5

3. I keep myself fully informed about 'futures', the fast-developing external environment which impacts on my business — the economy, the market place, the competition, our customers, technology, and the business sector in which we operate.   1   2   3   4   5

4. I attract, select, retain and develop staff of the highest calibre available.   1   2   3   4   5

Part A subtotal

Part B
Circle the relevant score

1. My main occupational interests are represented in my job, be they technical, computational, practical, medical, scientific, social, persuasive, literary, clerical, musical, outdoors or artistic.   1 2 3 4 5

2. My main capabilities — and those I enjoy using — are represented in my job, be they memory, verbal comprehension, numeracy, spatial ability, perception, fluency, reasoning ability, creativity, social ability, or clerical speed and accuracy.   1 2 3 4 5

3. My main values are represented in my job and work environment, be they security, integrity, social, community or environmental responsibility, personal or financial success, prestige or variety.   1 2 3 4 5

4. I have developed a sense of ownership, confidence and control over my own career destiny. I know where I am headed.   1 2 3 4 5

Part B subtotal

Part C
Circle the relevant score

1. I exhibit the competencies of adaptability, entrepreneurism, resilience and open two-way communication with managers and staff.   1 2 3 4 5

2. I understand and manage the various phases associated with organisational restructuring: planning, launch, break-up, recovery and re-fire.   1 2 3 4 5

3. At times of organisational change I emphasise the human factor, avoid 'slash and burn', 'hire and fire' and dismissals, and nuture talent.   1 2 3 4 5

4. I 'deliver' (the *process* of delivery, rather than the content) presentations and speeches.   1 2 3 4 5

Part C subtotal

Part D
Circle the relevant score

1. My motivational needs — material needs (remuneration, safety and security); structural needs (degree and type of structure, bureaucracy and systems); behavioural needs (management style and interpersonal relationships); and emotional needs (trust, social needs, esteem needs and sense of achievement) — are met by the organisation for which I work.   1 2 3 4 5

Part D *(continued)*   **Circle the relevant score**

2. I understand and apply what my organisation expects
   of me in terms of my leadership traits.   1   2   3   4   5

3. My operating style contributes to my team and
   adds value to teamwork.   1   2   3   4   5

4. I understand and respond to organisational politics,
   power and influence by selling myself, networking,
   and negotiating my way to success.   1   2   3   4   5

Part D subtotal

Score Guide

Part A relates to the first trigger of executive failure, **job performance**; Part B to the second trigger, **personal performance**; Part C to the third trigger, **change management**; and Part D to the fourth trigger, **chemistry and fit**.

The subtotals for each part suggest:
- 1-5:   high risk
- 6-10:   at risk
- 11-15:   unlikely to be at risk currently
- 16-20:   apparently safe for now.

Assess your greatest risk areas and then read the relevant chapters first.

Part A   **Part B**
Checklist Item 1: Chapter 3   Checklist Item 1: Chapter 4
          Item 2: Chapter 3   Item 2: Chapter 4
          Item 3: Chapter 3   Item 3: Chapter 4
          Item 4: Chapter 10   Item 4: Chapters 5, 11, 12, 13

Part C   **Part D**
Checklist Item 1: Chapter 8   Checklist Item 1: Chapter 7
          Item 2: Chapter 8   Item 2: Chapter 5
          Item 3: Chapters 8, 9, 10   Item 3: Chapter 6
          Item 4: Chapter 8   Item 4: Chapters 14, 15, 16

2.

Management Practices Survey

This section contains exercises for Chapters 3 and 8.

The survey document included in this section is copyright protected, but the first reader is authorised to photocopy it sufficient times for a one-off, multi-level personal survey.

Instructions for Use

Select three people working at a more senior level in your organisation than yourself, such as your boss and others to whom you report indirectly or with whom you liaise. In order for their participation in the survey to be worthwhile, they must be knowledgeable about your management practices.

Similarly, select three peers, three direct reports, and three others, if you wish, who comprise a similar grouping — for example, customer contacts, suppliers, or the direct reports of your own direct reports.

All the people you select to participate in your multi-level survey need to have known you for at least five to seven months.

Make a photocopy of the survey for each participant. On the first page of each copy, write your name, when you need the completed survey document returned, and the name of the person to whom you want it returned (usually yourself). Indicate the relationship of the person completing the survey to you by ticking the appropriate box.

Send the survey to the people you have selected, with a covering letter. (A sample letter follows.) Do *not* send out the Summary of Survey Results, which is for your own reference.

Complete one survey document yourself, about yourself.

When you receive the completed surveys back, complete the Summary of Survey Results by transferring your own 'eyeball average' scores to where shown on pages 208, 209 and 210, as well as the overall average of the 'eyeball average' scores for your senior colleagues, your peers, your direct reports, and the 'other' group you may have selected.

Finally, you can use the bar chart and diagram formats on pages 211–214 to provide graphic representations of all the scores on pages 208, 209 and 210.

Sample Letter to Multi-level Survey Respondents

Dear

Re: Confidential Multi-level Survey

I'm currently reading *The Bulletproof Executive*, by Peter Stephenson. This is a book about management effectiveness and career success, designed to help the reader analyse their own performance and areas for improvement. This includes a multi-level survey on my management practices and our organisation in a range of functional areas. The survey is to be completed by myself, my senior colleagues, my peers, my direct reports and others.

I am inviting you, along with quite a few others, to complete this multi-level survey about me.

Please complete the following checklists as accurately as possible and return them to me in confidence by [*insert date*].

I will provide general feedback relating to the management and organisation practice areas I have selected for further development in keeping with the results of the survey.

Many thanks indeed for your cooperation in this.

Yours sincerely,

Enclosed: Your confidential multi-level survey document.

The Bulletproof Executive Confidential Multi-level Survey

Confidential multi-level survey on
[*name of person whose management practices are the focus of this survey*]:

Respondent's relationship to the above person
[*tick one box*]:

Senior colleague ❑

Peer ❑

Direct report ❑

Self ❑

Other relationship ❑ Please specify: ....

....

....

....

Please answer the 11 checklists attached, and return the complete survey document by [*date*] ....../....../...... in confidence to ....

....

© *The Bulletproof Executive*

Checklist 1

In thinking about the management practices of the individual who is the focus of the survey, award points for each statement below by circling the relevant number as follows:

1 Never   **2** Sometimes   **3** 50% of the time   **4** Frequently   **5** Always

NB Be careful not to lapse into central, high score or low score tendency when you complete this checklist!

• is good at planning and objective setting, and establishing the strategies to accomplish these objectives	1	2	3	4	5
• anticipates problems in progressing from planning to implementation, and reviews progress	1	2	3	4	5
• updates plans according to progress and external conditions, making necessary changes to plans	1	2	3	4	5
• ensures that objectives are quantified and stretching, yet attainable, and that they address what, when, where and how	1	2	3	4	5
• ensures that staff are involved in the planning process and understand what is expected	1	2	3	4	5
• is proactive rather than reactive to external changes which impact on the organisation	1	2	3	4	5
• sees planning as continuous rather than one-off, ie not just an annual event	1	2	3	4	5
• displays a capacity to conceptualise, be creative, think 'outside the square' and take an external perspective	1	2	3	4	5
• ensures that planning receives top management commitment, priority attention, and the necessary time and resources	1	2	3	4	5
• ensures that planning focuses on effectiveness (outcomes and achievements) and efficiency (inputs and processes)	1	2	3	4	5
'Eyeball average' score	1	2	3	4	5

© *The Bulletproof Executive*

Checklist 2

In thinking about the management practices of the individual who is the focus of the survey, award points for each statement below by circling the relevant number as follows:

1 Never   **2** Sometimes   **3** 50% of the time   **4** Frequently   **5** Always

NB Be careful not to lapse into central, high score or low score tendency when you complete this checklist!

• in terms of organisation, ensures that all relevant parties understand the structure and reporting relationships	1	2	3	4	5
• ensures that people are organised in the most effective, efficient and flexible ways to attain desired objectives	1	2	3	4	5
• ensures that coordination is enhanced by all knowing who is responsible for what and accountable to whom	1	2	3	4	5
• ensures that jobs are well defined, but 'broad-banded' and flexible enough to adapt to changing operating conditions	1	2	3	4	5
• ensures that span of control — the number of job positions reporting to him/her — is neither too broad nor too narrow	1	2	3	4	5
• ensures that people are clear about with whom they need to liaise and to whom they report	1	2	3	4	5
• ensures that opportunities for delegation are maximised, but 'abdication' is avoided	1	2	3	4	5
• ensures that organisational arrangements maximise morale	1	2	3	4	5
• ensures that teams are composed of people with different operating styles, rather than 'clones' of the team leader	1	2	3	4	5
• ensures that teams are empowered and encouraged as far as possible to be self-directing	1	2	3	4	5
'Eyeball average' score	1	2	3	4	5

© The Bulletproof Executive

Checklist 3

In thinking about the management practices of the individual who is the focus of the survey, award points for each statement below by circling the relevant number as follows:

1 Never   **2** Sometimes   **3** 50% of the time   **4** Frequently   **5** Always

NB Be careful not to lapse into central, high score or low score tendency when you complete this checklist!

• in monitoring progress, ensures that goals and objectives are attained according to plan	1	2	3	4	5
• ensures that monitoring is oriented towards preventing problems, rather than having to resolve them	1	2	3	4	5
• ensures that preventative monitoring helps employees to know what is expected in terms of quality, quantity, time and cost	1	2	3	4	5
• ensures that employees know their job parameters, scope of responsibility, authority and accountability	1	2	3	4	5
• ensures that maintenance monitoring focuses on key result areas, signalling if progress to plan is adverse	1	2	3	4	5
• ensures that key result areas for staff are specific: orders, units, errors, complaints, dollar volumes and costs	1	2	3	4	5
• ensures that monitoring takes the form of on-the-job supervision and management by exception	1	2	3	4	5
• ensures that mutually agreed personal performance standards define the outcome of tasks satisfactorily performed	1	2	3	4	5
• ensures that appraisal processes regularly check performance against standards and development needs	1	2	3	4	5
• ensures that development needs are quickly and effectively addressed via counselling, coaching or training	1	2	3	4	5
'Eyeball average' score	1	2	3	4	5

© *The Bulletproof Executive*

Checklist 4

In thinking about the management practices of the individual who is the focus of the survey, award points for each statement below by circling the relevant number as follows:

1 Never   **2** Sometimes   **3** 50% of the time   **4** Frequently   **5** Always

NB Be careful not to lapse into central, high score or low score tendency when you complete this checklist!

• ensures that decision-making is sound, selecting a course of action from a range of alternatives	1	2	3	4	5
• ensures that decision-making starts via fully defining and understanding the problem or opportunity	1	2	3	4	5
• ensures that all facts are analysed, evaluated and interpreted in the context of the problem or opportunity	1	2	3	4	5
• ensures that a range of solutions or options is developed, and alternative potential decisions are addressed	1	2	3	4	5
• ensures that alternatives are compared and ranked, with the overall ranking determining the decision	1	2	3	4	5
• in defining problems, ensures that root causes — as opposed to symptoms — are addressed	1	2	3	4	5
• in collecting facts, ensures that they are true and valid facts, rather than guesses, opinions or lies	1	2	3	4	5
• in examining all possible solutions, ensures that creative, 'outside the square' thinking is encouraged	1	2	3	4	5
• ensures that problems and opportunities are shared, and that all parties contribute to decision-making	1	2	3	4	5
• ensures that a 'bottom up', as well as a 'top down', approach is taken in decision-making	1	2	3	4	5
'Eyeball average' score	1	2	3	4	5

© The Bulletproof Executive

Checklist 5

In thinking about the management practices of the individual who is the focus of the survey, award points for each statement below by circling the relevant number as follows:

1 Never   **2** Sometimes   **3** 50% of the time   **4** Frequently   **5** Always

NB Be careful not to lapse into central, high score or low score tendency when you complete this checklist!

• sees delegation as a priority area and decides what and how much can be delegated to whom	1	2	3	4	5
• explains the reasons for, and objectives of, the delegation and provides sufficient resources and authority for it	1	2	3	4	5
• is prepared to take some risks in delegating, minimised through effective monitoring	1	2	3	4	5
• puts in sufficient time and effort to make delegation work successfully	1	2	3	4	5
• delegates activities which do not use his/her major competencies; retains priority activities	1	2	3	4	5
• only delegates when he/she has confidence in direct reports to take up the delegation satisfactorily	1	2	3	4	5
• delegates to increase direct report involvement, motivation and personal performance	1	2	3	4	5
• provides sufficient authority to the direct report for carrying through the delegation satisfactorily	1	2	3	4	5
• establishes priorities and time-lines for progress reporting and completion of delegated tasks	1	2	3	4	5
• relinquishes sufficient control for the direct report to buy ownership of the delegation and to have freedom to act	1	2	3	4	5
'Eyeball average' score	1	2	3	4	5

© *The Bulletproof Executive*

Checklist 6

In thinking about the management practices of the individual who is the focus of the survey, award points for each statement below by circling the relevant number as follows:

1 Never **2** Sometimes **3** 50% of the time **4** Frequently **5** Always

***NB** Be careful not to lapse into central, high score or low score tendency when you complete this checklist!*

• selects and develops staff on the basis of their strong work ethic and high standards in terms of results	1	2	3	4	5
• creates challenging jobs which in themselves create satisfaction, enjoyment and self-motivation	1	2	3	4	5
• develops an external and internal organisational image based on clear and shared values and principles	1	2	3	4	5
• encourages employees to be involved in goal-setting, and offers freedom to attain goals	1	2	3	4	5
• creates a positive environment, with a sense of dynamism, excellence, self-direction and empowerment	1	2	3	4	5
• creates an environment where personal power and influence prevail, rather than formal authority	1	2	3	4	5
• consistently praises in public, and counsels and takes action for poor performance in private, when due	1	2	3	4	5
• tries to meet the motivational needs of individuals via remuneration, degree and type of structure	1	2	3	4	5
• tries to meet the motivational needs of individuals via management style, interpersonal relationships, trust and sense of achievement	1	2	3	4	5
• his/her management style is honest, democratic, consultative, participative and delegating	1	2	3	4	5
'Eyeball average' score	1	2	3	4	5

© *The Bulletproof Executive*

☞ Change of Survey Focus

Checklist 7

In thinking about the *organisation for which you work*, award points for each statement below by circling the relevant number as follows:

1 Never   **2** Sometimes   **3** 50% of the time   **4** Frequently   **5** Always

NB Be careful not to lapse into central, high score or low score tendency when you complete this checklist!

Reminder: Please score these statements on the basis of how you perceive the organisation for which you work rather than how you perceive the individual who is the focus of the survey in all other sections.

• status differences are minimised and staff at all levels are treated equally	1	2	3	4	5
• while reporting lines and authority are in place, cooperation and teamwork are given more priority	1	2	3	4	5
• open, two-way communication prevails both laterally and vertically	1	2	3	4	5
• job specifications and grades are broad-banded to maximise flexibility, cooperation and teamwork	1	2	3	4	5
• spans of control are never so narrow as to impose a regime of very close 'top down' management	1	2	3	4	5
• shared values and goals are emphasised, as is group-based decision-making	1	2	3	4	5
• a climate of trust, fairness and co-operation prevails — employees trust each other and managers	1	2	3	4	5
• mutually supportive teams help people to synergise and act co-operatively rather than independently	1	2	3	4	5
• the operational climate encourages personal development and advancement	1	2	3	4	5
• the management style in the organisation maximises self-motivation, morale and productivity	1	2	3	4	5
'Eyeball average' score	1	2	3	4	5

© *The Bulletproof Executive*

☞ Back to the Individual

Checklist 8

In thinking about the management practices of *the individual* who is the focus of the survey, award points for each statement below by circling the relevant number as follows:

1 Never   **2** Sometimes   **3** 50% of the time   **4** Frequently   **5** Always

***NB** Be careful not to lapse into central, high score or low score tendency when you complete this checklist.*

• communicates well with direct reports, keeping them involved as and whenever necessary	1	2	3	4	5
• communicates well with peers, keeping them informed as and whenever necessary	1	2	3	4	5
• communicates well with his/her more senior colleagues, keeping them informed as necessary	1	2	3	4	5
• listens twice as much as talks, and understands the other party's point of view before responding	1	2	3	4	5
• understands and minimises the physical barriers to effective communication — noise, outside interruptions, etc	1	2	3	4	5
• understands that others' expectations are often different from one's own and impact on what is heard	1	2	3	4	5
• communicates precisely and concisely in writing, by planning written communications	1	2	3	4	5
• plans formal oral presentations and is clear about what is to be achieved with the audience	1	2	3	4	5
• at times of change, communicates with all affected parties, both in person and in writing, repeatedly and regularly	1	2	3	4	5
• is seen as approachable, encouraging questions, and wanting to hear about bad, as well as good, news	1	2	3	4	5
'Eyeball average' score	1	2	3	4	5

© *The Bulletproof Executive*

Checklist 9

In thinking about the management practices of the individual who is the focus of the survey, award points for each statement below by circling the relevant number as follows:

1 Never   **2** Sometimes   **3** 50% of the time   **4** Frequently   **5** Always

NB Be careful not to lapse into central, high score or low score tendency when you complete this checklist!

• when confronted by challenges, takes a flexible approach to solutions rather than assumes 'business as usual'	1	2	3	4	5
• seeks variety and change at work, rather than routine	1	2	3	4	5
• when new situations arise at work, is curious and probing	1	2	3	4	5
• upholds corporate policy, but is seen by colleagues as non-conformist	1	2	3	4	5
• adapts to changing circumstances rather than resists them	1	2	3	4	5
• is comfortable with the unexpected at work and interested in the unconventional	1	2	3	4	5
• leadership style modifies according to the direct report's competence and the urgency of the task	1	2	3	4	5
• is seen by direct reports as flexible rather than rigid in day-to-day operations	1	2	3	4	5
• in problem-solving, thinks 'outside the square'	1	2	3	4	5
• actively seeks input from others when confronted by changes at work	1	2	3	4	5
'Eyeball average' score	1	2	3	4	5

© *The Bulletproof Executive*

Checklist 10

In thinking about the management practices of the individual who is the focus of the survey, award points for each statement below by circling the relevant number as follows:

1 Never   **2** Sometimes   **3** 50% of the time   **4** Frequently   **5** Always

NB Be careful not to lapse into central, high score or low score tendency when you complete this checklist!

• is good at experimenting with new ways of doing things at work	1	2	3	4	5
• is successful in innovation, be this in the form of new products, services, processes or systems	1	2	3	4	5
• displays a certain 'daring' and tries out brand-new concepts at work	1	2	3	4	5
• takes the initiative, but also accepts accountability for the results from the initiative — good or bad	1	2	3	4	5
• displays an independent style and acts autonomously	1	2	3	4	5
• is good at development, not just maintenance of ongoing operations	1	2	3	4	5
• is seen by others as entrepreneurial in approaches to work	1	2	3	4	5
• takes risks when the rewards are high	1	2	3	4	5
• understands the possible benefits *and* adverse consequences of taking risks	1	2	3	4	5
• is good at managing risks, applying appropriate preventative measures as needed	1	2	3	4	5
'Eyeball average' score	1	2	3	4	5

© The Bulletproof Executive

Checklist 11

In thinking about the management practices of the individual who is the focus of the survey, award points for each statement below by circling the relevant number as follows:

1 Never   **2** Sometimes   **3** 50% of the time   **4** Frequently   **5** Always

NB Be careful not to lapse into central, high score or low score tendency when you complete this checklist!

• avoids the negative impacts of stress at work	1	2	3	4	5
• leaves troubles at work rather than taking them home	1	2	3	4	5
• sleeps well and enjoys weekends, rather than worrying about work	1	2	3	4	5
• when the going gets rough, perseveres	1	2	3	4	5
• is considered to be tough; forges ahead, even at times of adversity	1	2	3	4	5
• gets desired results, even when confronted by difficult work situations	1	2	3	4	5
• confronts change as a way of life, rather than as a hindrance; accepts change positively	1	2	3	4	5
• when given a job to do or a task to accomplish, attains it, even though the challenge may be extreme	1	2	3	4	5
• is seen as a good ally by colleagues when the going gets difficult and when everyone is up against it	1	2	3	4	5
• has a dogged streak of resilience, particularly at times of change or uncertainty	1	2	3	4	5
'Eyeball average' score	1	2	3	4	5

© *The Bulletproof Executive*

SUMMARY OF SURVEY RESULTS

(Do not send this out ... Retain it for later.)

Scores						Range*	
						Highest average score	Lowest average score

Checklist 1 'Planning'

Self (eyeball average)	1	2	3	4	5	(Not for 'Self')
Direct reports (overall average)	1	2	3	4	5	
Peers (overall average)	1	2	3	4	5	
Senior colleagues (overall average)	1	2	3	4	5	
Others (overall average)	1	2	3	4	5	

Checklist 2 'Organising'

Self (eyeball average)	1	2	3	4	5	(Not for 'Self')
Direct reports (overall average)	1	2	3	4	5	
Peers (overall average)	1	2	3	4	5	
Senior colleagues (overall average)	1	2	3	4	5	
Others (overall average)	1	2	3	4	5	

Checklist 3 'Monitoring'

Self (eyeball average)	1	2	3	4	5	(Not for 'Self')
Direct reports (overall average)	1	2	3	4	5	
Peers (overall average)	1	2	3	4	5	
Senior colleagues (overall average)	1	2	3	4	5	
Others (overall average)	1	2	3	4	5	

> * Insert here the highest and lowest scores from the survey, which gives you a snapshot of the range of scores, as well as the averages.

Scores						Range*	
						Highest average score	Lowest average score

Checklist 4 'Decision-making'

Self (eyeball average)	1	2	3	4	5	(Not for 'Self')
Direct reports (overall average)	1	2	3	4	5	
Peers (overall average)	1	2	3	4	5	
Senior colleagues (overall average)	1	2	3	4	5	
Others (overall average)	1	2	3	4	5	

Checklist 5 'Delegating'

Self (eyeball average)	1	2	3	4	5	(Not for 'Self')
Direct reports (overall average)	1	2	3	4	5	
Peers (overall average)	1	2	3	4	5	
Senior colleagues (overall average)	1	2	3	4	5	
Others (overall average)	1	2	3	4	5	

Checklist 6 '*Individual* Motivating'

Self (eyeball average)	1	2	3	4	5	(Not for 'Self')
Direct reports (overall average)	1	2	3	4	5	
Peers (overall average)	1	2	3	4	5	
Senior colleagues (overall average)	1	2	3	4	5	
Others (overall average)	1	2	3	4	5	

Checklist 7 '*Organisation* Motivating'

Self (eyeball average)	1	2	3	4	5	(Not for 'Self')
Direct reports (overall average)	1	2	3	4	5	
Peers (overall average)	1	2	3	4	5	
Senior colleagues (overall average)	1	2	3	4	5	
Others (overall average)	1	2	3	4	5	

Scores						Range*	
						Highest average score	Lowest average score

Checklist 8 'Communicating'
Self (eyeball average)	1	2	3	4	5	(Not for 'Self')
Direct reports (overall average)	1	2	3	4	5	
Peers (overall average)	1	2	3	4	5	
Senior colleagues (overall average)	1	2	3	4	5	
Others (overall average)	1	2	3	4	5	

Checklist 9 'Adaptability'
Self (eyeball average)	1	2	3	4	5	(Not for 'Self')
Direct reports (overall average)	1	2	3	4	5	
Peers (overall average)	1	2	3	4	5	
Senior colleagues (overall average)	1	2	3	4	5	
Others (overall average)	1	2	3	4	5	

Checklist 10 'Entrepreneurism'
Self (eyeball average)	1	2	3	4	5	(Not for 'Self')
Direct reports (overall average)	1	2	3	4	5	
Peers (overall average)	1	2	3	4	5	
Senior colleagues (overall average)	1	2	3	4	5	
Others (overall average)	1	2	3	4	5	

Checklist 11 'Resilience'
Self (eyeball average)	1	2	3	4	5	(Not for 'Self')
Direct reports (overall average)	1	2	3	4	5	
Peers (overall average)	1	2	3	4	5	
Senior colleagues (overall average)	1	2	3	4	5	
Others (overall average)	1	2	3	4	5	

Now transfer these scores to the bar chart summaries on pages 212–214.

Management Practices Survey

Bar Chart Summary of Survey Results

Transfer the scores from pages 208, 209 and 210 to the following charts, using felt-tip highlighter pens. Use one colour for self, and other colours for each of direct reports, peers, senior colleagues and others. An example is set out below.

A. Basic Management Practices: Example

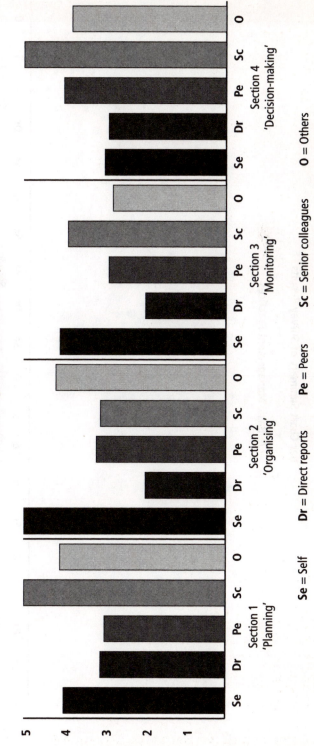

Se = Self **Dr** = Direct reports **Pe** = Peers **Sc** = Senior colleagues **O** = Others

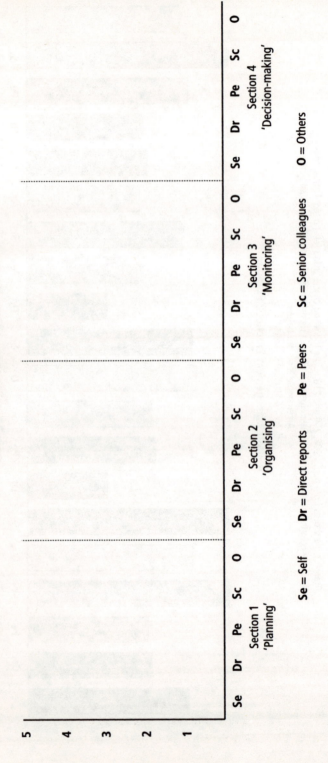

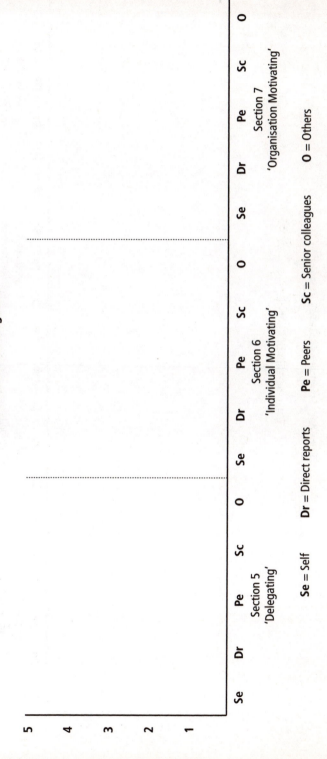

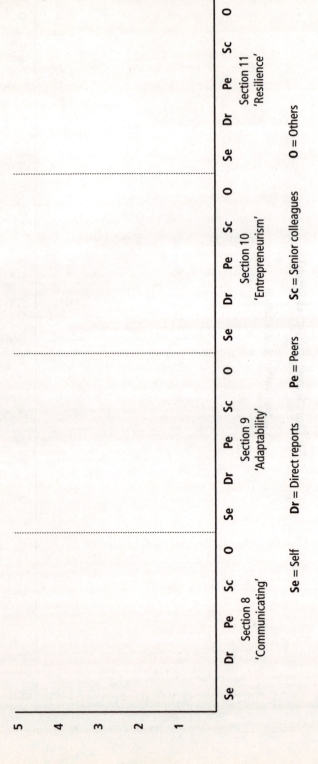

Completion of Survey Results

Analyse the results for each Checklist in the survey, concentrating initially on Checklists 1-4. In deciding which management practice areas you need to concentrate on, take particular note of the level of scores, the range of scores, and the differences in the levels between self, direct reports, peers, your senior colleagues and others. What does all this tell you? Whose perception is the most accurate, or the most relevant? Clearly, low scores need consideration, as do large differences in scores between 'self' and other classes of survey respondent.

Next, examine just your direct reports' results for Checklists 5-7 and transfer these results to the New Core Management Competence diagram on page 216. You will have to do this twice, using the results from Checklists 5 and 6 first — revealing the impact of your own motivating capabilities on motivational delegation — and then the results from Checklists 5 and 7 — revealing the impact of your organisation's motivating capabilities on motivational delegation. Record your scores on the diagram by drawing two lines between the two positions, denoting the scores on the vertical and horizontal lines, to form a square or rectangle (see the one example). Then draw a prominent dot or small circle on the corner furthest from the bottom left-hand corner of the existing diagram, which becomes your 'position-fix'. (If the two positions denoting the scores only each score 1, your position-fix will be the bottom left-hand corner itself of the existing diagram, and the previous instructions will not apply.)

If you are not perceived as a motivational delegator, what needs to be attended to most, your *own* motivational capabilities, or the *organisation's*, or *both*?

Next, review the results of Checklists 8-11, which relate to the competencies required for effective leadership of change.

Finally, target just the three areas where you perceive, from the survey results, you have the greatest need for personal development (or, in the case of Section 7, organisational development). Then turn to the relevant chapters for guidance, as noted below.

Checklist	1	Planning	Chapter	3
	2	Organising		3
	3	Monitoring		3
	4	Decision-making		3
	5	Delegating		3
	6	*Individual* motivating		3
	7	*Organisation* motivating		3
	8	Communicating		8
	9	Adaptability		8
	10	Entrepreneurism		8
	11	Resilience		8

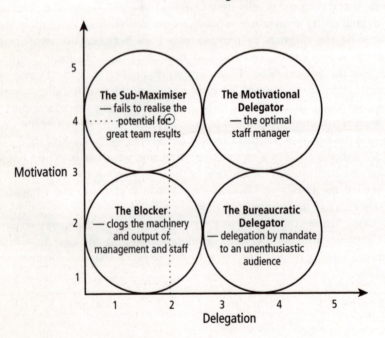

NB An example of plotting scores 4 and 2, the position-fix being shown by ⊙

3.

Primary Business Drivers

This section contains further information for Chapter 3.

By way of an example of primary business drivers, let us examine the case of Fred Poulos, the general manager of an autonomous division of a large manufacturing and distribution company. I helped Fred develop his hierarchy of drivers and expressed it in the form of a 'profit tree', as follows (in simplified format for example purposes). Although this example is a financial one, the same approach can be used with non-financial subjects.

The principal business objective in Fred's case is Return on Total Assets expressed as a percentage, as supported by the two main business drivers of Net Pre-tax Profit and Assets Employed in the Business. These two main drivers are supported by the secondary drivers of Sales, Operating Expenses, Fixed Assets and Current Assets, which in turn are supported by a range of supporting drivers.

Given the need to attain the principal business objective of maximising return on total assets, and by developing a complete hierarchy of drivers, Fred then determined which drivers were 'primary' — in other words, which drivers he was able to improve most and which had the greatest impact on improving his principal business objective, and which he therefore needed to prioritise. Fred's profit tree is shown in the following diagram. You may care to guess which drivers he considered primary (as defined above) at the time the profit tree was developed.

In addition to the profit tree, or hierarchy of drivers approach, enabling executives like Fred Poulos to determine their primary business drivers, and which ones to prioritise at any given time, the hierarchy can also be turned upside down and superimposed on the organisation structure of the business, with relevant subordinates and their teams being held accountable for results in primary business driver areas.

Fred Poulos did this with great success. He found that superimposing the profit tree on his organisation structure had a strongly unifying effect on his team — they all pulled together in the pursuit of maximising return on total assets, which they nearly doubled in three years!

The Profit Tree

Noting principal business objective
and main and secondary business drivers

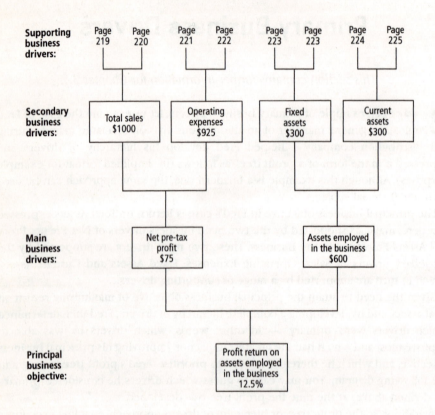

Primary Business Drivers

Supporting Business Drivers for Domestic Sales

Profit improvement action:	Redefine and expand total market	Prioritise selling and promotional activities towards 'growth' customer segments and products	Increase differential pricing	Pay incentives to sales force on basis of margin as well as sales
Profit improvement targets:	Increase market size by 7.5%	Increase market share by 1.0%	Increase prices by 7.5% on 20% of sales volume	Reduce discounts by 10%
$ value of profit improvement (based on sales of $1000):	$3.66	$4.88	$11.25	$10.00
Improves profit return on assets employed in the business by:	+0.6%	+0.8%	+1.9%	+1.7%

Supporting business drivers:

- Domestic market size: 500 units
- Domestic market share: 10%
- Average list price: $15
- Average discount: $2

Supporting business drivers:

- Domestic sales: 50 units
- Domestic price: $13

Supporting business driver:

- Domestic sales: $650 → To page 220

Secondary business driver:

- Total sales: $1000

From page 218

219

Supporting Business Drivers for Export Sales

Profit improvement action:	Appoint agents in new export markets	Concentrate on fastest growing export markets	Differentiate prices according to country potential	Provide 'free' product in place of discounts
Profit improvement targets:	Increase export market size by 40% at usual market share	Increase export market share by 0.5%	Increase prices by 6% on 20% of sales volume	Reduce $ effect of discounts by 10%
$ value of profit improvement (based on sales of $1000):	$1.04	$5.63	$5.46	$10.50
Improves profit return on assets employed in the business by:	+0.2%	+0.9%	+0.9%	+1.8%
Supporting business drivers:	Export market size 1500 units	Export market share 2.3%	Average list price $13	Average discount $3
Supporting business drivers:	Export sales 35 units		Export price $10	
Supporting business driver:		Export sales $350		
Secondary business driver:	Total sales $1000 (From page 218)			

From page 219

Primary Business Drivers

Supporting Business Drivers for Variable Expenses

Profit improvement action:	Reduce wastage and inprove yield	Set up 'joint gain' productivity program	Apply Pareto's principle: concentrate on the 20% which will generate 80% gain	Establish energy conservation program
Profit improvement targets:	Reduce raw material usage by 4%	Improve productivity by 4%	Profit improvement of 1.0% on sales	Reduce expenses by 8.5%
$ value of profit improvement (based on sales of $1000):	$7.00	$10.60	$10.00	$5.95
Improves profit return on assets employed in the business by:	+1.2%	+1.8%	+1.7%	+1.0%

Supporting business drivers:

- Raw materials $175
- Direct labour $265
- Research and development $15
- Other direct expenses $70

Supporting business driver:

Variable expenses $525

→ To page 222

Secondary business driver:

Operating expenses $925

From page 218

221

Supporting Business Drivers for Fixed Expenses

Profit improvement action:	Reorganise and reduce staffing	Reorganise and reduce staffing	Initiate cost reduction program
Profit improvement targets:	Reduce expenses by 10%	Reduce expenses by 7%	Reduce expenses by 8%
$ value of profit improvement (based on sales of $1000):	$11.50	$11.20	$10.00
Improves profit return on assets employed in the business by:	+1.9%	+1.9%	+1.7%

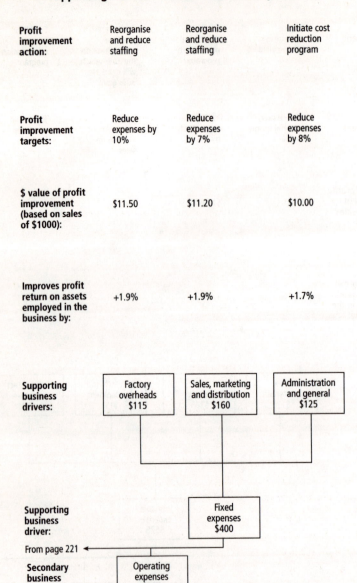

Supporting business drivers: Factory overheads $115 | Sales, marketing and distribution $160 | Administration and general $125

Supporting business driver: Fixed expenses $400

From page 221

Secondary business driver: Operating expenses $925

From page 218

Supporting Business Drivers for Fixed Assets

Asset reduction action:	Consolidate manufacturing and distribution and sell off excess equipment	Consolidate manufacturing, distribution and administration and sell off excess facilities
Asset reduction targets:	Reduce by 12.5%	Reduce by 15%
Value of asset reduction:	$22.50	$18.00
Improves profit return on assets employed in the business by:	+0.5%	+0.4%

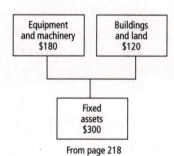

Supporting business drivers: Equipment and machinery $180 — Buildings and land $120

Secondary business driver: Fixed assets $300

From page 218

the bulletproof executive

Supporting Business Drivers for Current Assets

Asset reduction action:	Reduce collection period	Consolidate current accounts and centralise control	Install 'economic order quantity' ordering system	Improve production planning
Asset reduction targets:	Reduce by 22%	Cash reduction by 24%	Stock reduction by 25%	Work in progress reduction by 20%
Value of asset reduction:	$39.60	$14.40	$8.75	$10.00
Improves profit return on assets employed in the business by:	+0.9%	+0.3%	+0.2%	+0.2%

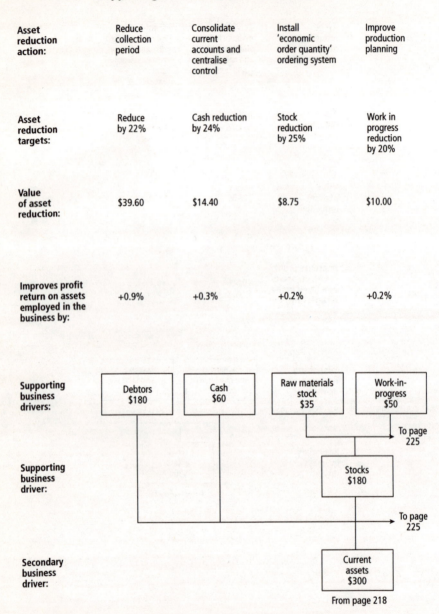

Supporting business drivers:
- Debtors $180
- Cash $60
- Raw materials stock $35
- Work-in-progress $50

To page 225

Supporting business driver:
- Stocks $180

To page 225

Secondary business driver:
- Current assets $300

From page 218

224

Primary Business Drivers

Supporting Business Drivers for Current Assets

Asset reduction action:	Improve the sell/make for stock decision-making process	Increase/renegotiate payment periods
Asset reduction targets:	Reduce by 20%	Increase by 15%
Value of asset reduction:	$19.00	$18.00
Improves profit return on assets employed in the business by:	+0.4%	+0.4%

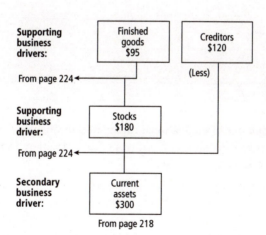

Supporting business drivers: Finished goods $95 — Creditors $120

From page 224

(Less)

Supporting business driver: Stocks $180

From page 224

Secondary business driver: Current assets $300

From page 218

4.

Optimising Job Fit, Self-motivation And Personal Performance

This section contains exercises for Chapter 4.

Refer to the definitions of occupational interests in Chapter 4, and rank them by order of your greatest interests first and your greatest disinterests last. Select your greatest interests, the ones you would particularly like to deploy in your job or work, and make a note of them here:

....
....
....
....
....
....
....
....
....
....
....
....

Refer to the definitions of motivational capabilities in Chapter 4, and rank them by order of your greatest capability first and your least capability last. Write down the full rank order of your capabilities here:

....
....
....
....
....
....
....
....
....
....
....
....
....
....

Now re-rank the above list of your motivational capabilities according to your level of enjoyment in using these capabilities.

....
....
....
....
....
....
....
....
....
....
....
....

Now turn to the Career Areas Matrix on page 228. Using a highlighter pen, draw horizontal lines across the page against your greatest interest areas and greatest motivational capabilities. Then check those career areas, listed A to L, which contain most of your interests and capabilities. Refer to the following code and Chapter 4 to ascertain which career areas seem to offer the closest match, referred to as 'job fit'.

- **A** Practical careers
- **B** Technical careers
- **C** Analytical careers
- **D** Scientific careers
- **E** Creative careers
- **F** Careers in design
- **G** People-oriented careers
- **H** Managerial careers
- **I** Enterprising careers
- **J** Entrepreneurial careers
- **K** Administrative careers
- **L** Professional services careers

Career Areas Matrix

Career Areas:	A	B	C	D	E	F	G	H	I	J	K	L
Interests:												
Scientific				✓								
Social				✓			✓	✓	✓		✓	
Persuasive					✓		✓	✓	✓	✓		✓
Literary					✓							
Artistic					✓	✓						
Clerical			✓								✓	✓
Practical	✓	✓			✓	✓	✓			✓		
Musical					✓							
Computational			✓	✓		✓					✓	✓
Outside	✓	✓										
Technical		✓				✓						
Medical		✓		✓			✓					
Motivational capabilities:												
Memory		✓	✓	✓		✓					✓	✓
Verbal					✓						✓	✓
Numeracy		✓	✓	✓		✓					✓	✓
Spatial	✓	✓	✓	✓	✓	✓			✓			
Perception		✓	✓	✓	✓	✓	✓	✓	✓	✓	✓	✓
Fluency					✓		✓	✓	✓	✓		✓
Reasoning		✓	✓	✓		✓	✓	✓	✓	✓	✓	✓
Creativity					✓	✓	✓			✓	✓	
Social					✓		✓	✓	✓		✓	✓
Clerical			✓								✓	

5.

Defining Leadership Traits

This section contains exercises for Chapter 5.

Refer to the definition and examples of leadership traits in Chapter 5. Next, on a scale of A to E (A representing output, and E representing people), where would you position yourself? Here is a further guide:

- A = largely output-oriented
- B = somewhat output-oriented
- C = output and people count equally (Try to avoid C unless it really sounds most like you!)
- D = somewhat people-oriented
- E = largely people-oriented

Now, on a scale of F to J (F representing control, and J representing creativity), where would you position yourself? This may help you further:

- F = largely controlling
- G = somewhat controlling
- H = control and creativity count equally
  (Try to avoid H unless it really sounds most like you!)
- I = somewhat creative
- J = largely creative

    Having positioned yourself on each scale honestly — and there are no right or wrong answers here — turn to the Leadership Traits: 'Position-fix' Matrix on page 230 and plot your positions. Draw two lines between your two positions on the vertical and horizontal lines, forming a square or a rectangle (see the example), and draw a prominent dot or small circle on the corner furthest from the centre, which becomes your 'position-fix'. (If your two positions are C and H, your position-fix will be the dead centre of the matrix and the previous instructions will not apply.) Next, transfer your position-fix to the Leadership Traits: 'Descriptions' Matrix on page 231.
    Study the matrix carefully; are the descriptions reflective of some of your leadership traits? Underline or highlight those descriptions which you feel are particularly reflective, and cross out those you disagree with.
    The third matrix, Leadership Traits: 'Labels' on page 232, provides name tags for the five main behaviour categories highlighted. Please don't feel affronted if you don't like the sound of your label!

the bulletproof executive

Having studied the matrices and assessed your own position-fix, an acid test is to undertake the same exercise, but from the perspective of the organisation for which you work, or most recently worked. What desirable leadership traits are sought by the organisation, and what traits are considered undesirable? What is the gap between the organisation's requirements and your own position-fix? What are you going to do to narrow the gap? As shown in Chapter 5, your options include *ignore it*, *attack it*, *change the organisation*, *change your attitude*, *change your traits* or *retreat*.

If you are considering joining a new organisation, does their perception of desirable leadership traits coincide with your position-fix? If so, then this bodes well for success. If not, it clearly signals 'danger'!

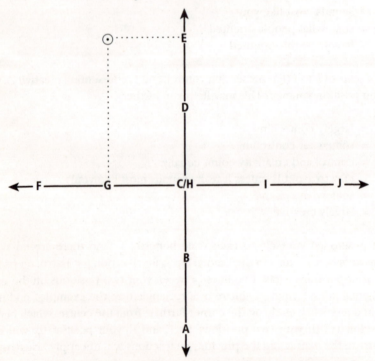

NB An example of plotting positions E and G, the position-fix being shown by ⊙

Leadership Traits: 'Descriptions' Matrix

People (↑) / **Output** (↓) / **Control** (←) / **Creativity** (→)

Upper-left (Control / People):
- paternalistic
- considerate of staff
- caring attitude
- natural attrition rather than retrenchment
- good staff benefits
- autocratic
- discipline
- not always trusting of staff
- tight control
- firm, directive management
- formal hierarchy
- controlled top-down communication
- self before team

Upper-right (Creativity / People):
- natural and inspirational leader
- customer-oriented
- empowerment of employees
- innovative
- flat organisational hierarchy
- open two-way communication
- learning and people development
- relates well to groups and individuals
- trusting of employees
- unstructured and non-directive
- team first, self second
- creative
- enthuses others

Lower-left (Control / Output):
- specialist
- tight control
- centralisation
- strategic business units
- administration
- local knowledge and perspective
- conforming to the rule-book
- continuation of the status quo
- conventional operations
- production-driven
- involved in detail
- logical problem-solver

Lower-right (Creativity / Output):
- global knowlege and perspective
- non-conformist
- entrepreneurial
- core competencies of organisation
- flexible
- decentralised control
- responsive to change
- pioneer and pathfinder
- financially astute
- uses initiative
- creative problem-solver
- broad-based general manager

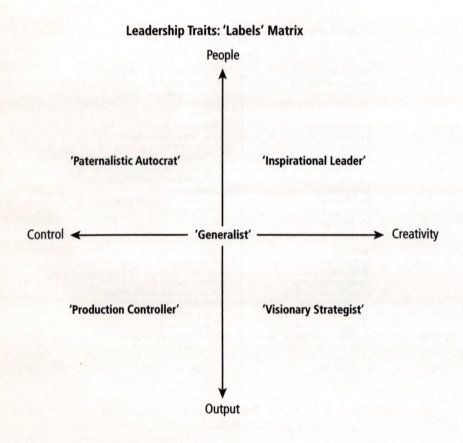

6.

Operating Style And Teamwork

This section contains exercises for Chapter 6.

The guidelines provided in this section of your Executive Armoury are designed to help you assess your own operating style and then the styles of your team members.

In Chapter 6, I pointed out that behaviour is the driver of operating style — check your behaviour by assessing the degree to which each of the following descriptions of behaviour sound like you.

Behaviour Category I

Hands-on, action-oriented, talks a lot, actively gives instructions, preoccupied with results, displays a strong output orientation, displays highly proactive behaviour.

Behaviour Category II

Hands-off, calm in nature, a good and active listener, friendly and approachable, reflective in evaluation of situations, invariably emphasises the human factor, exhibits highly receptive behaviour.

Now use the following answer guide for the above behaviour categories.

Behaviour Category I

- **A** Very like me
- **B** Quite like me
- **C** Some elements like me
- **D** Not particularly like me
- **E** Definitely not like me
- **Z** Sometimes I'm extremely like this, sometimes I'm extremely opposite to this

Behaviour Category II

- **F** Very like me
- **G** Quite like me
- **H** Some elements like me
- **I** Not particularly like me
- **J** Definitely not like me
- **Z** Sometimes I'm extremely like this, sometimes I'm extremely opposite to this

Now check how these letters of the alphabet relate to the following operating style categories, which are defined in Chapter 6. See if you agree with the definitions. If you do not, which of the operating style categories sound most like you? Some people have combinations of styles, sometimes with a main and subordinate style.

Commander/Doer:	A, B, I, J
Empathiser/Humanist:	D, E, F, G
Responder/Initiator:	A, B, F, G
Evaluator/Detailer:	D, E, I, J
Idea generator:	Z
All-rounder:	C, H

Now go through the same exercise for each of your team members and plot where you and each of the others are, by writing your and their initials on the Operating Styles Matrix in the relevant position for each team member.

The rest of Chapter 6 will reveal how to use all this information you have now derived.

Watch out for knights, rooks and clones, and try to help each team member to become a henchman!

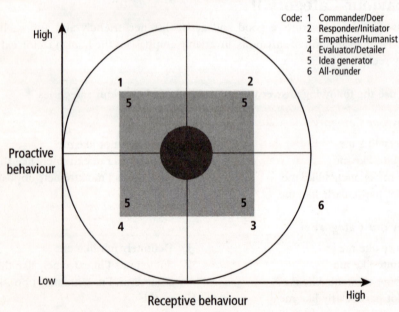

7.

Personal Chemistry And Fit

This section contains exercises for Chapter 7.

What are your 'atmospheric' needs, and to what extent does your existing or future organisation satisfy them? The following profile will help you to assess this, using Chapter 7 as a reference point for definitions and ideas. Read the chapter before completing the profile.

1. **Material needs:** *remuneration, safety and security*
   What I need:
   ....
   ....

   What the organisation provides:
   ....
   ....

   Gaps:
   ....
   ....

   How to close the gaps:
   ....
   ....
   ....

2. **Structural needs:** *degree and type of structure, bureaucracy and systems*
   What I need:
   ....
   ....

   What the organisation provides:
   ....
   ....

   Gaps:
   ....
   ....

   How to close the gaps:
   ....
   ....
   ....

3. **Behavioural needs:** *management style and interpersonal relationships*
   What I need:
   ....

   What the organisation provides:
   ....
   ....

   Gaps:
   ....
   ....

   How to close the gaps:
   ....
   ....
   ....

4. **Emotional needs:** *trust, social needs, esteem needs and sense of achievement*
   What I need:
   ....
   ....

   What the organisation provides:
   ....
   ....

   Gaps:
   ....
   ....

   How to close the gaps:
   ....
   ....
   ....

Summary

Overall perspective on gaps:
....
....
....
....
....

Overall perspective on how to close the gaps:
....
....
....
....
....

8.

How To Plan And Manage Restructures

This section contains exercises for Chapter 8.

The following represents a checklist of executive and manager actions required with their teams at each stage of the restructuring process, to ensure BP² — Best Principles and Best Practice.

Stage 1: Planning of Restructure

Planning can be either a good news or bad news story. Even the most confidential planning process imposes change on executive routines, and staff notice this. Those extra meetings, those off-site 'seminars', all generate signals and speculation that something is going on, 'probably another restructure'. The best planning environment is one where, through a climate of 'open management', staff all realise and accept that organisations have to respond to the changing external environment, and see this as representing opportunities.

Open management requires prioritising the *proactive leadership* of the restructuring process, *an open environment*, and the *encouragement of feedback* from direct reports.

Proactive leadership includes:
- a preparedness to discuss the needs for, and drivers of, change in organisational life today
- 'management by walking about' — rather than being office-bound behind closed doors
- frequent use of core statements emphasising the party line and the need for continuous adaptability in the face of ever-increasing external pressures.

An open environment requires that teams are encouraged to learn and to convert criticism to remedy — *making* necessary improvements rather than complaining about the need for improvements. Team meetings may also benefit from the chairmanship being rotated, and from participation in team meetings by others from elsewhere in the organisation experiencing change.

Encouragement of feedback requires further developing the means for upwards communication — feedback from the team and individuals about any issues or concerns. These matters need to be discussed and shared, and should be acted upon.

However, over the past few years when I have shared restructuring models of this nature with executives, I sometimes receive the initial response: 'If we suddenly start emphasising open management at the planning stage of a restructure, we are at risk of causing the worst case scenario — employees will read the signals that another restructure is being planned.'

My response is usually two-fold. First, you should graduate the open management approach and initiate it in the context of improving the organisation's management practices, rather than implying — or allowing it to be inferred — that a restructure is imminent. If one is imminent, the signals will be seen anyway and open management will improve the chances of success. Secondly, employees expect and prefer open management, and perform better as a result of it, and so executives should be practising it anyway. It's never too late or too soon to move further down the path of open management!

Stage 2: Launch of Restructure

The launch of a restructure will either be received with scepticism by staff, who feel they have seen it all before and believe it will not work, or it will be accepted positively and be seen as making sense. In order to ensure the latter, vision and principles need to be emphasised at this stage and the vision as to where the organisation is headed should be presented with impact. The principles — the guidelines on what is important to the organisation, and how it should operate — need to be shared and to gain group commitment.

The vision needs to emphasise benefits for all parties, and to be presented in a way that really means something to the listener. For example, rather than long-winded statements about continuous improvement, a short and sharp headline statement — such as, 'We will be the best in our industry' — is more effective. This may seem trite to senior management, but their intended audience, staff and customers, can understand and accept such headline statements.

Vision also needs to define how the organisation will look in terms of structure, as well as the impact the restructuring will have on teams and each individual. In fact, *all* the key elements of vision need to be emphasised — where, when, why and how: 'We will be the best in our industry within two years. Our customers deserve and expect this, and we will attain market leadership by providing uncompromising customer service and delivering best value for money. For this to happen we need to decentralise and work in independent business units based on each of our major product lines. You will be working in smaller work groups.'

Principles need to cascade down to individual teams, so the way each team should behave and operate should be discussed and agreed by team members. Behaviour is addressed at the individual level in terms of what is expected and what is unacceptable. The agreed principles and behaviours need to be referred to regularly, and represent the 'glue' between team members — 'the way we behave and operate around here'.

Stage 3: Break-up of the Old Structure

At the break-up stage and in the worst case scenario, resistance can often be fierce and a dogged determination not to accept the changes can prevail. However, a 'can-do' atmosphere can and needs to be created, by executives clearly detailing goals and roles. Goals should be specific and clearly understood, and new roles should be defined, sold to, and accepted by each affected individual.

To be meaningful, organisational vision and goals should be clearly linked to individual goals. Achievement or otherwise of individual goals needs to be monitored and any adverse variances quickly and positively addressed.

Roles are invariably altered at times of organisational change, usually with an emphasis on 'doing more with less, faster'. Therefore, it is a good opportunity to make jobs and work content more streamlined and thus more efficient. Efficiency improvements should be tested and modified as necessary on the run, to maximise effectiveness and productivity. No matter how well planned the restructure or the definition of new roles, modifications will always be necessary and are to be expected.

Stage 4: Recovery of the Organisation

As noted, it is estimated that two-thirds of restructures fail to achieve their goals within the desired timeframes. For recovery to happen more rapidly, teams need to start to feel empowered in their new roles in the new structure and be able to make decisions and act promptly. Self-improvement through education should continue to be encouraged. In this, the manager needs to delegate more, to enact the role of resource rather than controller, to monitor progress and to manage by exception.

Self-improvement also means that staff are encouraged to seek their own solutions, so that the work environment becomes more participative and less autocratic, and so that managers concentrate on leading from behind rather than 'micro-managing' from the front.

Stage 5: The Organisation Re-fires

For the organisation to re-fire, all parties need to 'win' at this stage, in the context of high levels of motivation, productivity and rewards. Motivation and productivity are optimised through a sense of achievement and commitment. For this to occur, staff need to own, believe in, and be inspired by the changes which have been implemented.

Rewards are two-way. The organisation derives bottom-line benefits, and so should individuals in order to create an 'I win-You win' situation. Individual rewards can be intrinsic, in the way that individual jobs have developed — inherently more interesting and satisfying — and extrinsic, via improved remuneration. Indeed, 'shared gain' needs to be the ethos as the organisation re-fires and benefits from improved productivity and bottom-line performance compared to pre-restructuring.

The diagram on page 240 highlights how to manage restructures successfully.

How to Plan and Manage Restructures

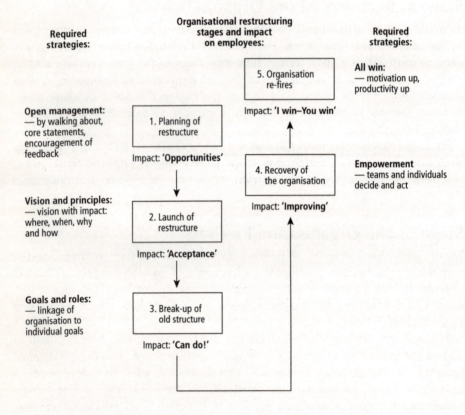

9.

How To Select An External Outplacement Provider

This section contains further exercises for Chapter 8.

Whenever I have outlined the essential elements of Best Principles, Best Practice (BP^2) with my client organisations, they have invariably agreed that BP^2 is the way to go, and yet have been unsure about how to ensure they are selecting the most appropriate provider to meet their needs. The following questions are helpful in this regard.

- *The values and principles of the downsizing organisation.* Is the organisation people-centred or dollar-driven? People-centred organisations believe that the ongoing profitability and sustained success of the organisation comes through putting people first — customers and employees. Such organisations are invariably progressive and profitable. Dollar-driven organisations prioritise the bottom line — the whole focus is on generating margin, cash flow and return on assets, particularly in the shorter term. People, particularly employees, are perceived as being an expendable resource in this regard — in other words, in making money — and staff turnover can be quite high ('burn and churn!').
- *The values and principles of the outplacement provider.* What type of firm would the downsizing organisation like to do business with — one which is also preoccupied with just making money in the shorter term, or one which prioritises 'making a difference' through the quality and performance of the consultants and the services it provides, and which makes a satisfactory return on investment as a result of this? Clearly, any sensible client organisation would wish to do business with a firm which is a viable and profitable business, but what is the preferred emphasis — an outplacement provider which is just dollar-driven, or a commercially astute and successful provider which genuinely wants to help people?

In order to check this out, the pedigrees of the owners, other stakeholders and leaders of the firm need to be evaluated. For example, are they just from entrepreneurial backgrounds, or have they a background in human resources management? Do they treat the business mainly as an investment, or are they in the business because they really want to make a difference to other people's lives (the fundamental principle behind real outplacement) and at the same time make a good living?

In making this assessment, what is their dividend and reinvestment policy? Do they distribute most of their profits to the shareholders or partners, or do they reinvest, say, 50 per cent of their profits on an ongoing basis for the continuous upgrade of their facilities and resources?

How are their consultants remunerated — by a commission or bonus related to sales (suggesting a preoccupation with generating business revenue, often at the expense of under-serviced outplacement candidates) or by a high base salary (allowing a preoccupation by consultants with generating outplacement candidate satisfaction)? What is the calibre (and therefore cost) of their consultants, office facilities and other resources (bearing in mind the axiom, 'you get what you pay for!')?

Next, the competitive characteristics of the outplacement provider need to be addressed.

- *The full service provider:* believes in and bases its whole operation on meeting the full outplacement needs of candidates in their career transitions. As a result, the *total* costs of downsizing and restructuring can be minimised.
  - Departing staff provided with full service outplacement are more inclined to leave the organisation favourably disposed towards it, in a good position to target and attain their next career steps within reasonable timeframes, and with self-esteem and dignity in better shape than might otherwise be the case.
  - This is transmitted back to the remaining staff, and the public image of the organisation is upheld: 'They had to downsize but they implemented it with sensitivity and really supported those leaving.'
  - The risks and costs associated with legal and court action are lessened, and the morale and productivity of remaining staff remain in good order.

- *The generic provider:* competes on price and is prepared to discount aggressively (and strip down the level of outplacement service), in order to win the work. Such providers simply cannot afford to take a full service approach, or they would go out of business. Working at the 'commodity' end of the outplacement industry, they can only afford, in effect, to go through the motions of outplacement — in other words, they provide a 'tick and flick', or production line, experience for candidates passing through their offices.

The generic provider can often turn out to be the most costly option.
  - Departing staff, sensing they are not getting good service, leave the organisation *unfavourably* disposed, and like customers with complaints, go around telling everybody how badly they have been treated.
  - Their first port of call is remaining staff, who become very concerned when they hear this. ('There, but for the grace of God, go I!' is often the response of remaining staff in such cases.) Morale and productivity drop, at a huge cost to the organisation, and talented staff (for whom there is always employment demand elsewhere) jump ship.
  - The second port of call of disaffected leavers can be the customer base, union representatives, industry contacts and the public at large. Customer and public perceptions of the organisation can nose-dive; sales can wane.
  - Some of the leavers increasingly seek to take individual or class action at the advice of the legal profession, at a potentially vast cost in terms of payouts, legal fees and management time on the part of the organisation, now caught on the back foot in defence mode.

Thus, the generic low-fee solution can often turn out to be the high-risk, high-cost and harmful solution.

In selecting the full service provider, on the other hand, and in selecting one whose values and principles focus on 'making a difference', the client organisation is virtually guaranteeing BP^2, *usually at lowest overall cost and risk*. This outcome is demonstrated in the following model.

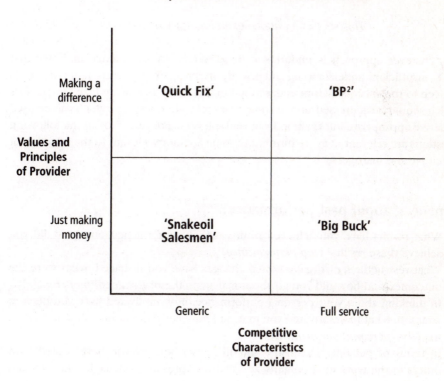

The consultancy that offers full service outplacement and prioritises 'making a difference' is the only provider to engage, whether your organisation is employee-centred *or* dollar-driven. This makes both humanistic *and* economic sense. 'Quick Fix' is too risky and potentially too costly if things go wrong. 'Big Buck' invariably channels too many dollars into the pockets of such providers. As for the travelling 'Snakeoil Salesmen' of the old Wild West, beware! They make their sales and know when to move on, before anyone can catch up with them and take them to task for their unfulfilled promises.

10.

Factors And Questions For Selection Interviews

This section contains exercises for Chapter 10.

Whatever approach is undertaken in selection, my experience indicates that insufficient understanding and priority attention in the selection of individuals is given to the success factors as described in this book. Below are listed the factors which should be addressed, and in some cases relevant questions which can be used to derive appropriate information from senior-level candidates. Not all the following questions are relevant in every hiring, and some are more relevant to the selection of executive and managers.

'Openers' about past performance:

- What results have you achieved from your job performance, and how did you achieve these results? *(job performance)*
- What restructures or organisational changes have you managed, what were the outcomes, and how did you go about managing them? *(leadership of change)*
- In thinking about your personal performance, how motivated have you been in your job, what has motivated you in it, and how has this caused you to behave in the job? *(personal performance)*
- In terms of personal 'chemistry' and 'fit', describe how you have related with others in the work environment, and with the prevailing management style and organisational culture. How would others have described your personal chemistry and fit? *(atmospherics)*

Job performance:

- Describe the management practices you have prioritised, how you have managed staff and the results from this. *(management practices)*
- What did you prioritise as the primary business drivers in your last job? How did you prioritise them? What outcomes were achieved, via what actions, in these areas? *(primary business drivers)*
- To what extent have you prioritised the tracking of 'futures' — the developing external environment? What has this entailed, how have you undertaken it, and what were the results? *(futures)*

Atmospherics:

- In thinking about your needs and expectations of any new job or employer, what levels of remuneration and other material items (eg car, office, leave and notice periods) do you need to satisfy you? *(material needs)*
- In terms of structure, what degree of formality or informality in terms of business processes and systems, work planning and the inevitable bureaucracy, suit you best? *(structural needs)*
- Regarding management style, describe the characteristics of the ideal line manager to whom you have reported. *(behavioural needs — management style)*
- Regarding interpersonal relationships, describe the ideal personal characteristics of those with whom you have worked. *(behavioural needs — interpersonal relationships)*
- In the past, to what degree have you felt there is two-way trust between employer and employee, a social working environment and a sense of achievement? Examples? *(emotional needs)*

Leadership traits:

- How controlling have you been as an executive or manager, and how have you controlled others? *(control)*
- How creative have you been? Describe any examples of your creativity in the past. *(creativity)*
- How output-oriented have you been, and how have you displayed any orientation towards output? *(output)*
- How people-oriented have you been, and how have you displayed any orientation towards people? *(people)*
- Have you been more oriented towards controlling or creativity, and how have you previously demonstrated this? *(This and the next question help to determine leadership traits.)*
- Have you been more oriented towards output or people, and how have you previously demonstrated this? *(leadership traits: production controller, paternalistic autocrat, inspirational leader, visionary strategist)*

Team make-up:

- Describe your usual operating style in a team environment.
- Of the following six descriptions, which best describes your operating style and how can you demonstrate this?
    — directing other people and working energetically to get results *(Commander/Doer)*
    — seeking to understand others, communicate well and lead enthusiastically *(Responder/Initiator)*
    — being amicable and people-oriented rather than production-oriented *(Empathiser/Humanist)*

- being analytical, logical, a planner and organiser *(Evaluator/Detailer)*
- developing concepts, being creative, seeing endless possibilities, and being renowned perhaps for occasionally showing some extremes in behaviour *(Idea generator)*
- exhibiting balance and flexibility, with predictable and consistent behaviour *(All-rounder)*

• Having decided on your primary style, give examples of what this has meant in practice, in the way you work with teams and other people.

Politics, power and influence:

• How have you handled organisational politics, power and influence in the past? Examples?
• How have you sold yourself, networked, developed allies (internal and external) and negotiated your way to personal success? Examples?

Leadership of change:

• How accommodating have you been of change? Examples?
• How adaptable have you been? Examples? *(adaptability)*
• How innovative and accommodating of risks have you been? Examples? *(entrepreneurism)*
• How resilient have you been? Examples? *(resilience)*
• How have you shown open and two-way communication? Examples? *(open, two-way communication)*
• How adept have you been at group presentations, and how have you gone about preparing and delivering them? *(group presentations — process of delivery)*

Job fit:

• How would you describe your main occupational interests? *(interests)*
• How would you describe those capabilities you possess which motivate you when they can be used in your work? *(motivational capabilities)*
• How would you describe your values — those 'non-negotiables' in the way you work and live? *(values)*

Career ownership:

• What are your longer-term career objectives and directions, and to what degree do you believe it is the organisation's responsibility or your own responsibility that these are met?

Attraction, retention and development of talent:

• To what degree in the past have you been able to align your personal goals with the goals of the organisation for which you worked? Describe how you have attained any alignment. *(personal career alignment)*

- To what degree have you ensured that the personal goals of those whom you are hiring can be aligned to the goals of the organisation? Examples? *(career alignment of new hires)*

Dismissal avoidance:

- What experience have you had of being part of a formal performance appraisal and management process which includes performance improvement programs when job performance is less than satisfactory? How have you reacted to such processes and programs? Examples? *(performance appraisal and improvement processes)*

All the above are examples of areas potentially needing assessment, and the types of questions potentially to be asked of candidates. The needs of differing job positions and organisations will vary, and so the factors to be included and the types of questions to be asked will need to be adjusted on a case-by-case basis.

11.

A Bulletproof Career Planning And Strategy Development Process

This section contains exercises for Chapter 11.

The process of career planning and strategy development is much like business planning. The stages are very similar, and most executives and managers should feel very comfortable with this. Instead of guiding the direction of the business, you are guiding your own career direction. This section explains the steps in a Bulletproof career planning process.

Bulletproof Career Planning

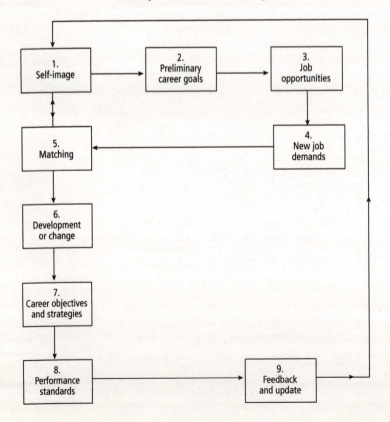

We begin in the top left corner of the diagram with our *self-image*, derived from our honest self and career assessment in Chapter 11. We should also try to get feedback from as many sources as possible in order to reality-check and finalise this self-image.

Derived from this self-image and a study of the career environment, we need to come up with a list of activity choices — jobs or activities which we would like to be involved in, in the future. These form your preliminary *career goals*. These activities may be sought within your present job, or may only be available outside your present job. You should be as specific as possible. For example, 'move sideways to a new job position' or 'move up to a higher executive level' are too vague. 'Attaining a chief executive position within four years' is much better — it helps you to work out specific strategies to achieve your goal.

Defining your *job opportunities* comes next. Decide which job positions, relating and leading to your career goals in step 2, are available to you. You will need to do some research to find out which desired opportunities may be available within your own job or organisation, and which are only available externally. Draw on your own experience, and on the experiences of others, as well as on relevant articles, professional publications, and other desk and library research.

You will now need to analyse the *demands of the new jobs* you have picked out for consideration. What kind of aptitudes, competencies, operating styles, and so forth are required to fulfil these new jobs? Examine this issue in three ways: (1) the demands of the new jobs as you see them; (2) the demands of the new jobs as seen by others in your organisation or contact network; and (3) the demands of the new jobs as seen by people who are actually performing them now, perhaps elsewhere. These three views may differ, and you will need to reconcile them somehow in your mind, in order to arrive at a realistic assessment of your ideal new job position.

Next comes *matching* the new job demands in step 4 with your own self-image. You will either need to develop the skills and attributes necessary to grow into the new job role, or you may have to abandon it in favour of something with a better match to your self-image.

If you have identified areas of mismatch and conflict, either your career goals must be adjusted, your values and priorities reconsidered, or your skills and capabilities in certain areas upgraded, ie *development or change*. In some cases, external conditions, such as organisational policies or the attitudes of family and friends, may be causing the conflict. Sometimes these external blocks can be changed, but often they cannot. In the latter case, accept this as a reality, and find other ways of satisfying your career goals, or adjust your goals accordingly.

Now you are ready to formulate your *career objectives and strategies*. These are both your specific career objectives based on steps 1 to 6 of the career planning process, and the methods and actions you will use to achieve these objectives. I will address career strategies in more detail later.

Commitment to performance comes next. You must set *performance standards* for yourself, and monitor your progress towards achieving your career objectives. Make these standards specific and measurable, such as 'a 15 per cent increase in my sales force's performance within one year', or 'a salary increase of 7.5 per cent by next

March'. Try to make this performance commitment to those who have some stake in it — your chairman or CEO, or your partner.

Establishing specific performance standards will serve as a basis on which to provide you with necessary *feedback*. Seek from those around you at work, and take heed of, their feedback on how you are progressing, and integrate it into your store of experience. Also, use it to modify your career development strategies or your self-image.

Now we have come full circle in a continuous career planning process.

Where to from Here? Strategy Development

Once you have completed the stages of self-assessment and goal-setting, identified opportunities and job requirements, matched job demands with your self-image, and identified areas of harmony and conflict, you are ready to work on specific strategies.

Looking at where you are now in terms of your career, you must decide where you want to go, and how you will get there. What are your options in working towards the achievement of your career objective? Here are some general career strategies which may be available to you: *'status quo'*, *moving within your existing organisation*, *moving within your business sector*, *changing your career* and *self-employment*.

'Status quo' means staying put, at least for the time being, for positive reasons which you have worked out. It does not mean passive resignation or 'giving up' on your career objective. For example, you may decide that your career objective can be met within your present position, or perhaps you decide to decrease your career expectations temporarily, in light of present circumstances, and obtain more satisfaction from your present job, or from your family or home life.

Another possibility is that you may want to 'bide your time' until the economy improves, or until you can obtain more information on alternative career development possibilities. Don't neglect this as a very real option to be considered — just make sure you consider it in a positive way, and not as an excuse for doing nothing.

The second strategy is to *move within your existing organisation*. This can involve a move centrally, upwards, sideways or even downwards. A move centrally means expanding the professional boundaries of your existing job, thereby increasing your value to the organisation and becoming perceived as a greater 'centre of excellence' — with this central expansion often comes additional influence and even power. Don't underestimate the potential for central expansion!

A sideways move, offering new responsibilities, may be just what you need to meet your goals. It may not be possible to move upwards at the present time — and this may have to be a longer-term, rather than shorter-term objective. Upwards promotion is a tough proposition in today's smaller, flatter organisations.

A sideways move usually means a transfer to another area, to take up a position at the same level as your present one. This may be a viable option for you if you want to remain with your existing organisation but feel you are better suited to another functional or geographical area, or department, or you just cannot get along with the people with whom you currently work.

A downwards move involves giving up some responsibility. This may seem to be a step backwards, but for some people it is really what they need in order to meet their career objective. An example is technical executives who have been promoted to senior management positions and find they can no longer practise what they do best. Not everyone is cut out for management, and such people may actually serve their needs and career objective best by moving downwards.

The third strategy is to *move within your business sector*. Perhaps you find your career advancement blocked in your present organisation, or you foresee problems in the form of business downsizing, mergers, reorganisations, and so forth. Sometimes the only way to move, is to move out. This option is becoming increasingly popular, with executives and managers switching jobs or companies on average every three to five years.

Perhaps the move is an involuntary one — you have no choice in the matter. We are going through an unprecedented period of restructuring and downsizing. If you find yourself in this situation, your options have been reduced in number, but you can still have several to work with. Indeed, in some cases it may be the best thing that can have happened.

An involuntary move can motivate you, as it motivated me, to undertake this process of self and career assessment. There is every possibility that, with greater understanding and use of effective career planning, you will go on to bigger and better things!

The fourth strategy is to *change your career*. This option is also for those who want to leave their present career path and do something completely different. This may seem quite drastic, but it is being undertaken more and more by people who have spent many years at one job and who find they are bored. It may also be an appropriate option if you are on the receiving end of a dismissal, as was my case, when I received my 'bullet'! After recovering, regrouping and reframing my career thinking, and having now served my apprenticeship in my new chosen career, I will never look back, even though getting to this point has been painful for myself and for my family. Out of adversity comes strength!

Like me, many executives may want to start using skills and abilities they know they possess, but have not been able to use in their present line of work. A complete career change, if planned carefully, can be the answer to career objective attainment for some.

Switching careers may also be a strategic move on your part, if you foresee that the demand for your present capabilities will drop off drastically in the years ahead, and if you want to position yourself in a sector with growth potential. Choosing this option demands a careful investigation of career opportunities and careful matching, as discussed earlier, and, like the previous option, will entail a comprehensive job search.

The final strategy is *self-employment*. There is a growing interest in the option of self-employment. 'Going it alone', 'taking the plunge' — whatever you may call it — is definitely not for everyone! It involves a certain degree of risk, and demands certain personal characteristics, in order to carry it off successfully. The other side of the coin is that it can be highly rewarding, and one way to achieve many of your career and personal goals.

Many people cannot conceive of wanting to take that risk. Many others cannot conceive of working for anyone but themselves. Only you can decide if this is the option to take, to satisfy your goals. If this option is interesting to you, make sure you do some careful investigation of such things as the market for your product or service, the costs of starting up and getting established, the demands on your time and energy, and the personal characteristics required for such a role.

An alternative, lower-risk form of self-employment may be contracting or consulting, for which the growth in demand is exponential. However, so is the growth in supply of available talent, and so make sure that you really do have something to offer, over and above the sea of faces competing with you for the contracting or consulting options.

Of the five general options we have looked at, one may seem to jump out at you as the obvious choice. Resist the temptation to ignore all the other options in favour of one right now. Your 'hunch' may prove to be correct, but you are trying to reduce your chances of making a costly error.

Establishing a career objective which is attainable within your existing employer organisation — rather than assuming that the grass is greener in another organisation — in all likelihood makes a lot of sense and may well be an appropriate strategy for most of us. On the other hand, if you can really believe your career objective cannot be met within your existing employer organisation, then you may well need to consider alternative employment environments and develop an appropriate career development plan. This may be difficult to compile at first. However, rigorous investigation of the career areas you are targeting, as well as of potential employer organisations, should assist in this process.

12.

Financial Planning

This section contains further information for Chapter 11.

There has to be an ultimate aim or use for your money you earn from working. That ultimate purpose may be to enjoy a chosen lifestyle, both now (which is relatively simple) and in the future. Just as you have a corporate plan, you should also have a personal plan. This should cover items such as:
- when you want to retire
- what help, if any, you want to give your children
- what you want to do about lifestyle decisions such as upgrading your home, moving house or buying a weekender
- what cars, boats, antiques, holidays and other items you want, and whether you will save for them or provide for them out of your earnings, now and in retirement.

A personal plan can help you to work out the best way of saving. For instance, superannuation is very tax-efficient, but it is totally useless to a 45-year-old who wants to buy a boat at age 50. Similarly, negative gearing is not to be recommended for someone two or three years from retirement, and do you really need a discretionary trust if you are single?

By discussing with a financial planner some of your lifestyle objectives and goals, you have a realistic chance of them recommending an appropriate structure for saving, whether this is in your own or your spouse's name, or in the form of a family trust, superannuation fund or company, as well as various suitable investments. For instance, if you wanted to buy a boat in a year's time, shares or property are inappropriate investments as they can move down as well as up in value and have significant costs of acquisition and disposal. However, if the money is to be used in 20 years' time, shares or property can provide potential gains.

In financial planning, it is important to consider your objectives in the following order: (1) your lifestyle — what you are trying to achieve with your money; (2) investments; and (3) taxation. Plans often fail because taxation is the primary purpose of investment. Remember that for every dollar that is lost, the Tax Office only pays the first 48.7¢. Frankly, it is better to make a dollar and pay the tax than to lose the dollar and only have half the loss subsidised.

It is interesting to consider how some relatively wealthy people in their fifties and sixties acquired their funds (apart from inheritances). Often it has been through saving regularly, possibly fairly small amounts, by selecting the right growth assets and by taking advantage of legitimate tax breaks such as imputation credits or depreciation allowances; rarely is it through going into a scheme that is tax-driven.

As a contrast, some people who have been on very high incomes (say, more than $200 000 a year) have a conspicuous lifestyle, but own very few net assets and have a fairly poverty-stricken retirement to look forward to. This is often due to high levels of borrowing, investment in assets that don't perform or fail, and excessive expenditure. Careful compounding and growth provide good wealth creation, although this is no 'get rich quick' scheme. It is more a slow but sure method of building up assets.

If you are retrenched, you may not know when you will be working again. New employment may be as a contractor, in a job with a large corporation or a small company, or you might set up your own business. Normally, I recommend the following strategy:

1. Use the redundancy payment and possibly part of your superannuation to repay your mortgage. This is conditional on the mortgage being redrawable — in other words, it can be increased should you run out of cash. If that option is not available, then there needs to be some emergency cash until a new job is obtained.
2. Check on any Social Security benefits that may be available. This includes Job Search Allowance and Family Allowances. The strategy in step 1 above can also often maximise benefits.
3. Ensure that you have adequate life insurance cover until your position is settled. Using your old employer's scheme on some form of continuation policy is often the easiest method.
4. In the short term place your superannuation money and, in some cases, the *ex-gratia* part of your redundancy payout into one or more no-entry/no-exit fee, cash approved deposit funds. The money can remain there until age 65. This is not a good long-term investment, but it takes the pressure off and will earn roughly the same rate of return as an interest-earning bank account. Frankly, your best investment is a new job; once a new position is secured, long-term investments can be considered. At that stage the options are as follows:

    (i) Use the new employer's superannuation fund. Some employers have very good funds, and it may be worthwhile rolling money over into that fund. Or you may be better off making your own arrangements. Frequently, with a defined benefit scheme, it is worthwhile considering buying prior years of service.

    (ii) Withdraw the money if, say, you are moving abroad or need it to set up a business (subject to superannuation preservation constraints). Some taxation, depending on age, will be payable.

    (iii) Use growth rollovers — that is, approved deposit funds and deferred annuities. These have portfolios comprising some or all of local and overseas shares, local and overseas fixed interest, property and cash. Usually these are a very good long-term investment, although they can move up and down in the short term.

    (iv) Set up your own superannuation fund. This is often recommended for contractors or the self-employed, or for people who want to have direct investments such as property or shares.

(v) Use your superannuation money to provide an income. This can be done if benefits are unpreserved and could be useful where a business has been set up but income is required in the first year. The superannuation money will not grow in value; however, lump sum tax will not be payable to access the income in this way and, at the end of term, it can always be placed into a rollover or superannuation fund or withdrawn, as mentioned above.

Quite simply, when you are retrenched, your first priority should be to concentrate on your best investment, which is to secure a new position, rather than start worrying about superannuation money or whether one fund manager is better than a direct share, or vice versa. Once that has been secured, then long-term financial planning should take place.

Contributed by Robert Schaverien, Bleakleys Limited, Sydney City Office, Australia.

13.

Your Own Business

This section contains further exercises for Chapter 11.

Self-evaluation

To determine how your personal background relates to success in independent business, complete the following table by ticking the appropriate column.

	Somewhat (✓)	No (✓)	Yes (✓)
I feel that I'm confident, conscientious resilient and decisive.	☐	☐	☐
I'm usually quite active, certainly self-motivated, ambitious and hard-working.	☐	☐	☐
People might describe me as practical, perceptive, good at reasoning, fairly creative and able to get on well with others.	☐	☐	☐
They might also describe me as fluent, persuasive, fairly independent and quick-witted.	☐	☐	☐
I am experienced in such functions as selling, marketing, staff management, accounting and finance.	☐	☐	☐
I want to start a business in a field where I have had substantial experience.	☐	☐	☐
I have one-and-a-half to two times the personal resources I need to tide me over, in the event that the business takes longer to get going than I had anticipated.	☐	☐	☐
I have managed a small business successfully before.	☐	☐	☐
I have experience working in a small business at the non-managerial level.	☐	☐	☐
I have always been successful in my career.	☐	☐	☐
TOTALS:			

Multiply the total of your 'Yes's by three, and add this subtotal to your subtotal of 'Somewhat's. A score of over 25 is very encouraging, and over 20 is fairly encouraging; a score below 15 should send out danger signals!

Business Feasibility

The following are the main steps for evaluating the feasibility of a new business.

Marketplace:
- What is the total demand for similar products or services in the market you will be serving?
- Based on your business's competitive strengths and weaknesses, how much are you likely to sell?
- How tough will it be, and how long will it take, to get established?

Operational matters:
- What facilities and equipment do you need? At what cost?
- What supplies and staff do you need, and at what cost?
- Are all these available, at a cost you can afford?

Financial matters:
- What sales revenue are you likely to generate in the short, mid and longer term?
- What are your direct expenses — for supplies and staff — and what margin on sales does this leave you?
- What are your indirect expenses — for overheads and administration — and how much profit does this leave you?
- How much cash outflow will you experience before you start breaking even? When will you break even?
- Where do you get financing, and at what cost and risk? Do you really want to put at risk your savings or the equity in your home?

Business planning:
- Is all the above succinctly written up in a plan in order to help you evaluate business feasibility and raise finance (if necessary)?

Overall assessment:
- Given the risks associated with independent business, does it generate a sufficient financial return on your investment in it, and on your time and effort?
- Does it utilise your strengths and avoid your weaknesses?
- Can it be financed economically and at a satisfactory level of risk?
- Should you go ahead, or should you try something else?

Buying a Business

Rationale for buying:
- At least *one* of the following should apply:
  - Buying a business is the only way to enter the market.
  - It is the best way to acquire a new product or service.
  - It is easier/less risky than starting a new business.
  - It eliminates a major competitor.
  - An established business operation is a prerequisite for success.

- *All* of the following should apply:
  — The business is a good personal 'fit'.
  — The business is/will be profitable.
  — The business has good management or will respond well to new management.
  — The business is/will be generating cash.

Selection:
- Which business sectors offer greatest profitable growth potential?
- Which customers, and products or services sold, offer greatest potential?
- Which businesses offer the potential for utilising your strengths and avoiding your weaknesses in such areas as sales and marketing, operations, personnel and organisation, finance and planning?
- Which businesses fit best in terms of size, profitability, location, management and operating performance, given all the foregoing?

Approaching possible sellers:
- Tailor-make your approach to each shortlisted business:
  — Why may they wish to sell their business?
  — How can they benefit by selling it to you?
- Arrange an initial 'exploratory' meeting with the owner and find out as much as you can about the business and the level of interest in selling it to you.

Detailed evaluation:
- Assuming interest exists, ask for copies of the last three to five years' financial statements of the business and discuss them with an independent accountant who is experienced in small business.
- With the accountant, physically inspect the business, meet with customers and suppliers, and interview staff to gain additional insights.
- Familiarise yourself with local, state and federal government regulations and licence requirements.

Negotiating:
- Try to agree first with the seller, the underlying main principles to be followed in the purchase:
  — the formula for valuing the business
  — how long they will stay during the handover to you
  — how and when the purchase of the business will be paid for.
- Exchange letters of intent, summarising these principles.
- Conduct a very detailed review of the business, including legal aspects, asset valuation (writing down old stock), and a full risk assessment of liabilities. Engage the services of an appropriately experienced lawyer and accountant to advise and assist in this.
- Draw up a formal agreement with a solicitor and an accountant experienced in buy/sell agreements.

The Business Plan

Business planning is like developing and following a road map. Without one, it will take longer and be more risky and costly to arrive at your destination — in other words, to achieve your business goals and aspirations. Business planning forces you to think through the options for profitable growth, and to consolidate these thoughts into a blueprint for the way ahead.

If you receive start-up or growth financing, your banker will be more positive if you can demonstrate well-developed objectives and strategies, in the form of a concise and readable business plan. Typical contents might include:

A brief executive summary:
- a description of the business
- the finance required and for what purpose
- the security you will offer
- a summary of earnings and projections.

Prepare this summary *last*, but present it *first* in your business plan.

Background:
- the history of the existing business
- its legal status of proprietorship, partnership or limited company, and the date of commencement or incorporation
- the names and addresses of the owners and the percentage of the business they own.

Sales and marketing:
- the total market for the business
- the business's target market
- its competition and relative market share
- its competitive marketing strengths
- past sales and future positions
- risks perceived and how to manage/offset these
- pricing policy
- payment terms and credit policy
- promotional plans
- methods of selling and distribution.

Products and services:
- a description of the products and services, with an assessment of their competitive strengths and weaknesses
- patents, trade secrets and other technical advantages
- special processes or technologies used
- a review of the market, customers, business sector and outlook.

Operational aspects:
- provide diagrams of work flow if applicable
- quality control
- inventory control
- availability of supplies and materials, costs and terms
- job descriptions of managers and staff, along with an organisation chart
- salaries and wages
- production cost estimates
- operations time schedule
- key events and decision points.

Facilities:
- description of location
- reason for location
- land and site plan, value of land and buildings, including any necessary installation of services
- machinery and equipment required
- costs and installation charges
- from whom and where purchases are to be made.

Organisation and management:
- how the business is organised and managed
- brief biographies of key personnel
- remuneration of managers and staff.

Financial plan:
- capital requirements and sources of financing
- profit and loss statements, and balance sheets for the present and preceding three years
- three-year projections, cash flow budgets, pro forma profit and loss statements, pro forma balance sheet, and break-even chart.

Summary of assumptions and critical risks:
- Attachments should include resumés of key personnel, benefits to the community, and any other supporting documents, depending on the nature of the business.
- In your written presentation, be thorough but concise. The more relevant details supplied to support the application, the more likely you are to achieve your business objectives and raise the required finance.

References:
- your bank and others with whom you have had financial dealings, including types of previous loans, terms, etc
- your accountant, lawyer and other professionals with whom you have had business relationships.

14.

Career- And Capability-oriented Resume/Profile

This section contains further information for Chapter 12.

Career-oriented Profile

CONFIDENTIAL RESUME/PROFILE

JOHN BASSETT
Phone: 9999–9999 (BH); 8888–8888 (AH)

CAREER OBJECTIVE
To combine my substantial senior line management, human resources and management consulting experience into a **senior human resources executive and change-agent role**, with the objective of moving major organisations and their operating subsidiaries into customer-oriented, competitive and progressive operating entities.

CAREER SUMMARY
Some 10 years of diverse line management experience culminating in the general managership of a medium-sized group of manufacturing and marketing companies.

During this time, accomplishments in all aspects of human resources management and development, particularly while a member of the personnel department of one of the most progressive employee-centred groups of companies in the world.

Over 10 years' management consulting experience, with a particular emphasis on change management from both human resources and return on investment perspectives, including periods of contract management as CEO of both service and manufacturing organisations.

CAREER HIGHLIGHTS

1986 to now   **Foremost Consulting Pty Ltd, Sydney**
Managing Director and Management Consultant

Responsible for the profitable growth and development of this medium-sized practice which employs 19 consultants and 10 administration staff, and which provides strategy and operations improvement consulting and contracting services to mid- to larger-sized organisations.

- Turned around a consulting practice from substantial loss to more than 20 per cent net profit on sales, and doubled sales revenue — all over a two-year period, through effective marketing and cohesive team leadership.

- Developed and implemented a patient-oriented and innovative form of health care delivery, and created significant cultural, organisational and operational change in private health funds, government departments and major hospitals.

- Led the management consulting division of a 'Big 6' accountancy firm from responsive 'all things to all people' consulting, to more proactive methodology-driven consulting.

- Moved a substantial operating division of a major food group from a production orientation to a key account service orientation.

- Via customer service surveys and training, coupled with organisational change and operating systems development, converted a computer data centre from a supply/technical orientation into a customer service/functional orientation.

- Acted as a catalyst for the fusion of strategic direction into organisational change, in terms of the management, organisation and motivation of managers and staff, for a major computer company.

1978–1985   **Canadian Oilfield Manufacturers Association, Canada**
Business Development Director and Independent Management Consultant

Responsible for the strategic and membership development activities of this medium-sized trade association, along with government liaison and export market development.

- More than doubled the membership base and income of the association through cost-effective targeted direct marketing and member services development.

- Changed the way the oilfield manufacturing sector viewed its market position and revenue source, by converting its focus and operational activity from domestic supply and sales, to that of export and technology transfer, with significant results in the Asia–Pacific region.

- Developed and implemented numerous change management, human resources planning, organisational restructuring, job evaluation, performance appraisal and skills training programs in diverse industrial and business settings.

1975–1977   **Lucas Marine Ltd, UK**
            Director and General Manager

Responsible for the development and implementation of strategic direction and performance improvement of this medium-sized group of five businesses.

- Turned around this medium-sized group of manufacturing and marketing companies from significant loss/no direction to positive cash flow/clear strategic direction.

Pre-1975   **The Mars Group, UK, Jameson's Chocolates, UK, and Hassan Abdal Cadet College, Pakistan**

Various line and staff management roles, having commenced my career as a volunteer teacher overseas.

ACADEMIC QUALIFICATIONS

Institute of Management Consultants of Alberta, Canada
Certified Management Consultant, by examination: marketing major; private study.

Slough College of Technology, UK
Postgraduate Diploma in Management Studies: behavioural studies, business analysis, marketing and management accountancy majors; evening class course.

Hendon & Waltham Forest Technical Colleges, UK
Distinction in the Higher National Certificate in Business Studies: economics and accounting majors; evening class course.

Eastbourne College, UK
2 'A' levels in English and German and 11 'O' levels; Royal Air Force Flying Scholarship also awarded.

PROFESSIONAL AFFILIATIONS AND TRAINING

- Fellow of the Australian Institute of Management and Institute of Company Directors.
- Member of the Australian Human Resources Institute.
- As a human resources professional, trained and proficient in numerous techniques, including organisation and customer services surveys, focus groups, management assessment, psychological testing, career planning, downsizing, and change and revitalisation management.

PERSONAL DETAILS
Languages: some French, some German.
Interests: sailing, skiing and family activities.

Address:

Phone numbers: Home:

                  Business:

Capability-oriented Profile

CONFIDENTIAL RESUME/PROFILE

JOHN BASSETT
Phone: 9999–9999 (BH); 8888–8888 (AH)

CAREER OBJECTIVE
To combine my substantial senior line management, human resources and management consulting experience into a **senior management consultant and change-agent role**, with the objective of moving major organisations and their operating subsidiaries into customer-oriented, competitive and progressive operating entities.

CAREER SUMMARY
Some 10 years of diverse line management experience culminating in the general managership of a medium-sized group of manufacturing and marketing companies.

During this time, accomplishments in all aspects of human resources management and development, particularly while a member of the personnel department of one of the most progressive employee-centred groups of companies in the world.

Over 10 years' management consulting experience, with a particular emphasis on change management from both human resources and return on investment perspectives, including periods of contract management as CEO of both service and manufacturing organisations.

Management Consulting and Change-Agent Experience:
- Moved a substantial operating division of a major food group from a production orientation to a key account service orientation.
- Via customer service surveys and training, coupled with organisational change and operating systems development, converted a computer data centre from a supply/technical orientation into a customer service/functional orientation.
- Changed the way an important manufacturing sector viewed its market position and revenue source, by converting its focus and operational activity from domestic supply and sales, to that of export and technology transfer, with significant results.

- Developed and implemented a patient-oriented and innovative form of health care delivery, and created significant cultural, organisational and operational change in private health funds, government departments and major hospitals.

Senior Business Management Experience:
- Turned around a consulting practice from substantial loss to more than 20 per cent net profit on sales, and doubled sales revenue — all over a two-year period, through effective marketing and cohesive team leadership.
- Led the management consulting division of a 'Big 6' accountancy firm from responsive 'all things to all people' consulting, to more proactive methodology-driven consulting.
- Turned around a medium-sized group of manufacturing and marketing companies from significant loss/no direction to positive cash flow/clear strategic direction.

Human Resources Technical Skills:
- Acted as a catalyst for the fusion of strategic direction into organisational change, in terms of the management, organisation and motivation of managers and staff, for a major computer company.
- Developed and implemented numerous human resources planning, organisation restructuring, job evaluation, performance appraisal and skills training programs in diverse industrial and business settings.
- Designed and conducted numerous recruitment, management assessment and development, and downsizing programs, internationally.

CAREER HIGHLIGHTS

1986 to now	**Foremost Consulting Pty Ltd, Sydney** Managing Director and Management Consultant
1978–1985	**Canadian Oilfield Manufacturers Association, Canada** Business Development Director and Independent Management Consultant
1975–1977	**Lucas Marine Ltd, UK** Director and General Manager
Pre-1975	**The Mars Group, UK, Jameson's Chocolates, UK, and Hassan Abdal Cadet College, Pakistan** Various line and staff management roles, having commenced my career as a volunteer teacher overseas.

ACADEMIC QUALIFICATIONS

Institute of Management Consultants of Alberta, Canada
Certified Management Consultant, by examination: marketing major; private study.

Slough College of Technology, UK
Postgraduate Diploma in Management Studies: behavioural studies, business analysis, marketing and management accountancy majors; evening class course.

Hendon & Waltham Forest Technical Colleges, UK
Distinction in the Higher National Certificate in Business Studies: economics and accounting majors; evening class course.

Eastbourne College, UK
2 'A' levels in English and German and 11 'O' levels; Royal Air Force Flying Scholarship also awarded.

PROFESSIONAL AFFILIATIONS AND TRAINING

- Fellow of the Australian Institute of Management and Institute of Company Directors.
- Member of the Australian Human Resources Institute.
- As a human resources professional, trained and proficient in numerous techniques, including organisation and customer services surveys, focus groups, management assessment, psychological testing, career planning, downsizing, and change and revitalisation management.

PERSONAL DETAILS
Languages: some French, some German.
Interests: sailing, skiing and family activities.

Address:

Phone numbers: Home:

                   Business:

15.

A Bulletproof Networking System For Career Search

This section contains further exercises for Chapter 12.

Chapter 12 addresses the importance of networking in your career search, and this section of your Executive Armoury provides you with a complete system to use.

But first, why do we call it a 'network'? Think of it this way. Imagine you are standing at one side of a tennis court by one of the posts holding up the net. Look across the net to the other post. See how the net with its strands of twine links itself between the posts. Networking for career search purposes is just like that. The post this side of the net is you, with your job and career targets in place. The post on the other side represents your target business sectors and organisations, and the tennis net between the two posts represents your developing network as you progress from your closest and most accessible contacts, through word-of-mouth referral, to other contacts, and so on, until you are referred into an organisation where a job or career position exists or can be developed for you.

Networkers usually find that they need between three and five 'levels' of referrals (three to five 'links' in that tennis net) from a reasonably sized initial range of close and accessible contacts (say 20 to 30, preferably 40), in order to uncover career openings in target business sectors and organisations. And, of course, such openings are usually 'invisible', which means they are often far less competitive for you to attain in the form of a job offer.

On pages 271–272 you will find a ten-stage networking system which you can use, as defined below:

1. Your job and career targets

Here you can write your job and career targets, which may have been developed by using the Bulletproof Career Planning Process outlined in Section 11.

2. Your stated reason for making contact

Remember, you are not asking your contacts for a job, or specifically to find you a job (both of which requests may put them off). Rather, you may use the following stated reasons, or others of your choice, and write them in boxes A to E in the ten-stage networking table:

- I'm doing some market research about career opportunities in the XYZ business sector.
- I'm seeking advice about whom I should contact to find out more about working in the XYZ business sector.

- I'm thinking of making a career change into the XYZ business sector, and I'd like to speak to people who are knowledgeable about this sector.
- We've not spoken for a while, and I'd appreciate catching up with you. I'm making some changes in my career.
- I need to know whom I should speak with who can advise me if my experience lends itself to the XYZ business sector.
- I'm thinking of changing my job — moving into an entirely new type of job function — and I need to know more about my options and how realistic it is to do this.

3. Your 'carrots'

The best way to succeed in networking is not just to ask for advice, but also to give it! In other words, develop some rationale as to why network contacts might benefit from a meeting with you, as a result of information or insights you can provide which are of interest to them — a 'two-way trade'. Write your carrots in boxes F to J in the table.

Here are some examples of 'carrots':

- Offer to introduce them to other contacts.
- Provide information about what you have been doing in your recent or past work which may be of interest to them.
- Help them to keep up to date with what's happening elsewhere.
- Provide them with other forms of information which may be of interest to them.

4. Your desired outcomes in addition to referrals

In addition to referrals to other contacts, there may be other outcomes you specifically seek from a network meeting. Write them in boxes K to O. For example:

- Their reaction to your resumé and suggestions for further improvement
- Their reaction to your career plans (Do they react positively, or do they indicate you are being unrealistic in your goals? NB You can listen to such advice, but you don't have to follow it!)
- For the contact to become a member of your ongoing contact network — once you start networking, keep it alive as you never know when you will need it!
- Advice about alternative possible job and career targets
- Permission from them to act as a referee for you (and at the same time, receive their help in the networking process)
- Advice about specific opportunities of which they are aware.

5. Your closest and most accessible personal/family/business contacts

These are people you feel you can approach for a networking meeting or discussion with relative ease. They can literally be anyone you know, because we all have contacts. Many would-be networkers get stuck at this stage by assuming these initial contacts should only be business contacts. Wrong! We all have contacts, and it's surprising who knows whom! Write their names against numbers 1 to 20 in the table (you may need more space).

6. Institutional contacts

These include the various professional bodies, trade associations, business groups, sporting or social clubs, church and community groups, executive search firms, recruiters, management consultants, government departments, and so forth, who themselves have a range of relevant and good contacts to whom you seek to be referred. Write their names against numbers 21 to 40.

7, 8, 9. Next closest contacts and referrals

Here you write the names of the various next levels of contacts, referred by your earlier contacts (columns 5, 6, 7 and 8), and other contacts that you believe are not close enough to you, or accessible enough, to be included initially in column 5. Write their names against numbers 41 to 100.

10. Your target business sectors and typical organisations

Note here your target business sectors and, underneath, write down typical organisations within these sectors which may be attractive to you for employment purposes.

On the last page of this section, you will find a pro forma Network Contact Record which may be photocopied by the first reader of this book in sufficient quantities for one record per contact. These can then be kept alphabetically for ease of reference. By way of definitions:

- The word 'number' refers to the numbers (1-100) in the vertical columns of the ten-stage networking table.
- Against 'R', record A to E, depending on which reason was used for making contact.
- Against 'C', record F to J, similarly.
- Against 'O', record K to O, similarly.
- 'Referror' is the person (record name and number) who referred you to this contact.
- 'Referred' are the people (record names and numbers) to whom this contact referred you.
- 'Notes' capture the essence of what transpired in your network meeting or conversation.

You now have a complete networking system available for your use. Good luck!

Note: The Networking Template and Network Contact Record are copyright protected, but the first reader is authorised to photocopy them and use them solely for their own personal networking.

A Bulletproof Networking System For Career Search

Your Network into the Invisible Job Market

1. Your Job and Career Targets

Immediate:
I
II
III

Longer term:
I
II
III

2. Your Stated Reason for Making Contact (R)

A
B
C
D
E

3. Your 'Carrots' (C)

F
G
H
I
J

4. Your Desired Outcomes (O) in Addition to Referrals

K
L
M
N
O

5. Your Closest and Most Accessible Personal/Family/Business Contacts

1
2
3
4
5
6
7
8
9
10
11
12
13
14
15
16
17
18
19
20

© *The Bulletproof Executive*

271

the bulletproof executive

6. Institutional Contacts	7. Next Closest Contacts and Referrals	8. Next Closest Contacts and Referrals	9. Next Closest Contacts and Referrals	10. Your Target Business Sectors and Typical Organisations
21	41	61	81	Sector 1 ....
22	42	62	82	....
23	43	63	83	....
24	44	64	84	....
25	45	65	85	....
26	46	66	86	....
27	47	67	87	Sector 2 ....
28	48	68	88	....
29	49	69	89	....
30	50	70	90	....
31	51	71	91	....
32	52	72	92	....
33	53	73	93	Sector 3 ....
34	54	74	94	....
35	55	75	95	....
36	56	76	96	....
37	57	77	97	....
38	58	78	98	....
39	59	79	99	....
40	60	80	100	....

© *The Bulletproof Executive*

NETWORK CONTACT RECORD

Contact Name and Network Reference Number: ....

Address: ....

Phone/Fax: ....

R: .... Referror & Number: ....

C: .... Referred & Numbers: ....

O: ....

Dates of meeting (*insert* 'M') or
phone conversation (*insert* 'P')

Notes: .... Follow-up Dates: ....

....

....

....

© The Bulletproof Executive

16.

The Convincing Communications Clinic: 39 Steps To Success

This section contains exercises for Chapters 14, 15 and 16.

The following 39 statements represent a do-it-yourself diagnosis of any communication problems you may have experienced or opportunities for further personal development. Prescriptions for success are also included. If a diagnosis doesn't 'ring a bell' in this context, just move on to the next one. If a particular diagnosis does sound relevant, read the notes and try out the concepts.

1. **Diagnosis:** *You would like to speak as clearly and as articulately as some of the top newscasters, who seem to be able to make the most of every word.*
   Prescription: *You may need an elocution lesson — read on.*

Speakers are in the business of using words and their voices, in order to get their message across. You will now find out what happens in an elocution lesson!

I will start with the vowels: A E I O U. Say these vowels as though in conversation and you will find that your mouth is only half open, with little movement between saying each vowel. Now shout them in a pronounced fashion, moving your mouth, lips and tongue to really 'make a meal' of them. The effect is interesting; you can notice how different and pronounced they sound by comparison to saying them conversationally. Good speakers go for a mid-way style of delivery, mid-way between conversational and pronounced, and in this way project their voices to those seated at the back of the room.

Let us move on to the consonants: B C D F G H J K L M N P Q R S T V W X Y Z. Again, say these conversationally and then shout them out in a pronounced way, moving your mouth, lips and tongue exaggeratedly. Now try the mid-way style of delivery as though projecting them to those seated at the back of the room.

Finally, practice the combination consonants: Br Ch Cl Dr Fr Gr Ng Pr Pl Sh Sl Th. Say them conversationally first, then shout them in a pronounced fashion as before. Now try the mid-way style, though still projecting them.

In summary, good speakers aim for a mid-way style between conversational volume and pronounced shouting, and they aim to project their voices so as to be heard by those seated at the back of the room.

2. **Diagnosis:** *You sometimes have difficulty in getting the other party to open up, converse with you, or tell you what is on their mind.*
   Prescription: *Ask questions.*

Effective personal selling requires effective communication, and questioning is a vital part of the communication process. In selling, the main purpose of questioning is to uncover the contact's interests, to confirm that your messages have been understood as you intended, and to encourage contact participation in the discussion process. It is through questioning that you find out the information necessary to help you do this — the trick is to know what you are looking for, and to ask the right questions in the right way.

The 'traditional' method of personal selling spends a lot of time on 'small talk', but little on real information-gathering. 'Professional' personal selling shuns meaningless chit-chat, and focuses instead on drawing out the contact for the purpose of learning how best to address the contact's interests and needs. Most contacts today appreciate business networkers who, after a few brief opening statements, come right to the point and show some interest and concern for their needs by asking well-phrased, pertinent questions. The art of effective questioning is thus a crucial part of the personal selling process.

3. **Diagnosis:** *You have an important speech coming up and you have to cover a lot of content accurately, in quite a short time. You don't want to read it. What can you do?*
Prescription: *Memorise it.*

This process can be used at any time, providing you have the time to memorise it! It is again best used for formal occasions or for when you are 'going on record'. It is also suitable for use with larger audiences — just as actors memorise their scripts.

In terms of preparation, the starting point is the fully-typed script, as previously described. The learning-by-heart process then follows, which is best undertaken phrase by phrase, sentence by sentence, and paragraph by paragraph — as mentioned, this can take some time to learn.

Another way of assisting memorisation is to tape the transcript and to recite the speech as the tape plays it back.

Regarding delivery, don't deliver your memorised speech as though you are reading it. Animation is the key, along with developing and maintaining good eye contact with the audience.

The advantages of the memorised script relate mainly to accuracy of content — providing you have memorised it correctly. The disadvantages relate to the time taken to memorise the script, and the fact that the system is by no means infallible. Many a previously word-perfect speaker has forgotten all in the face of a large audience. Another disadvantage is that the speech can become a recital — too stilted and too formal.

4. **Diagnosis:** *You sometimes have difficulty, lack impact, or feel you are lacking something else as you start, or 'open', your presentation, speech or meeting.*
Prescription: *Use creative opening statements.*

- *Background.* Here the speaker starts with a rapid introduction to some element of the history of the subject. Brevity, relevance and appeal are all key ingredients. For example: 'Last August your board of directors asked me to undertake a

preliminary analysis of the comparative productivity of your plant. After six months' work, I now have my preliminary results.'
- *The personal 'opener'*. For example: 'I was just talking to Mr Saunders here at the head table and he mentioned to me that most of you would be interested to hear about ...' This is a very relaxed style of opening, with good appeal to the audience and some impact.
- *The news-item opener*. For example: 'So the Liberals are in for another term — does this bode well for the poor?' This can have good appeal, particularly if used with a question.
- *Provocative openers*. For example: 'Government programs of support to industry are ineffective. Firms simply do not bother to source them and utilise them — to their own misfortune.' This type of opener is particularly useful when you include your audience in the first apparently negative statement — they certainly sit up and listen! Try this form of opener with the after-dinner audience, or where the audience seems somewhat aloof or distant. Another example: 'Management training is useless, unless it is delivered in a specific fashion that relates to the development of a competency, rather than simply the acquisition of knowledge.'

5. **Diagnosis:** *You sometimes have difficulty in closing your presentation, speech, meeting or personal selling endeavour. (By 'closing', I am referring to attaining your intended outcomes.)*
   Prescription: *Ask, and try test closing.*

As obvious as it may seem, many networkers and presenters fail to close because they forget to ask for what they seek, or don't know they are supposed to ask for this. Successful completion of the personal selling process requires the networker or presenter to initiate the closing stage. Very few prospects will actually ask you what you need, even if they are interested. No matter how involved the contact has been up to that point, it is up to you to initiate the close by asking for what you seek.

Test closing is also important and helps to offset the chances of a poor closing. One method of test closing is to offer several options:

'Which of the three approaches appears most to meet your needs?'
'The second.'
'So you would like to move forward into that approach?'
'Yes!'

Another method is to answer a question with a question 'boomerang':

'Are your colleagues available to meet now?'
'You would like to meet them now?'
'Yes!'

Yet another method is to make an assumption with an error (you may have made the error on purpose):

'And so it was the second approach which you preferred?'
'No, the first!'
'Let me make a note about that.'

6. **Diagnosis:** *You find it difficult to end your speech or presentation.*
   Prescription: *Understand what can go wrong and learn by these mistakes.*

Some of the greatest mistakes at the end of presentations are:

- *Fade-out.* Perhaps time is up, or the speaker has said all they want to say. Fade-out can result in an abrupt end, or an end that literally fades out like a song that has no real ending — the recording studio just turns the volume down to zero while the musicians are still in full swing.
- *Grasping for life-lines.* Many speakers feel they have not done justice to their speech or presentation by the time they have to close. They try to throw in last-minute statements designed to rectify this situation. They go down fighting!
- *Off-topic.* Some speakers, having made their main points, wander off-topic during the closing seconds or minutes. It is as if they have become super-confident in front of the audience and decide to impart new content and ideas at the last minute, off the 'top of their head'.
- *Repeaters.* A repetition of your speech, even if considered useful for 'padding', is not the way to close. A summary of some of the key points or arguments is needed, but not too much repetition.
- *'Well, um, there may be some questions?'* Never be half-hearted about questions at the end of your speech. Decide beforehand whether or not you are going to invite questions. If you are, encourage the audience to ask them.

7. **Diagnosis:** *You have to make a really impressive presentation at a conference coming up and you want to use visuals which are more impressive and professional than overheads. You don't have computer graphics. You don't know what to use.*
   Prescription: *Try 35 millimetre slides.*

Thirty-five millimetre slides can be front- or rear-projected on to a screen — the latter requiring less dimming of the overhead lights. They need to be operated by a remote control at the lectern. The projector should be turned off and/or be placed out of sight when not in use, and you should practise using your slides in such a way that enhances your professionalism.

The advantages of 35 millimetre slides are that they offer full colour and high impact, particularly when multiple projectors and screens are used. They can be very effective visual aids.

One disadvantage is that you cannot point to them easily to stress a point. Whereas you can point to an overhead slide in front of you, with a 35 millimetre slide you are forced to move over to the screen and use a pointer, or a hand-held mini-laser light, which entails turning away from the audience.

Several companies offer 35 millimetre slide production services, as well as 'do-it-yourself' kits for use with computer graphics.

8. **Diagnosis:** *Only half your audience arrives, and they all sit at the back of the room!*
   Prescription: *Fill the room from the front.*

There is nothing worse than having to talk to empty chairs. Always encourage your audience to fill the auditorium, hall or room, from the front. Assistants can help here, but don't be afraid to encourage your audience to do this, from the lectern. This can help your nervous tension, too.

9. **Diagnosis:** *You feel that when you speak at meetings or presentations you come across in somewhat of a monotone and fail to inspire your audiences.*
   Prescription: *Use voice control.*

- Vary your volume — sometimes loud, sometimes soft.
- Pause occasionally — as Ralph Richardson, the actor, once said 'Acting is all about the pause.' You can pause for quite a long time with good effect.
- Vary your delivery from time to time by slowing down, speeding up, speaking louder or speaking softer.
- Emphasise key words.
- Deliver the bulk of your speech at your normal level or pitch — not too high, not too low.
- Occasionally vary this level, for emphasis or variety, to keep the audience interested.
- Watch your quality of voice, or tone. Attempt to go for a rounded, almost musical tone — a resonant tone — rather than a rasping tone or a thin voice.
- Don't overact or sound false — your voice control must sound natural.

To practise voice control, read aloud from a book or newspaper on a regular basis. Take one element at a time that you wish to build into your speech-making and practise it in this way by reading aloud regularly. In reading aloud, remember to project your voice to those seated at the back of the room.

10. **Diagnosis:** *You sometimes feel the conversation is not going your way, or that you need to somehow exert more control.*
    Prescription: *Ask 'closed' questions.*

This type of question limits the contact's response in that it can usually be answered by means of a simple 'Yes' or 'No'. Closed questions are therefore also known as 'directive' questions. Some examples are:

'Are you happy with your present supplier?'
'Are you having any problems with the system you had installed last year?'
'Will you be needing to renegotiate contracts soon?'
'Do you feel the investment is too high?'
'Are you worried about the availability of top professional staff?'

Closed questions are not usually effective in drawing out the feelings and needs of the other party, but they can be used effectively to:

- steer the conversation towards a specific topic
- uncover hidden queries or objections
- control the time spent at the meeting
- involve the contact who is unresponsive to open questions.

11. **Diagnosis:** *You sometimes feel you lack impact part-way through your speech or presentation, and need somehow to liven it up and generate greater audience interest.*
    Prescription: *Use creative continuity statements.*

There are many continuity statements which can enhance the main body of your speech or presentation. They include:

- *Anecdotes or stories* — factual or fictional — that relate directly to the subject as well as to audience needs and appeal. By bringing yourself into the story, the audience automatically becomes more interested in what you have to say. If you can make yourself the loser in the story, the audience will start to align themselves with you. If you are the winner, the audience may react negatively.

  The story must be well-polished, and be related in a way that arouses the attention of the audience. Relating it slowly usually will have a better effect than relating it quickly. For example: 'When I was an apprentice welder, I worked in a plant headed up by a rather domineering type of manager. I was progressing quite well, until one day . . .'

- *Quoting a well-known saying and giving its source.* This works well if the saying relates directly to the main thrust of your speech and if its source is an authoritative one. The best form of quotation is one that is short, to the point, and that appeals to the emotions rather than logic. For example: '"Inventiveness is 10 per cent inspiration and 90 per cent perspiration," Thomas Edison said.'

- *Asking the audience a question.* This can have dramatic impact, particularly if the answer to the question relates directly to the main thrust of your speech. The question should be framed so that the audience doesn't answer. You, the speaker, then proceed to answer it in a way that you know will appeal to the audience and grasp their attention. The problem with encouraging the audience to answer, is that you might get a wrong or less than desirable answer, which will throw you off your stride. For example: 'As a manufacturing plant, how can we compete better against plants operating in lower labour cost countries?'

- *'You' and 'we' appeal.* By building 'you' or 'we' into statements, audience involvement is enhanced from the outset. For example: 'You are here today to find out how council's long-term transportation plan might affect your neighbourhood . . .' 'We all want to see our neighbourhood's natural features preserved . . .'

In summary, you select your continuity statements according to the main thrust of your speech, the type of audience and your personal style. These statements must be well-rehearsed and well-delivered, and represent important opportunities for generating good audience impact.

12. **Diagnosis:** *You have a really difficult presentation coming up and it's a complex subject at which you're not an expert. You don't know what to do.*
    Prescription: *Use computer graphics or a video.*

Computer graphics and videos can make excellent visual aids, but they can be expensive to prepare. There are many videos available for rental that address all kinds of subjects — for example, management topics and employee training. However, it is sometimes difficult to find one that relates to your particular speech or presentation.

When using computer graphics or videos, make sure that you have sufficient monitors for your audience — a rough guide is that one 51cm screen will be needed for each 20 to 25 viewers.

13. **Diagnosis:** *When you try to close your presentation, speech or meeting, you sometimes wish you had something tangible to which you could refer.*
Prescription: *Use a closing aid.*

Closing aids include the tools needed to help you close, such as:

- *Testimonials* — verification that others have found your input beneficial. These testimonials can be in writing from the satisfied contact, or even tape-recorded. The latter is far more powerful. Record it as though it is an interview: ask pertinent questions, and lead the speaker into saying the sorts of things that will help you close.
- *Paperwork* — reports, brochures or business cards. These, as needed, should all be at hand in a paper pad holder/folder. All paperwork must be kept clean and uncreased. The total package of paperwork must be out of the briefcase and instantly accessible — perhaps on your lap, under your arm, or on the desk or table in front of you — to allow you to move smoothly into the next sequence.
- *Hardware* — the electronic organiser or diary. This must also be instantly accessible for logging follow-up meetings.

14. **Diagnosis:** *You sometimes get put off your speech or presentation by noises 'off'.*
Prescription: *Insist on no external interruptions.*

While you may want a participative and sometimes boisterous audience, you don't want outside noises such as waiters, or speakers next door, interrupting your speech. Don't try to overpower such distractions by raising your voice. Simply instruct an assistant to monitor and control all such interruptions. In the final analysis, it is better to stop or delay starting your speech until such interruptions cease.

15. **Diagnosis:** *You have heard presenters or speakers do too much 'umming' or repeat annoying pet phrases too often. You think you do this.*
Prescription: *Keep 'repeaters' under control.*

Try to eliminate repeaters, such words and phrases as:

- 'Um'
- 'Er'
- 'Ah'
- 'Well'
- 'Now'
- 'the point is'
- 'to be honest'
- 'that reminds me'
- 'simply said'
- 'in plain language'

These are the more common repeaters, but each of us has our pet repeaters, such as:

- the cough
- the nervous laugh
- 'huh'
- 'and so on'
- 'in other words'
- 'the question is'

16. Diagnosis: *Sometimes you feel you haven't identified the needs and interests of the other party, or that you have failed somehow to draw them out.*
Prescription: *Ask open-ended questions.*

Open-ended question are ones which allow more freedom of response. Open questions are therefore also known as 'non-directive' questions. Some contacts prefer this type of questioning, since they feel they are volunteering information, rather than merely responding to your demands.

Open questioning, or probing, lets the other party express what is on their mind. As such, it tends to bring needs and objections out into the open where they can be dealt with, rather than keeping them hidden, where they continue to act as 'blocks' to accommodating what you seek.

Some comments from the other party serve as signals that an open question should be used. For example:

Other party: 'I really don't think that approach is suitable for our needs.'
You: 'Why don't you tell me about your needs?'
Other party: 'We are in a position to change courses right now.'
You: 'Why is that?'

Open questions which begin with:

- 'Tell me about . . .'
- 'What do you think of . . . ?'
- 'How do you feel about . . . ?'

Give people a chance to open up, air their concerns, and ask a few questions of their own.

Most networkers use a combination of both closed and open questions at meetings.

17. Diagnosis: *You often get caught out at conferences, and find yourself having to make impromptu speeches with almost no notice. You want to improve your performance.*
Prescription: *Use notes on the 'back of envelopes'.*

This approach should be used only for impromptu speeches. Make sure you address, as always, the start of the speech (how you are going to open it), the development of curiosity and trust, the main thrust, and the ending — it must have impact and leave the audience on a high.

Sometimes there simply isn't time to make proper notes. Jot down what comes into your mind as you listen to another speaker, or as you are introduced. In this case, go back over these notes and write the order of delivery beside them by noting

(1), (2), (3), etc. With notes on the 'back of envelopes', make sure your writing is large and legible, and ensure that the notes are complete enough to be useful.

Regarding delivery, don't worry or feel embarrassed about being seen to be using your notes — you have gone to the trouble of thinking through your speech for your audience (large or small) and this is a favour to them. Again, an animated delivery is the order of the day.

The advantages of 'back of envelope' notes relate to speed and confidence. They can be prepared very quickly and help to develop your confidence — you have a guide to follow and, providing the notes are complete, you will cover all you wanted to say.

The disadvantages relate to the limited time available to organise these notes. Legibility can be a problem also. Remember, 'back of envelope' refers to any suitable-sized cards or pieces of paper that will fit in a shirt, blouse or jacket pocket.

18. Diagnosis: *You sometimes feel the audience is flat, uninvolved or, worse still, falling asleep.*
   Prescription: *Get the audience to participate.*

Getting the audience to participate helps them to:
- stay awake and interested
- assimilate what you are attempting to present
- retain what you are attempting to present.

Such participation can be enhanced by use of:
- Socratic approaches — asking them questions
- group discussions
- role playing
- simulation — case studies
- individual exercises — self-help checklists
- audience assistance with demonstrations, etc.

Audience participation increases their retention of your speech or presentation to as much as 60–70 per cent when used in conjunction with visuals and your spoken presentation.

19. Diagnosis: *You sometimes have problems with choosing appropriate words and/or pronunciation the audience understands.*
   Prescriptions: *Watch for the pitfalls.*

Pitfalls regarding words used are:
- wrong use or choice of words
- use of slang or technical jargon
- wrong pronunciation
- inadequate vocabulary (try expanding your vocabulary with a thesaurus — a must for any speaker)
- use of difficult words
- use of stereotyped or hackneyed phrases, or clichés.

20. Diagnosis: *You feel you lack the polish or professionalism of other speakers or presenters, who seem to have their 'act together' better than you.*
Prescription: *Develop positive speaker traits.*

Good speakers:

- are punctual in terms of starting and finishing times
- appear to be sincere, say what they believe, and carry it out with conviction
- are enthusiastic, otherwise they are not likely to enthuse the audience
- use tact and sensitivity, and orientate their speech or presentation to the audience
- allow their emotions to show, but never let them get out of control. Sorrow, anger and hatred are powerful emotions which can get out of control at the lectern.
- rarely criticise; if they do, then they make the criticism constructive and try to keep it positive
- offer praise where it is due
- show they are not perfect and make the occasional mistake in their speech. They are human, too.
- make the audience feel they are important and appreciated
- keep their ego under control — audience first, self second
- use 'you' appeal — talk to the audience as 'you' to keep them involved and interested
- use 'we' appeal — address the audience as 'we' when they need to gain their acceptance and approval
- keep 'I' to a minimum.

21. Diagnosis: *You sometimes have problems gauging the other party's or audience's reactions to your questions.*
Prescription: *Test the temperature.*

Contact or audience reactions can be classified in the following four ways:

1. *Hot.* This includes such contact responses as clearly positive statements about the topics under discussion, or agreement with what you are saying.
2. *Cold.* Here, the contact makes clearly negative statements about the topic in question, disagrees with what you are saying, or otherwise responds in a deliberate, negative way.
3. *Warm.* Reactions which are *probably* positive include smiling and nodding, leaning forward in a chair, or examining something you have shown them, very closely. However, the prospect or contact *may*, be reacting negatively.
4. *Cool.* Reactions which are *probably* negative include wandering attention, fidgeting, crossing the arms or moving away. However, the prospect or contact *may* be reacting positively. Be alert for these reactions, and adjust your questioning technique to them.

22. Diagnosis: *You sometimes find it difficult to grasp the audience's attention when you make a speech or presentation.*
Prescription: *Try these 'do's' and 'don'ts'.*

Do:

- make sure that the top half of your body, including your hands, starts in control and remains in control
- take a second or two to look at the audience, sense their mood, empathise with them and *smile*
- commence with confidence, which will be the case if you are well-prepared
- make the opening of your speech or presentation interesting and novel.

Don't:

- start in the stereotype fashion of: 'Thank you for inviting me to speak to you today', or 'I am honoured at the privilege of being able to address you', or 'May I say how delighted I am to be here today.'
- start with too much emphasis, which may put the audience off — build up to your key issues and ending impact, rather than start too 'high' and end too 'low'
- be too lengthy in your opening remarks — 10 per cent of the available time is a rough guide.

23. Diagnosis: *You sometimes have problems answering difficult questions.*
  Prescription: *Learn and deploy appropriate techniques.*

You can answer a difficult question with a question. For example:

- 'Please explain what you mean?'
- 'Why do you say that?'
- 'Why?'
- 'What for?'
- 'How?'

This gives you time to think about an answer — it also throws the questioner off guard, and makes them think, too.

Another technique is to agree with the critical questioner. For example: 'I think you're absolutely right in your contention, but if you take the so and so circumstances into consideration, I think you'll find...', or 'I agree with you, but we're not working in isolation and other factors have to be taken into consideration. For example...' This tends to quieten the critical questioner somewhat, and allows them to feel they have made a good point. It allows them to retain their self-esteem.

Another technique is the reversal. For example: 'If you develop that new industrial estate, it will adversely impact on our parkland and leisure pursuits.' 'If we don't develop that industrial estate, there won't be enough jobs to allow people to enjoy their leisure pursuits.'

Stupid questions that are either too frivolous or too far off the subject to consider seriously may usefully be responded to by saying, 'You really don't want me to answer that, do you?' and then laughing it off.

When you really don't know the answer to a question, don't be afraid to say, 'I don't know, sorry!' — but don't say it too often. A little humility can win over the other party or an audience.

24. Diagnosis: *You have difficulties using microphones.*
   Prescription: *Remember these guidelines.*

Do:

- try to test the microphone before the meeting
- check whether it has an on-off switch and that it is on before you speak. If in doubt, gently tap it and take your time
- adjust the volume level so that you don't hear your own voice booming back to you
- watch out for negative feedback or microphone whine. Lower the volume level, stand further back from the microphone, and/or rearrange the speakers if you experience feedback.
- moderate your own speaking volume. Let the microphone do the work of projection for you.
- stand still in front of the microphone
- stand about 50 centimetres from the microphone
- ensure the microphone is just below your mouth level
- use a lapel microphone whenever possible — but remember that when it is switched on it will amplify every noise you make in its vicinity.

Don't:

- play with the microphone while speaking — hands off!
- fiddle with pens or papers near the microphone — these sounds may be amplified
- speak too close to the microphone, as this will distort your voice
- speak too far away from the microphone, as you won't be heard
- continue speaking while you turn your head away from the microphone and move away to use a visual aid — you won't be heard
- speak to the microphone. Speak to the audience, the object of your speech.

25. Diagnosis: *You sometimes feel you are doing too much of the talking and telling.*
   Prescription: *Question rather than inform.*

You can tell people things, or you can ask them questions. Which is preferable? Asking questions is always preferable because when you inform someone about something, you are often pushing; when you ask them questions, you are pulling. When you say something, the other party may doubt it; when the other party says something, it is usually true in their minds. In summary, you should spend about twice as much time questioning as you spend informing.

In order to choose the correct type of question for the moment at hand, you must know what you are trying to achieve with your questions (uncover interests or needs, get the other party talking, zero in on a particular topic), and temper this with the other party's level of responsiveness at the time.

Don't ask complicated questions with technical 'jargon'. The other party may be embarrassed to admit their ignorance, and thus may react in an abrupt or hostile way.

In any case, straightforward questions, using language and terms which are easily understood, will be more likely to put the other party at ease and elicit an honest response. Also, it is better to present one idea at a time, gradually building as you go, rather than confuse people with several questions at once.

Never ask others bluntly if they can help you, or if they have time. This just puts them on the defensive, and you may get an answer which is far from the truth. Instead, explain the reasons why it would help to have some idea of their interest in or ability to spend some time with you, or to accommodate what you seek.

'Will your input be sufficient? I'm sure you understand — I need to really do my homework and market research fully' is better than 'Who's the best person to talk to around here?' Most people will not object to such questions if you explain why you need to know.

In general, it is better to begin with fairly general questions and then proceed to more specific ones, as you get a better idea of the other party's concerns and requirements. You may find, through effective questioning, that you have been trying to address an inappropriate topic — better to find out sooner rather than later!

Build on previous responses, rather than 'jump around' from one topic to another — stay with one issue until you are sure the other party has been satisfied. Organising your questions will help you to keep the meeting focused, and thus you will maintain a sense of control as you lead the other party through the stages discussed previously — attention, interest, desire, commitment and action.

26. Diagnosis: *You have had problems with hecklers.*
Prescription: *Learn to handle them.*

The best approach with hecklers is to ignore them and let the audience take care of them. Be polite and hope the heckling will pass. The alternative is to answer a remark from a heckler with a remark that delights the audience. For example:

Heckler: 'You don't know what you're talking about.'
Speaker: 'That's why I'm up here and you're down there!'
Heckler: 'Boring!'
Speaker: 'Yes, you are!'
Heckler: Abusive language.
Speaker: 'In future, please bleep. There are youngsters in the audience!'
Heckler: Insult.
Speaker: Either ignore it or go quiet, and then ask the insulter to repeat the remark. Most people will normally go quiet as the audience focuses their attention on them.

27. Diagnosis: *You can't be bothered using visual aids with your presentations, and you can't see their value, although people say they can be very effective.*
Prescription: *Try using them for the following reasons.*

Visual aids are important tools to use in your speech or group presentation.

- They enhance audience understanding because they call on two senses — sound and sight.

- They enhance the organisation of your speech or presentation — you have to organise your thoughts in an orderly fashion before you can develop or use visuals.
- We are all visually oriented — sight plays an important role in our education, learning and communication.
- Visuals increase audience retention — from a low of 20-30 per cent retention of the spoken speech or presentation, to a high of 40-50 per cent retention when supplementary visual aids are used.

28. **Diagnosis:** *You sometimes have problems with your use of grammar.*
    Prescription: *Watch out for common mistakes.*

Good grammar is a prerequisite to successful speech-making. Watch out for the following common mistakes:

- mixing tenses
- using the wrong sequence of words and phrases, particularly adjectives and adverbs — they are usually in the order of time, manner and place
- mixing plural and singular words in a sentence
- using 'who' instead of 'whom'
- using 'neither . . . or', instead of 'neither . . . nor'.

There are hundreds of books available to assist you with your grammar.

29. **Diagnosis:** *You sometimes feel your appearance lets you down when making group presentations.*
    Prescription: *Follow these guidelines.*

The audience sees mainly the top half of a speaker's body. But the top half of the body can get out of control:

- tie knot slipped
- jacket open and flapping, or with bulky objects in the pockets
- hands on lapels, armpits or clutching the lectern
- hands in the pockets playing with keys or cash
- hands pulling or scratching the ears, nose or chin.

Keep the top half of your body under control by:

- previously adjusting your tie or scarf, emptying your pockets, and buttoning your jacket
- keeping your hands in front of you, behind you, by your side, or even keeping one hand in your pocket and the other free for gesticulating (particularly for informal presentations or speeches)
- keeping balanced by placing your feet slightly apart, with one foot angled slightly in front of the other.

Now that we have the top half of the body under control, keep it under control by *not*:

- coughing or blowing your nose — do this before you arrive at the lectern
- looking at your watch
- playing with pens or paperclips

- swaying, slouching or leaning
- looking around the room at anything but the audience.

30. **Diagnosis:** *Your audience or the other party sometimes give nothing away and remain poker-faced.*
    Prescription: *Use engaging phraseology.*

Engaging phraseology is designed to generate positive responses from the other party or audience and is based on the use of such words as 'isn't', 'wouldn't', 'doesn't' and 'haven't'. For example:

'Quality of service is important to you, *isn't it?*'
'You would like improved professional input, *wouldn't you?*'
'Continuity of association makes sense, *doesn't it?*'
'They've been more evident in the industry, *haven't they?*'

Using engaging phraseology at the start of the question tends to be even more personal. For example:

'*Isn't* quality of advice important?'
'*Wouldn't* you like improved professional input?'
'*Won't* specialised input be to your advantage?'
'*Doesn't* continuity of association make sense?'
'*Haven't* they been more evident in the industry?'

31. **Diagnosis:** *You wish to improve your performance in running meetings.*
    Prescription: *Concentrate on these key meeting guidelines.*

You may be asked to chair meetings, or this may be part of your ongoing duties. Bear in mind the following key guidelines:

- Chairing meetings requires good chairing ability, less so good speaking ability.
- Become knowledgeable about the speakers and the subject(s) to be addressed.
- Don't shatter the confidence of your speakers or meeting participants by actively demonstrating greater knowledge than theirs, by giving them too great a build-up before their speeches, or by being too autocratic in directing them in what they will and won't say or discuss.
- Be fair, firm and amicable — the chairperson is the host and needs to treat the speakers or meeting participants as guests. However, the chairperson controls the length of the meeting and doesn't let behaviour get out of hand. The chairperson is quite clear on why the meeting is being held, and on the meeting's objectives and agenda.
- A good chairperson keeps their ego under control and doesn't try to steal the show.
- They keep everything in control and are good time-managers.
- They empathise with speakers or meeting participants and don't show favouritism.
- They show interest, and are courteous and helpful to all attending the meeting.
- They thank all for their input when the meeting is closed.

- They show impartiality and encourage balanced input by all attendees.
- They remain dignified throughout the meeting and don't allow offensive behaviour.
- They make sure the meeting keeps on track and disallow (in a courteous and positive manner) questions that are irrelevant.

32. **Diagnosis:** *You feel you are presenting to just a crowd, rather than personalising your presentation and developing rapport with individuals, especially at large meetings.*
    Prescription: *Use eye control.*

Eye-to-eye contact, or eye control, is important in good speech-making. Three golden rules apply here:

1. During your presentation or speech, only speak when you have direct eye contact with one of your audience or, in the case of larger audiences, when you are apparently looking at the face of someone in the audience (even if you cannot focus on them).
2. Don't scan your audience rapidly while speaking; concentrate on individuals and give each of them five to ten seconds at a time.
3. Try to ensure you concentrate on each individual in the audience in this way during the speech. With larger audiences this can be achieved by picking out an individual from each group around the room and looking at him or her. Those sitting in the vicinity of these individuals will feel that you have been directing your words to each of them individually. This is a very powerful technique, because it personalises your presentation — you appear to be talking to each and every member of your audience.

33. **Diagnosis:** *You get too many flat rejections.*
    Prescription: *Ask questions with options.*

A good way of ensuring positive responses is to ask questions with two options. In other words, instead of:

You: 'I'm in town today and wonder if I can meet you?'
The other party: 'No.'
try:
You: 'I'm in town today and wonder if I can meet you late morning or early afternoon?'
The other party: 'Early afternoon.'
Instead of:
You: 'When would you like to come and visit us?'
The other party: 'I'll have to think about it.'
try:
You: 'Would you like us to visit say, next week, or the week after next?'
The other party: 'The week after next.'

Instead of:
You: 'Would you like to join me at that luncheon?'
The other party: 'No.'
try:
You: 'Would you like to join me at that luncheon or take in their function next month?'
The other party: 'Next month.'

34. **Diagnosis:** *You feel that you need to end your sales pitch, speech or presentation with more impact.*
    Prescription: *Try these creative endings.*

- *Emotional ending.* Some people end very effectively by appealing to the emotions of the audience, rather than by citing facts and figures. For example: 'By funding this waterwell project, our club will not only be saving the village from certain disaster, but we will also be taking the lead in our district. Yet again, we will be the number one club in international service projects.'
- *Last chance ending.* This is where you can make a convincing case that the audience has one last chance to act. It is a powerful ending, with considerable impact. For example: 'If we don't go ahead now, then we will have missed our chance forever.'
- *Premium ending.* With this technique you keep one last selling point or benefit in reserve until the very end of your speech. This is designed to sway the audience over to you. It is a useful technique where you are speaking about a somewhat contentious issue. For example: 'Not only will all your stated requirements be satisfied, but we are also prepared to throw in a new purpose-designed community hall as part of the complex.'
- *Summarise.* A *brief* summary of the main elements of the speech can offer impact and reinforcement at the end of it. For example: 'We can afford it, we need it, we like it, and it will enhance our image as a community. We must go ahead.'
- *Options.* Some speakers leave two options before the audience, giving greater emphasis to the one the speaker supports. The danger is that the audience may select the other option. For example: 'We can build this year, when construction costs are at their lowest level, or we can delay building until the economy gets rolling again and construction costs go through the roof. We have the money. The choice is yours.'

35. **Diagnosis:** *Your humour falls flat.*
    Prescription: *If you must use humour, follow these guidelines.*

When in doubt, don't try to be funny! If you feel you have to be funny, make sure you source your jokes and witticisms from such publications as the *Reader's Digest*, or other speakers or joke books — but always adapt the material to suit the speech. This is preferable to trying to make up your own jokes.

Always tell third-party jokes — jokes about yourself or your family can be very flat and go over badly.

Don't give notice that you are about to tell a joke. Just get on with it — in other words, eliminate lead-ins such as:
'I told a marvellous tale last week . . .'
'I think this tale is relevant . . .'
'Stop me if you have been told the joke about . . .'
'One of the most amusing tales I've been told is . . .'.

Many people have problems with foreign accents — don't feel you have to include accents in tales involving foreigners, unless you can mimic the accents well. Never tell obscene jokes, or jokes that could be considered offensive to others. On informal occasions, you can certainly include the names of members of the audience in your jokes to good effect, but be sensitive.

Quoting from a publication or book is a good way to lead into a joke — this tends to give your story a topical flavour or an air of integrity.

If you have trouble telling jokes, slow down your pace of delivery. This always helps. Always practise telling your jokes beforehand and always make sure that they relate to your speech.

36. Diagnosis: *Your presentation or speech develops 'log-jams', doesn't go smoothly or appears unprepared.*
   Prescription: *Prepare thoroughly.*

Become familiar with your presentation or speech content, visual aids and related aspects. Practise your speech and rehearse it aloud, using your visual aids. The more prepared you are, the better will be your performance.

37. Diagnosis: *You get nervous when you have to speak in public or present to groups.*
   Prescription: *Take heart.*

Most public speakers suffer nerves from time to time. Take the approach that you are doing this for your family or your firm and that you both will benefit from a task that can cause a little anguish. Remember the battle cry, 'for God and my country!' Your battle cry may be, 'for my wife/husband and family!' Go through the same animations as the warrior — literally clench your fists and go for it 'for the greater glory!' Try it — it can work well.

A confident speaker also knows that breathing correctly is also important. Before your speech, inhale and exhale deeply and slowly several times to help you relax. During the speech, pace yourself and pause sufficiently to keep your breathing even. When you are nervous, it is easy to speak quickly and continuously until you have exhaled all your breath and have to gulp for air! Without breath control, your speech will be interrupted by these distracting gasps.

38. Diagnosis: *You have difficulty 'closing' in meetings — that is, getting the other party to accommodate what you seek.*
   Prescription: *Try different closing techniques.*

- *Options.* With this common method of closing, you give the other party a choice of two or three options. This forces them to make a decision — for example, not whether to assist you but whether to assist you regarding 'A', 'B' or even 'C'. Once they make such a choice, they have made a commitment to meet your needs. If they hedge, they will have to give reasons why a choice cannot be made, in which case you have an opportunity to expand further, based on their concerns.
- *Hidden close.* In the hidden close, you state and assume the decision to accommodate what you seek and then ask a question with two options, the question relating to a less significant aspect. For example: 'Well, it seems to me that it makes sense to continue meeting. Should we meet in each of our locations, or should I continue visiting you here?'
- *Summary close.* With this technique, you review the key benefits to the other party of helping you meet your objectives — you are appealing to logic here. This technique can be very effective, especially if you pause occasionally during the summary to elicit some form of agreement from them.
- *Emotional close.* It is a mistake to assume that most people make decisions about accommodating what you seek, based on logic. While logic does play a major role in the decisions of some people, emotional factors which appeal to pride, status and security can often provide the impetus to help you, even when logic dictates otherwise.

  This type of close should be used carefully, as decisions made solely on emotional impulses can come back to haunt you later. Make sure that in helping you to meet your objectives, the other party's interests or needs are also satisfied. There should also be a logical basis for helping you; an appeal to emotion can then be effective if the other party is hesitant to make the decision.
- *Silent close.* Stop talking, look at the other party and wait. This is most effective if done immediately following the presentation of a major benefit, after successfully answering an objection, or after a visual presentation relating to the topic.

  The length of the pause will depend on the other person's response. If they fidget, tense up or appear to be thinking things over carefully, don't break the silence — the signal is positive! If, however, they stare right back at you and don't change their body language at all, you haven't been convincing enough and will need to expand further on your presentation.

39. Diagnosis: *You hate cold calling by telephone.*
   Prescription: *Try these do's and don'ts.*

Do:
- script out what you want to say and keep it at hand next to the phone
- introduce yourself and state the purpose of your call
- ask if it is convenient to talk now, or arrange a time to call back
- try to uncover an interest or a need which relates to your reason for calling and bring that to the surface
- ask questions
- stimulate interest by offering an opportunity to satisfy the interest or need
- close on an agreement to meet at a specific time and place to discuss details.

Don't:
- reveal too much, as this risks getting a turndown right away
- use a 'canned' approach, as this takes away from the personal qualities of the telephone
- launch into a 'monologue', as this doesn't get the other party involved. Rather, ask some open-ended questions.
- try to block objections or overcome them on the phone — use them instead as a reason to get together
- give up if the other party stalls about a personal visit. If this happens, go back to where you started and reconfirm the interest or need. It may also help to suggest a different time for the appointment.
- be rigid about the time and place to meet.

17.

Eleven-point Plan For Preparing Group Presentations

This section contains further exercises for Chapter 15.

Let us now look at how to prepare a speech or presentation, based on the '11-point plan'.

1. Try to get a good understanding of who the audience is and what they are expecting from you.
2. Develop your objectives: what are you trying to achieve with your presentation?
3. Collect appropriate information in order to attain these objectives.
4. Develop the structure and sequence of your presentation.
5. Develop the script or notes.
6. Review your script or notes to check that they all coincide with your understanding of the audience and their expectations.
7. Develop your visual aids.
8. Check that they coincide with your understanding of the audience and their expectations.
9. Rehearse your presentation.
10. Deliver your presentation.
11. Critically appraise your performance — you should be seeking continuous improvement.

An example of a presentation plan for a one-hour presentation follows. This outline assumes you have one hour to make your presentation (including set-up and questions). The times noted will need to be changed for longer or shorter presentations.

Presentation Plan Outline
(Assumes one hour available)

Lapsed time (in minutes)	Stage	Notes
0-5	Set-up	
5-10	Attention	
10-15	Curiosity	
15-20	Trust	
20-40	Main thrust	
40-45	Ending impact	
45-60	Questions and close down	

18.

Meeting Room Layouts

This section contains further information for Chapter 16.

The layout of meeting rooms is important in group presentations. This includes the seating arrangement and the positioning of such equipment as the projector, screen and lectern. The following diagrams show the right and wrong ways to organise these.

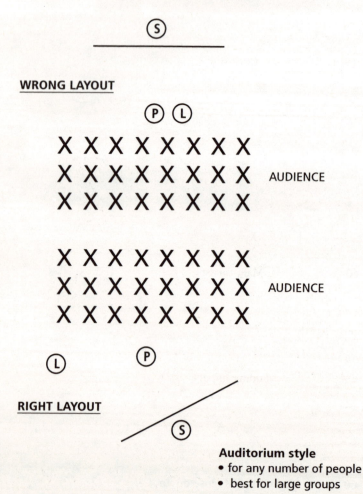

Auditorium style
- for any number of people
- best for large groups

Meeting Room Layouts

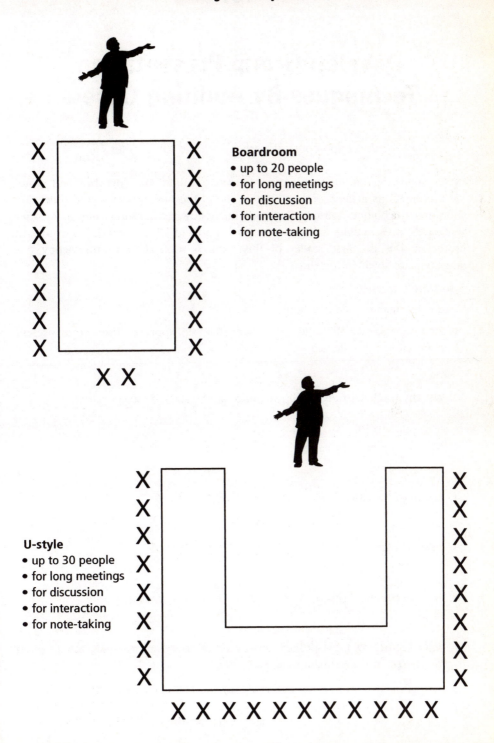

Boardroom
- up to 20 people
- for long meetings
- for discussion
- for interaction
- for note-taking

U-style
- up to 30 people
- for long meetings
- for discussion
- for interaction
- for note-taking

19.

Develop Group Presentation Techniques By Auditing Others

This section contains further exercises for Chapter 16.

The following questionnaire can be used to 'audit' the speeches and group presentations made by others. This is one of the best ways for you to develop your own techniques. Simply run over the following questions during or after someone's presentation and make notes accordingly. This material is copyright protected, but the first reader of this book is authorised to photocopy this questionnaire solely for personal use.

Speaker's name:

Make notes against each question.

1. First impressions? How did the speaker stand up, approach the lectern, present themself to the audience?

2. Was the top half of their body in control at the start of the speech?

3. Was the top half of their body in control during the speech?

4. Any negative styles?

5. Positive styles?

6. Pronunciation of vowels, consonants and combined consonants?

7. Voice control? Did the speaker pause, vary the speed and volume, vary the pitch for interest, use a resonant tone, etc?

© The Bulletproof Executive

8. Word control? Was the speaker's use of words suitable for the audience?

9. Grammar? Did the speaker make correct use of tenses, order of words, etc?

10. Breath control and eye-to-eye contact? Did the speaker concentrate on individuals when talking?

11. **Don'ts**. Did the speaker delay the start too long? Was the speaker negative, stereotyped, too emphatic or too lengthy?

12. **Do's**. Did the speaker adjust their chair and microphone correctly, approach the lectern well, sense audience mood, empathise and smile?

13. What type of opening statement did the speaker use? Did it suit the audience and the speaker? Was it well-delivered and polished?

14. Did the speaker win or lose the audience in the first 30 seconds? Why?

15. During the curiosity phase, did the speaker make you curious?

16. Comment on the speaker's use (or the absence) of positive audience reaction techniques, eg 'you' and then 'we' appeal.

17. During the trust phase, did you trust the speaker?

18. Comment on the use (or absence) of sincerity and truth, believability, audience concern, verification, voice, word and breath control.

19. Did the speaker modify their communication style according to the operating styles of the audience?

20. Any signs of active listening?

21. Which operating style did the speaker use?

22. Was the speaker's main operating style dominant, or did the speaker vary this style?

23. Did the speaker end with impact?

24. What type of technique for ending with impact did the speaker use?

25. How could the ending have been improved?

26. What other ending technique may have been more suitable under the circumstances?

27. Comment on how the speaker used scripts, prompter cards or 'envelopes'.

28. Did the speaker read them, or just glance — the latter being the desired approach?

29. Were they unobtrusive?

30. Were overheads legible, in colour, simple and well-formatted?

31. Did the speaker point well, and turn off the projector when not in use?

32. Was the flip chart used effectively?

33. When writing on the flip chart, did the speaker minimise turning their back to the audience and talking to the chart?

The Executive Panel

An Executive Panel was formed to check and comment on my assessment of career success and failure factors for executives and managers. The panel was established by inviting 200 senior executives and managers across a broad cross-section of business sectors in Australia, the United States, the United Kingdom, Canada, Hong Kong, Singapore and New Zealand to participate. More than 85 (over 40 per cent) elected to respond to the survey and, in so doing, became part of the Executive Panel. (Some will have changed their job positions and companies by the time this book is published.) They were:

Ian Moore, General Manager Human Resources, James Hardie Industries Ltd.

Ken Boag, Managing Director, Tower Life Australia Limited.

John Marlay, Chief General Manager, Australian Building Materials Division, Pioneer International.

Ron Enestrom, Senior Adviser, AIG Financial Products Ltd and Associate Director of Davidson & Associates, previously Senior Vice President and Regional Head of the First National Bank of Chicago.

Alan Popham, Human Resources Director of Rothman International BV, London.

Jay Lowrey, Human Resources Director, AMP, and previously Senior Vice President, Chase Manhattan Bank.

Rob McPaul, Human Resources Director Australasia, Reckitt and Colman.

Donald Ross, General Manager Sydney Ports Corporation, and previously Managing Director of Stegbar.

David W Benn, Managing Director Australasia, Korn/Ferry International.

Rodney Lester, Managing Director, AMP General Insurance.

Mark C Kershisnik, Managing Director, Eli Lilly Australia Pty Ltd, and formerly Director of Manufacturing, Lilly Germany.

Dick Austen, Chairman of Savage Resources Ltd and Holyman Ltd.

Stuart Hamilton, Executive Director of the Australian Vice-Chancellors Committee, previously Secretary (CEO) of the Commonwealth Department of the Environment.

Philip Twyman, Finance Director of General Accident plc, Scotland, previously Chief General Manager, AMP Society.

John Baker, independent consultant and Associate of Davidson & Associates, previously President Australia and New Zealand of Marion Merell Dow Pty Limited.

Robert C Stephenson, Local Divisional Manager of SCA Molnlycke AB in the United Kingdom, and previously Managing Director, Sancella Ltd and Northfleet Terminal of Scott Ltd.

Kenneth J Roberts, Company Director of ATG, CSL and AGEN, and formerly Chairman and Managing Director, Wellcome Australia.

Dr Lionel Wilson, Managing Director, Qual-Med Pty Ltd.

Christopher Conybeare, independent consultant and Associate Director of Davidson & Associates, previously Secretary (CEO) of the Australian Department of Immigration and Ethnic Affairs.

Martin Prentice, Vice President Training and Education of a major consumer product manufacturing and marketing organisation in the United States.

Sue Bussell, General Manager Employee Relations of Qantas.

Bruce Coates, General Manager Employee Relations, Ampol (Australian Petroleum P/L).

R V Matthews, Human Resources Director of Goodman Fielder International.

Jon Isaacs, Chief Executive Officer of the Royal Blind Society.

Tim Hessell, Human Resources Director of Frito-lay Australia.

Tony Thirlwell, Chief Executive of Tourism New South Wales, previously Managing Director of the Australian Tourism Commission.

Peter Herborn, Group General Manager, Development, of Tower Corporation Holding Limited in New Zealand, previously Partner of Deloitte Touche Tohmatsu.

Bob Paterson, Director Human Resources, Unisys Australia Limited, previously Chief Manager, Card Services, Westpac Banking Corporation.

James Cogan, Managing Director Finance and Administration of Credit Suisse First Boston.

Peeyush Gupta, Chief Executive Officer of IPAC Securities.

Ken Harris, Managing Director, ADI Limited.

Oleh Butchatsky, Director of Ward Howell International, and co-author of *Leadership, Australia's Top CEOs: Finding out what makes them best* (published by HarperBusiness).

Rob Lourey, Director of Human Resources, BOC Gases Australia Ltd, and previously Director of Human Resources, McIntosh Security.

Scott Reid, Managing Director of Chase Manhattan Bank Australia.

Maree Taylor, Human Resources Director, Asia Pacific, Apple Computer Pty Ltd.

Graeme Galt, a leading Sydney businessman and one of Australia's foremost senior level headhunters, co-founder of Australia's largest executive search firm, now known as Amrop International, former Chairman of Korn Ferry International in Australia, and former Chairman of Sydney Football and the Sydney Dance Company.

Tony Harbour, independent management consultant and formerly Group Personnel Director of the Ocean Group PLC in the United Kingdom.

The Executive Panel

David Learmond, Personnel Director of Unilever Australia.

Graeme Duhs, Managing Director, Davidson & Associates Limited New Zealand, and formerly Director of Cook Duhs & Associates Ltd, a recruitment consultancy.

Meredith Hellicar, Managing Director, TNT Logistics Asia, previously Executive Director of the NSW Coal Association.

Bruce Robertson, Trustee of the Royal Botanical Gardens and Director of a number of community and sports Boards, and previously Chairman of the Zoological Parks Board of NSW and Executive General Manager, Divisional General Manager and Subsidiary Director of James Hardie Industries.

Moira Holmes, Director Human Resources, Hitachi Data Systems.

Greg Brinkley, State Director Queensland, Davidson & Associates, and previously Deputy General Manager, Queensland Confederation of Industry.

Geoff Wright, former State Director Western Australia, Davidson & Associates.

Michael T Duffy, Senior Manager Group Human Resources at the Commonwealth Bank of Australia.

Carol Limmer, Chief Manager, Executive Development and Recognition, Commonwealth Bank of Australia.

Kit Middleton, General Manager Human Resources, Tandem Computers.

Paul Lilley, General Manager Human Resources, (Australian Banking Group) Westpac, formerly Human Resources Director, Rothmans Asia.

Brett Haly, General Manager Customer Relations and Organisation Development, Tower Life.

Joe Fischer, Manager Human Resources Department and Regional Staff Coordination of Nestlé Australia Ltd.

Phillip Hart, Executive Director, Red Cross New South Wales.

Karen Robinson, Director Human Resources, BZW Australia Ltd.

Brian Armour, Employee Development Manager of ADI Technology Group.

John Walmsley, Production and Engineering Manager, Masport Pty Ltd, and formerly Chief Design and Development Engineer of Gas and Fuel Corporation.

Vic Betteridge, General Manager Corporate Services of GIO Australia Ltd.

David Habler, National Manager Human Resources of the Australian Stock Exchange.

Alan Bateman, Information Technology Manager, Aristocrat Leisure Industries Pty Ltd.

Aaron Broadway, Career and Leadership Development Facilitator, Citibank.

John Matthews, Deputy General Manager Group Human Resources, Commonwealth Bank.

Ron Hopwood, Director of Human Resources, 3M Australia Pty Ltd.

Lyn Cobley, Strategic Planning and Marketing Manager of Citibank and formerly Head of Securitisation.

Lawrie Horder, Head of Human Resources, Business Financial Services NSW and ACT, National Australia Bank.

Philip Johnston, Director Cabarita Operations, Glaxo Wellcome Australia Ltd.

Michael Nadler, independent consultant, and previously Chief Executive of the Australian Institute of Management in New South Wales.

J G (John) Koch, Chief Representative of the Forma Group, formerly a General Manager with the Commonwealth Bank of Australia.

Michael Rowan, formerly Chief Manager Commercial and Agribusiness Banking, NSW Country and ACT, Westpac.

Colin Bateman, Principal Engineer, Maunsell.

Mike Burdett, previously Executive Chief Manager of a major banking and financial services organisation.

Paul Martin, State Director Western Australia, Davidson & Associates.

Cameron Bott, Human Resources Manager of Stramit Industries.

Kerri Burgess, Chief of Staff, Citibank Ltd.

Scott Pagan, Human Resources Director, The Smith's Snackfood Co. Ltd, formerly National Employee Relations Manager at Coco-Cola Amatil.

Others

A management consultant in London specialising in investment management software for banks, insurance companies and asset management companies.

A senior information technology manager based in Ireland.

Director of a specialist management consulting practice.

CEO of an engineering research and development organisation.

Chairman of a significant brewing company.

General manager human resources of a major insurance company.

Managing director of a medium-sized company.

Head of human resources of a major building products group, with international operations.

Managing director of a substantial resources development company.

Managing director of a major food group.

Director of a major division within a large telecommunications group.

Managing director of a major division within another large telecommunications group.

Human resources director of a large instrumentation and technical services group.

Vice president personnel and organisation of a major consumer product manufacturing and marketing organisation in the United States.

Director, human resources and public relations, of a major international bank, headquartered in the United States.

Bibliography

1996 AMA Survey 1996, *Corporate Downsizing, Job Elimination, and Job Creation* by Eric Rolfe Greenberg from AMA Survey Report, American Management Association, New York.

Birchall, David & Lyons, Laurence 1995, *Creating Tomorrow's Organisation*, Henley Pitman Publishing, London.

Birkman, Roger, *Birkman Career Management Profile*[sm].

Brass, Charles, 'Life Without Jobs', *HR Monthly*, April 1995.

Bridges, William 1995, *Job Shift: How to prosper in a workplace without jobs*, Nicholas Brealey Publishing, London.

Cascio, Professor Wayne F, 'The Cost of Downsizing', *HR Monthly*, February 1994.

Covey, Stephen R 1990, *The 7 Habits of Highly Effective People*, Information Australia, Melbourne.

Dent, Jr, Harry S 1995, *Job Shock: Four new principles transforming our work and business*, Bookman Press, Melbourne.

Freeman, Richard D 1996, 'Growth and Corporate Behaviour', *Centre Piece*, Centre for Economic Performance Newsletter, London School of Economics, London.

Gertz, Dwight L & Baptista, João P A 1995, *Grow to be Great: Breaking the downsizing cycle*, The Free Press/Simon & Schuster, New York.

Gordon, David M 1996, *Fat and Mean: The corporate squeeze of working Americans and the myth of managerial downsizing*, The Free Press/Simon & Schuster, New York.

Hamel, Gary & Prahalad, C K 1994, *Competing for the Future*, Harvard Business School Press, UK.

Handy, Charles 1994, *The Age of Unreason*, Arrow Books, Random House International, UK.

Handy, Charles 1994, *The Empty Raincoat*, Arrow Books, Random House International, UK.

The Karpin Report — Renewing Australia's Managers to Meet the Challenges of the Asia-Pacific Century 1994, Australian Government Publishing Service, Canberra.

Koch, Richard & Godden, Ian 1996, *Managing Without Management: A Post-Management Manifesto for Business Simplicity*, Nicholas Brealey Publishing London.

Korn/Ferry and the Economist Intelligence Unit 1996, *Developing Leadership for the 21st Century*, Korn/Ferry International, New York.

Kotter, John P 1995, *The New Rules*, The Free Press/Simon & Schuster, New York.

Lans, Jenni 1996, *If It Wasn't for the Money, I Wouldn't be Doing This*, HarperCollins Publishers, Sydney.

Leana, Carrie R and Feldman, Daniel C 1992, *Coping with Job Loss: How individuals, organisations, and communities respond to layoffs*, Lexington Books/Simon & Schuster, New York.

Levering, Robert 1993, *The 100 Best Companies to Work for in America*, Doubleday, New York.

Mackay, Harvey B 1995, *Sharkproof: Get the job you want, keep the job you love ... in today's frenzied job market*, HarperCollins Publishers, New York.

Meyer, G J 1995, *Executive Blues*, Franklin Square Press, United States.

Porras, Jerry I, *Built to Last: Successful habits of visionary companies*, Stanford Business School/HarperCollins, United States.

Rifkin, Jeremy 1995, *The End of Work: The decline of the global labour force and the dawn of the post-market era*, Jeremy P Tarcher/G P Putnam's Sons Publishers, New York.

Sarros, James C & Butchatsky, Oleh 1996, *Leadership, Australia's Top CEOs: Finding what makes them the best*, HarperCollins Publishers, Sydney.

Scott-Morgan, Peter 1994, *The Unwritten Rules of the Game: Master them, shatter them, and break through the barriers of organisational change*, Arthur D Little Inc., US.

Sloan, Allan, 'The Hit Men', *The Bulletin*, 27 February 1996.

Stewart, Thomas A, 'Looking out for Number 1', *Fortune*, January 1996.

Thompson, John A & Hennigsen, Catharine A, *The Portable Executive*, Simon & Schuster, New York.

Tichy, Noel M and Stratford, Sherman 1993, *Control Your Destiny or Someone Else Will*, Transworld Publishers/Doubleday, New York.

Waterman, Jr, Robert H 1996, *What America Does Right*, Norton Publishing (International Association of Career Management Professionals (IACMP) Future Focus Committees, Trends and Issues Affecting the Career Management Industry) United States.

Index

A

ability 36-37
achievement, personal 61
acquisitions, company 4, 129
adaptability 14, 59, 70
administrative careers 40
advertisements 170
allies 164-168
    see also contact network
    external 141-143
    for referrals 143
All-rounder operating style 51
analytical careers 39
appearance, personal 287-288
applying for jobs 110-112
appointments 152
appraisal 87, 96
approach planning 150-152
artistic interest 35
assets, business drivers for 223-225
atmospherics
    career assessment 102
    effect on chemistry and fit 57, 61
    egalitarian 24, 26
    'fit' problems 14-15
    motivational 27
    selection interview questions 245
attrition 83
audience
    attention 283-284
    motivating 150-163
    participation 282
    raising interest 288
    reactions 283
    seating 277-278, 296-297
    winning 158-163
autonomy 38

B

behaviour
    operating style 49-52, 233-234
    stress-related 124-125
behavioural needs 58
beliefs *see* values
'Best Principles, Best Practice' 73-75, 78-79
brochures, corporate 169-170
burnout 124
business drivers *see* primary business
    drivers
business objectives 29
business plan 259-260
business variables *see* variables
buying a business 257-258

C

capabilities
    career assessment 102
    dismissal avoidance 82, 85-90
    executive failure 13
capability-oriented profile 111-112, 265-267
career
    alignment 93-97
    consulting 95-96
    employment market 105-107
    environment 103-104
    management counselling 88-89
    objectives and strategies 249
    opportunities 107-109
    ownership 246
    planning 13, 101-109, 248-252
    ranking 181-187
    search 268-273
    stages 126-129
    taking stock 102-103
    types 39-40
career-oriented profile 111, 261-264
challenge 26
change
    as business driver 29
    leadership *see* change leadership
    management failure 13-14
    technological 30
change leadership 65-80
    executive success 14, 181
    selection interview questions 246
chemistry and fit
    see also job fit; organisational fit
    career alignment 96
    career problem 7
    dismissal avoidance 82, 85-90
    failure 14-15
    improving 56-62
    profile 235-236
clerical work
    ability 37
    interest in 35
'closing' meetings and presentations
    155-156, 276, 280, 291-292

clubs 144
cold calling 151, 292-293
Commander/Doer operating style 49
commitment 20
communication
   change leadership 14, 68-69, 71-72
   creating a motivational environment 26
   management style 59
   selling yourself 144-147
   tips for success 274-293
communications *see* telecommunications
competencies
   career problem 7
   for change leadership 70-71
   staff management 25-28
   success factors 183
competition as business driver 32
comprehension 36
computer graphics 174-175, 279-280
computers 65
conferences 144
conflict management 46
contact network
   for career search 268-273
   job seeking 115-116
   personal selling 138-140
continuity statements 279
contracting out 68
contracts 87
control
   leadership trait 45-46
   span of 11, 21, 26, 28
conventions 144
cooperation 26
coordination 21
coping skills 79
corporate brochures 169-170
counselling
   avoiding dismissals 88-90
   creating a motivational environment 26
   for restructuring 78, 79
covering letters 113-114
creative careers 39
creativity
   leadership trait 45-46
   motivation 37
   planning 20
culture, organisational *see* atmospherics
curiosity 159-160
current assets, business drivers for 224-225
customers as business driver 32

D

decision-making
   group-based 26
   improving 22-23
   management style 58
delegation
   improving 21, 24-25
   management style 59
   motivational 25-28
demographic impact on career development 104-105
design careers 39
discussion technique 151
dismissals
   avoidance 75, 81-91
   outcomes and implications 90
   reasons for 82-87
   selection interview questions 247
dissatisfaction 13
divestments 4, 129
downsizing 65, 67-68, 72-75
   outplacement providers 241
drivers *see* primary business drivers

E

economy
   impact on career development 103-104
   reasons for dismissal 82, 83-85
   variables as business driver 31
education 129
egalitarianism 24, 26
elocution 274
emotional needs 60-61
Empathiser/Humanist operating style 49-50
employees *see* staff
employment conditions 37
employment market 105-107
empowerment 21
ending speeches and presentations 277
enterprising careers 40
entrepreneurism
   careers 40
   change management 14, 70-71
   management style 59
esteem needs 61
Evaluator/Detailer operating style 50
expectations 183
expenses, business drivers for 221-223
external environment 28-29, 181
eye control 289

Index

F
fact-finding for presentations 157-158
failure, reasons for 10-16, 181-187
feedback 237
financial planning, personal 253-255
fit *see* chemistry and fit; job fit; organisational fit
fixed assets, business drivers for 223
flexible work arrangements 129
flip charts 175
fluency 37
forecasting 29-30
fulfilment 37
future
  as business driver 29-30
  planning and strategy 101-109

G
generalists 34-35
globalisation 4, 65
goals
  achievement 23
  restructures 239
  setting 26, 137
government influence 31, 103
grammar 287
grooming 287-288
group communication 145-147
group presentations 164-176
  see also speaking
  developing techniques 156-163, 298-300
  preparation 294-295
  tips for success 274-293
  visual aids 174-175

H
hecklers 286
hiring 92-93
  interviews 244-247
  for operating style 52
humour 290-291

I
Idea generator operating style 50
identification with the organisation 185
importance of the job 37
impromptu speeches 281-282
influence 133-149
  expanding 165
  'fit' problems 15
  motivational environment 26
  selection interview questions 246

survival skills 181
information
  contact network 139
  impact on career development 103
information packages 170
information technology
  effect of restructure 65
  the future 129
  threat to job tenure 4-5
innovation 31
integrity 184
interests, occupational *see* occupational interests
interpersonal relationships 60
interviews
  for a job 117-121
  selection 224-247

J
job
  applications 110-112
  demise of 5-6
  future changes 129
  interviews 117-121
  loss 10
  opportunities, defining 249
  seeking 105-107
  sharing 84
  specifications and grades 26
  tracking down 110-122
job fit 34-40
  career alignment 95
  career success factor 181, 185
  counselling 88, 89
  optimising 226-228
  selection interview questions 246
job performance *see* performance
jokes 290-291

L
layoffs *see* dismissals
leadership of change *see* change leadership
leadership traits
  career assessment 102
  career success factor 181
  defining 229-232
  developing 42-47
  'fit' problems 15
  selection interview questions 245
leave of absence 84
legislation 31
leisure time 129

letters
  of appreciation 153
  job applications 113-114
lifestyle 38
listening 71
literary interest 35
loyalty
  bonuses 75, 85
  building 164-165

M

magazines 144
maintenance monitoring 22
management
  effect of restructuring 65
  open 237-238
  practices 194-216
  staff 25-28, 181
  style 23, 58-59 (*see also* operating style)
management practices 19-25
managerial careers 40
marketing yourself *see* selling yourself
marriages, dual-career 129
material needs 58
mathematical abilities 36
media releases 170
medical interest 36
meetings 150-153, 288-289
  room layouts 296-297
memorising 275
memory 36
mergers 4, 129
microphones 285
mid-career counselling 89-90
middle management 34-35
'mirror-image' hiring 52
monitoring 20, 21-22, 58
motivating 23-24, 26-28
  see also self-motivation
  audiences 150-163
  management style 59
motivational capabilities 36-37
motivational delegation 25-28
musical interest 36

N

natural attrition 83
needs 57-58, 60-61
  recognition 139
nerves 291
networking *see* contact network

newspapers 144
numeracy 36

O

occupational interests 35-36
  career assessment 102
  executive failure 12
open management 237-238
openness 184, 237
operating environment 12
operating style
  career assessment 102
  interpersonal relationships 60
  management 23, 58-59
  public speaking 147-148
  teamwork 49-52, 233-234
organisational fit 181, 185
  teams 53-55
organising 21, 58
outdoor interests 36
outplacement provider, selecting 75-78, 241-243
output orientation 45-46
overhead transparencies 174-175

P

part-time work 84
people management practices 19
people orientation 37, 45-46
people-oriented careers 39-40
perception 37
performance
  appraisal 87, 96
  failure 10-12, 12-13
  improvement programs 88, 96
  improving 19-33, 34-41
  management 93-94
  optimising 226-228
  praising and counselling 26
  selection interview questions 244
  standards 22, 249-250
perseverance 14
personal chemistry *see* chemistry and fit
personal performance *see* performance
personal profile 106, 110-113, 261-267
personal selling *see* selling yourself
persuasiveness 35
planning
  business 259-260
  downsizing 74
  improving 20-21
  management style 58

Index

restructures 237-240
politics, national
   as business driver 31
   impact on career development 103
politics, organisational 133-149
   'fit' problems 15
   selection interview questions 246
   survival skills 181
poor performance 26
power 133-149
   'fit' problems 15
   motivational environment 26
   selection interview questions 246
   success factor 183
practical careers 39
practicalness 35
praising 26
presentations *see* group presentations
preventative monitoring 22
primary business drivers 28-32, 217-225
   executive failure 11
   success factor 181
prioritisation 140-141, 186-187
proactiveness 20, 49-52, 237
problems
   prevention 22
   solving 23
productivity 130
professional services careers 40
profile (resume) 106, 110-113, 261-267
profile, personal *see* personal profile
profit tree 218
promotional techniques 168-170
prompter cards 173-174
prospects 37
public records 144
public speaking *see* speaking
publications, promotional 168-169, 170

Q

questions
   answering 284
   asking 162, 274, 278, 281, 285-286

R

reasoning ability 37
rebuilding 78-79
receptiveness 49-52
recession 4
recruitment 92-93
redeployment 85-86
redundancy, voluntary 75, 84-85

rejections 289-290
relationships 60
resignation 86-87
resilience 59, 71
Responder/Initiator operating style 50
responsibility 28, 37
restructures 65-80
   see also downsizing
   executive failure 14
   the future 129
   planning and managing 237-240
   scenarios 66-70
resume 106, 110-113, 261-267
retirement
   early 84
   financial planning for 253-255
risk assessment 191-193

S

salary freeze or reduction 83-84
sales, business drivers for 219-220
science
   careers in 39
   interest in 35
seating arrangements for meetings 277-278, 296-297
secondment 84
selection interviews 244-247
self-confidence 184
self-development 13
self-employment 107-109, 256-260
self-expression 37
self-knowledge 184
self-motivation 34-41
   career problem 7
   dismissal avoidance 82, 85-90
   executive failure 12
   optimising 226-228
self-promotion *see* selling yourself
selling yourself
   within the organisation 136-143
   outside the organisation 141-144, 150-163
   techniques 164-176
   winning a new job 110-122
service 165
service organisations 144
skills *see* competencies
small business 256-260
sociability 35, 37
social contacts 144

social demography, impact on career development 104–105
social needs 60
social variables as business driver 32
span of control 11, 21, 26, 28
spatial ability 36
speaking 156–163
- aids 172–175
- fluency 37
- styles 147–148
- tips for success 274–293

specialisation 104
'square-peg-in-round-hole' counselling 88–89
staff
- see also talent
- development 22
- management 25–28, 181
- selection 92–93

strategy, career 250–252
stress 123–130
- career problem 7
- managing 125–126

structural needs 58
structure 21
- see also restructures
success factors 181–187

T

talent
- attracting 12
- future use 129
- nurturing 92–98, 181

teams 48–55
- career success 181
- composition 21
- executive success 52–55
- 'fit' problems 15
- members' styles 233–234
- rebuilding 79
- selection interview questions 245–246
- supportive 27

technical careers 39
technology
- see also information technology
- as business driver 30–31
- impact on career development 103
- interest in 36

telecommunications
- the future 129
- impact on career development 103
- threat to job tenure 4–5

telemarketing 170
telephone calls 151, 292–293
term contracts 87
termination see dismissal
testimonials 280
thank you letters 153
time management 140–141
trade shows 144
trust
- building 159–160
- emotional needs 60–61
- motivational environment 27

U

'umming' 280–281
'unique marketing differentiators' 128

V

values
- career assessment 102
- job fit 37–38
- motivational environment 26
- personal performance 13

variables
- business drivers 31–32
- impact on career development 103–104

videos 170, 279–280
vision
- leadership trait 46
- restructures 238, 239
- success factor 185

visual aids 154–155, 174, 277, 286–287
voice control 278
voluntary redundancy 75, 84–85

W

whiteboards 175
- writing techniques 170–172

4 Adult Audio Cassette Programs

Narrated by Peter Stephenson

For Adults. Each program $99.95 plus postage.

1. Career Success!
Planning, revitalising and succeeding in your career.

2. Career Alignment
Maximising staff commitment, job performance and their value to the organisation, by aligning personal and organisational goals, through career development counselling.

3. Sell Yourself, Network and Succeed
Selling yourself assertively, networking and negotiating your way to success.

4. Knock the Socks Off Your Audiences!
Developing confidence, polish and impact on your feet.

Each program:
- provides the equivalent of a three day professional training course, but is designed to be taken at home at a more convenient time
- comprises six audio cassettes of high impact training content and features an expansive training manual with descriptive diagrams and charts demonstrating key points, self-help checklists and action planning guides.

For more information or to place your order, please contact:

Barbara Stephenson
ADVANTAGE 2000 Pty Ltd
ACN 003 131 744
PO Box 367 Balgowlah NSW 2093 Australia
Phone/Fax No.: (02) 9949 4507
Email: canuck@Bigpond.com

4 Student Audio Cassette Programs

Narrated by Peter Stephenson

For Students and Young Adults. Each program $29.95 plus postage. ($99.95 plus postage for the full set of four programs — a saving of nearly $20.00).

Part 1: How To Choose Your Career

The complete self-help program on how to evaluate and select your ideal career path, based on your interests, abilities, values and behavioural style. Your complete home-based career guidance system!

Part 2: How To Find And Apply For Jobs Successfully

How to develop impressive resumes and application letters; how to track down the ideal job; how to present yourself well at interviews and answer difficult questions, with confidence.

Part 3: How To Succeed In Your New Job And Career

How to settle into a new job successfully and plan and develop your career; how to obtain a salary increase, new job position or promotion; how to deal with conflict and stress.

Part 4: How To Help Your Teenage Children And Other Young Adults Choose And Succeed In Their Careers

The complete guide on how to help your teenage children, students, graduates and other young adults, decide on an appropriate career path, find and apply for jobs successfully, and succeed in their chosen jobs and careers. (For optional use when your children or other young adults are using Parts 1, 2 and/or 3 of the 'Career Success!' series.)

Each program:
- represents a one day training course, yet can be taken at home at a convenient time
- comprises an audio cassette/workbook package, crammed full with vital information, examples, checklists, diagrams, tools and tasks, all designed to enhance career success

---

For more information or to place your order, please contact:

Barbara Stephenson
ADVANTAGE 2000 Pty Ltd
ACN 003 131 744
PO Box 367 Balgowlah NSW 2093 Australia
Phone/Fax No.: (02) 9949 4507
Email: canuck@Bigpond.com

Other titles from
HarperBusiness

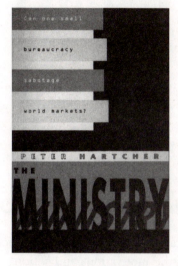

$24.95
ISBN 0 7322 5772 7

THE MINISTRY

Imagine a key government department which acknowledges no political master. Japan's Ministry of Finance is a political, intellectual and economic force that traces its lineage from the 7th century AD. Yet from 1985 to 1995, Japan's economy veered from calamity to calamity. Lives were ruined; world markets were embattled. But where are the reforms? What does the future hold?

In this startling exposé journalist and former foreign correspondent Peter Hartcher probes the ministry's culture of control — its recruitment patterns; its 'colonising' of other ministries and key corporations; and its utter disdain for market forces.

'A timely work on how the Ministry of Finance is promoting the crash of Japan's entire financial system.'

— Kenichi Ohmae

An imprint of HarperCollins*Publishers*

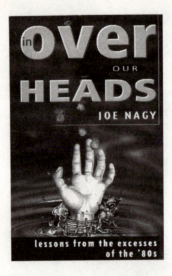

$19.95
ISBN 0 7322 5767 0

IN OVER OUR HEADS

In Over Our Heads takes a frank and engaging look at the excesses of the 1980s, exploring the motivations and actions of some of the high fliers, the banks, the organisations, the legal system and the media in an attempt to work out what went wrong. Ex-banker and financial consultant Joe Nagy examines in detail the individuals and entities that contributed to creating Australia's decade of shame.

Building on years of research, Nagy extracts from the disasters of the '80s some valuable lessons in leadership, ethics and strategic management, and suggests how business leaders in the 1990s can benefit from those lessons to take their organisations successfully into the 21st century.

Harper*Business*
An imprint of HarperCollins*Publishers*

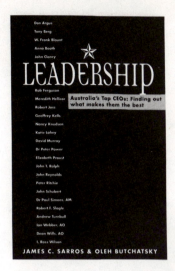

$24.95
ISBN 0 7322 5776 X

LEADERSHIP:
Australia's Top CEOs — Finding Out What Makes Them The Best

Is leadership an innate quality or a learned skill? Does your educational and family background influence your style as a leader? How is leadership different from management? What values are important in the way our best CEOs guide and develop major businesses?

Leadership is an in-depth study of Australia's most successful and respected Chief Executives, which explores these questions and other issues as Australian business increasingly adopts Learning Organisation principles to address the competitive challenges of the next century.

This unique and timely book gathers together and intensively documents the views of our top CEOs, as nominated by their peers, and develops a new model of leadership — Breakthrough Leadership. Learn from the interview transcripts and Handbook exercises how the principles of Breakthrough Leadership can be applied to your own Leadership challenges.

Harper*Business*
An imprint of HarperCollins*Publishers*